The
Reference Shelf®

Representative American Speeches 2012–2013

The Reference Shelf
Volume 85 • Number 6
H. W. Wilson
A Division of EBSCO Information Services
Ipswich, Massachusetts
2013

GREY HOUSE PUBLISHING

The Reference Shelf

The books in this series contain reprints of articles, excerpts from books, addresses on current issues, and studies of social trends in the United States and other countries. There are six separately bound numbers in each volume, all of which are usually published in the same calendar year. Numbers one through five are each devoted to a single subject, providing background information and discussion from various points of view and concluding with an index and comprehensive bibliography that lists books, pamphlets, and articles on the subject. The final number of each volume is a collection of recent speeches. Books in the series may be purchased individually or on subscription.

Library of Congress Cataloging-in-Publication Data

Representative American Speeches 2012-2013.
    pages cm. -- (The Reference Shelf ; Volume 85, Number 6)
  Includes bibliographical references and index.
  ISBN 978-0-8242-1211-7 (volume 85) -- ISBN 978-0-8242-1217-9 (issue 6) 1. Speeches, addresses, etc., American.
  PS668.2.R48 2013
  815.008--dc23

                        2013040302

Cover: Jim Yong Kim © Nicholas Kamm/AFP/Getty Images

The Reference Shelf, 2013, published by Grey House Publishing, Inc., Amenia, NY, under exclusive license from EBSCO Information Services, Inc.

Printed in the United States of America

Contents

3

The Debate on Gun Control

4

Immigration Reform

5

Remaking Business

Preface

Representative American Speeches

This edition of *Representative American Speeches*, a long-running series from H. W. Wilson, turns to important debates in American society that represent some of the most contested subjects in recent years. Consequently, many speakers are passionate in their hope and vision for what the future holds for Americans. Something should be said about the status of speeches in a period where video is the dominant medium. By collecting these speeches, we hope that the printed word offers readers the chance to capture nuances that might be missed in video and perhaps better understand the speaker's intent. The speeches in this volume, covering the years 2012–2013, welcome your undivided attention.

Following the enormity of events in World War II, member countries of the United Nations adopted the Universal Declaration of Human Rights in 1948. Taken as a whole, the thirty articles define a condition of equality and inalienable rights to which all people are entitled. Many of the concerns first addressed in the Declaration continue to demand our attention, as speeches in this chapter on human rights address the ongoing problem of war crimes, the rights of wartime prisoners, and human trafficking. Speeches by Navi Pillay, United Nations high commissioner, and Stephen J. Rapp, ambassador-at-large from the Office of Global Crime Justice, speak to the urgency of a concerted response to the problems that plague people and communities throughout the world. Both speakers reflect on the continuing need by policy makers to act aggressively and thus effectively resolve these and other issues today.

These speeches also remind readers that what constitutes a human right remains open to debate. Testimony by Anthony Graves, a man formerly on death row in Texas, describes his life and the life of other prisoners living in solitary confinement. From the vantage point of a free man, Graves argues that the treatment of prisoners in solitary confinement amounts to inhumane treatment. President Bill Clinton, in a speech before GLADD, an organization promoting LGBT equality, remarks that the recognition of gay rights is the test of America's conception of rights. The broad range of issues covered in this chapter offer insight into the work of rights activists close at home and abroad.

Speeches on the status of health care today take a broad view of the challenges and possibilities that lie ahead for Americans and the world. Everyone is familiar with the problems in our current system, particularly those who must negotiate these issues firsthand, whether as a result of a family health crisis or working in the industry. These same issues appear on the global scale, as many countries struggle to respond to health crises brought on by poverty, an aging population, and skyrocketing health care costs. Speeches by Jim Yong Kim, president of World Bank, and Margaret Chan, director-general of the World Health Organization, argue the importance of primary care as an essential element of a viable health care strategy, a model rooted in a community's health, social, and cultural needs.

One of the great challenges these speakers identify is the interconnected nature of poverty and health across the globe. Studies reveal a dramatic income disparity in health care. Inequality, Chan points out, is greater today than ever before. Former Secretary of State Hillary Clinton also responds to the global challenge in health care in the area of AIDS. Clinton provides a broad picture of America's contributions to the fight against the transmission of HIV, a virus that is particularly pernicious in the lives of women in some parts of the world. Finally, First Lady Michelle Obama celebrated the two-year anniversary of her "Let's Move On" campaign to end childhood obesity in America by delivering a series of speeches in the spring of 2012. In a speech in Longwood, Florida, Obama surveys the successes of the campaign to change the habits of not only families, but also the food industry to promote a healthier lifestyle. As is the case in the other speeches in this chapter, a progressive culture of community sets the terms for change in the future.

The winter of 2013 marked the return of one of the most hotly contested debates in America: the question of gun control. The mass shooting of twenty children and six adults at Sandy Hook Elementary School in December 2012 captured the attention of Americans in a way that stood apart from the ever-growing list of massacres, initiating a debate that had entirely disappeared during the preceding presidential election year. This chapter offers a view from multiple perspectives—from those in favor and those against federal and state regulation of guns.

While most of the speeches in this volume were written before their public delivery, a number were given extemporaneously, with little preparation. The delivery of these speeches can be in rough form, yet they may hold a sense of urgency missing in other speeches. The testimony of Neil Heslin before the Connecticut state legislature, was given just weeks following the murder of his son, Jessie Lewis, at Sandy Hook Elementary School. His emotional testimony would have received national attention in any case, but the interruption of his testimony by audience members opposed to gun control highlighted the stark divisions surrounding these debates. Mark E. Kelly, husband of former Congresswoman Gabrielle Giffords, who was shot with others by a gunman while at a political event in 2011, adds another voice from those whose loved ones experienced gun violence. Accompanying speeches by legislators and one by a law enforcement officer, this chapter provides a cross-section of the different perspectives and places from which the gun debate unfolds.

Divisiveness in American politics usually follows conventional liberal-conservative lines. Yet one debate appears to depart from the convention—the question of America's immigration policy. One reason may be that immigration presents multiple parts, not defined by the apparent clarity of black and white perspectives accompanying gun control. This chapter covers several angles of this issue, from the needs of business for a strong workforce to the rights of students living between citizenship and undocumented status. Business leaders, usually strong supporters of Republican politics, are generally in favor of immigration reform, aware of the contributions by immigrant workers to a healthy economy. Speeches by Republican senators Marco Rubio and Rand Paul point to these and other issues where political lines become increasingly blurred.

Jose Antonio Vargas, a Pulitzer Prize–winning *New York Times* reporter, in a speech before a Senate judiciary committee, offers a compelling perspective on immigration that captures the human side of many of the issues covered in this chapter. In a 2011 *Times* article, Vargas revealed his life as an "undocumented immigrant" who experienced the conflicted role immigrants hold in American society, remarking upon his success as a student and writer, while living a life of invisibility as an undocumented immigrant. His speech suggests how the debate on immigration can be, in the final analysis, a question of how one views the American ideal of an inclusive and diverse society.

The final chapter, "Remaking Business," looks to the future for a robust (in some cases, progressive) realm of work and business, after the economic crisis of the 2000s. Joanne Wilson implores women to, as Sheryl Sandburg succinctly put it, "lean in" when in the world of work, business, and opportunity. Wilson captures a line of thought in many of these speeches—the necessity of having a personal stake in making changes in the corporate and work-a-day world of business. Remarks by FTC Chair Edith Ramirez turn to the relationship between everyday consumption and online privacy, while Luis Arbulu describes his experience as a visa-sponsored immigrant worker who has contributed his skills of entrepreneurship to engineering projects in California. Each speech offers something to say about the future of American business.

The thirty-six speeches in this volume provide a diverse representation of speech as a vital form of public discourse, which depart in interesting ways from the writer's voice in newspapers and magazines. Accompanying each speech is a brief overview that sets the context; a biographical summary of the speaker follows.

1

Defending Human Rights

People dressed as detainees of Guantanamo Bay detention facility protest outside the White House, June 14, 2013. Human rights groups have criticized the Obama administration for failing to close Guantanamo, which Obama originally promised to do in his first year in office.

Rights in Crisis

By Ivan Šimonović

In this speech delivered before a meeting of experts from the United Nations Office of the High Commissioner for Human Rights, Assistant Secretary-General for Human Rights Ivan Šimonović explores the idea that formulating economic policies with human rights standards in mind can foster economic growth and sustainability. Global human rights are inextricably linked to global financial stability, Šimonović says. As worldwide social movements like Occupy Wall Street have shown, public opinion is behind a rights-based approach to economic and regulatory policies, according to Šimonović. Furthermore, Šimonović cites UN General Assembly reports that found systemic flaws, ever-widening inequalities, and a general lack of institutional accountability to be the underlying cause of the global financial crisis of 2008 and the recession that followed. He discusses the impact of austerity measures on human rights, citing World Bank numbers that found 114 million more people to be living below the poverty line since the onset of the downturn, and UN Department of Economic and Social Affairs statistics showing a deficit of 64 million jobs worldwide. A more thorough understanding of the way macroeconomic activity and human rights interweave is necessary to address the current crisis and to prevent similar problems in the future, says Šimonović, before urging states to act in individual and collective capacities to ensure the right to development for all enshrined in the UN Charter.

Excellencies, Distinguished participants, Ladies and Gentlemen,

It is my pleasure to welcome you here today at the opening of OHCHR's expert meeting, Rights in Crisis. We organized this meeting to explore how basing economic policies on human rights standards can help to make economic recovery and growth more sustainable.

I am pleased to be joined today by Her Excellency Ambassador Yanerit Morgan, Deputy Permanent Representative of Mexico to the United Nations. We have with us also a distinguished and diverse group of speakers from universities, international organizations, civil society, and governments—all of them leaders in their respective fields. And of course we have an equally distinguished audience. I encourage you all to actively participate in discussions.

Ladies and Gentlemen,

The issue before us is of critical importance. The impact of economic crises, financial regulations and economic policies on human rights is often neglected. The gravity of the global financial crisis and its human rights impacts show the need for

---

Delivered April 24, 2013, at OHCHR's expert meeting on Rights in Crisis, New York, New York, by Ivan Simonovic.

a new approach. Over the course of this meeting I would ask you to consider what this new approach should look like.

In order to answer this question, we must also discuss several others, among them: what caused the financial crisis, what were its human rights and social impacts and how do we mitigate them? I look forward to hearing your thoughts on these issues and will offer a few of my own.

What caused the crisis? According to General Assembly resolution 63/303, the crisis arose from systemic flaws in national and international monetary and financial architecture, de-regulation, the failure of existing systems to adapt to an increasingly complex and interconnected global financial system, rising inequalities, lack of accountability and global imbalances. These are substantial problems. Problems that can and should be examined from multiple angles and continue to be the subject of debates, including earlier this week at the annual meeting of ECOSOC with the Bretton Woods Institutions.

These debates reflect a growing consensus that financial institutions, economic policy decisions and global economic governance should be more transparent, accountable and democratically representative. These are not only expert opinions. Growing disaffection of many people with the status quo has led to the rise of popular protest movements like 'Occupy" and "Los Indignados." If there is no change in a right direction, in addition to economic we are risking social and political global crisis as well.

Transparency, accountability and participation in decision-making are fundamental human rights principles and their neglect raises another question for you to consider today: how do we translate the growing consensus for rights-based reform of financial systems into concrete measures that will promote economic stability and growth?

A second area that requires further examination is the nexus between financial crises, austerity measures, financial regulation and human rights. What are the impacts of the financial crisis and austerity measures on human rights? Our background paper, which Mr. Bat-Erdene Ayush will introduce in further detail, notes that at least 15 special procedures of the Human Rights Council have examined the human rights impacts of financial crises and/or austerity measures in addition to several human rights treaty bodies. The reports and concluding observations of these mechanisms find that many people have lost access to work, social welfare programs, and affordable food, housing, water and other basic necessities due to the crisis and austerity measures. Furthermore, they find that these impacts have been disproportionately borne by women, children, and vulnerable and marginalized persons.

How can we powerfully articulate these impacts to galvanize rights-based action? It can be difficult to put numbers to the human rights impacts of the crisis but there are indicators that suggest they are significant. According to the World Bank, 114 million more people are living below the poverty line than before the crisis. According to DESA, in 2011, there was a still-growing global employment deficit of 64 million jobs just to reach pre-crisis levels of employment. The forthcoming report of the High

Commissioner to ECOSOC examines the impacts of the crisis and austerity measures on the enjoyment of the rights to employment and social security.

Ladies and Gentlemen,

We must continue to further our understanding of the connection between human rights and economic and regulatory policies. Such an improved understanding is a necessary basis for future advocacy efforts to promote human rights considerations in macroeconomic policies and financial regulations.

According to the World Bank, 114 million more people are living below the poverty line than before the crisis. According to DESA, in 2011, there was a still-growing global employment deficit of 64 million jobs just to reach pre-crisis levels of employment.

One potential response that economists and human rights activists alike support is progressive and human rights sensitive macroeconomic policies that give all persons equal opportunities for development. In this regard, the Special Rapporteurs on food and extreme poverty have called for the establishment of a social protection floor, a call that has been welcomed by the European Parliament. How can we design measures that promote inclusive growth and equality? How to best establish a social protection floor in the face of austerity measures that threaten even basic social services in many States?

Ladies and Gentlemen,

I also believe that we must take action to address the root causes of the crisis, to prevent its recurrence, and to address its impacts on the most vulnerable. Human rights norms, articulated in the UN Charter, the Declaration on the Right to Development and the International Covenant on Economic, Social and Cultural Rights require that States act individually and collectively to guarantee the fulfillment of human rights and to create an enabling environment for development.

In this regard, the regulation of financial markets and actors through national mechanisms and international financial institutions is an exercise of State power that should promote the realization of human rights and be guided by the human rights principles of transparency, participation and accountability.

As the High Commissioner said at this year's World Economic Forum in Davos, "The rule of law must extend to the financial sector as well." How to achieve this?

Ladies and gentlemen, let me conclude.

In the current crisis lie both challenges and opportunities. The United Nations and the contemporary human rights regime emerged from the ashes of World War II to help us build a more just and peaceful world. The lessons learned from this crisis may lead to a more inclusive, sustainable development paradigm, a paradigm in which all human rights and fundamental freedoms, including the right to development, are within the reach of all persons.

Ladies and gentlemen, let us grab the opportunity!

About Ivan Šimonović

Ivan Šimonović of Croatia is the current Assistant Secretary-General for Human Rights in the United Nations Office of the High Commissioner for Human Rights. He assumed his role with the United Nations on July 17, 2010. Previously, he served as Croatia's minister of justice, starting in 2008. Before that, he was deputy minister in Croatia's Ministry of Foreign Affairs, having joined the ministry in 1992, working in various capacities including assistant foreign minister and first assistant minister. In 1997, Šimonović became Croatia's ambassador and permanent representative to the United Nations in New York. In 2000, he was appointed agent of the Republic of Croatia in the International Court of Justice trial against the Federal Republic of Yugoslavia on genocide charges. Šimonović served as senior vice president and president of the UN's Economic and Social Council from 2001 to 2003. Šimonović was born in 1959 in Zagreb. He has a law degree and a master's degree in public administration and politics. He earned his PhD from the University of Zagreb.

Reassessing Solitary Confinement

By Anthony Graves

In testimony presented to the Senate Judiciary Committee's Subcommittee on the Constitution, Civil Rights, and Human Rights, exonerated Texas death row inmate Anthony Graves describes life in solitary confinement and advocates for prison reform. Graves provides detailed accounts of his life in solitary confinement. Of the eighteen-and-a-half years he was on death row, Graves says at least ten elapsed without having any physical contact with another human being. He speaks of his eight-by-twelve-foot cell, sleep deprivation, and nutritionally-lacking meals that left him with over thirteen percent plaque in his arteries. Graves, whose 1994 conviction was dismissed in 2010, says he has known fellow death row inmates who dropped their appeals just to escape the conditions of life in solitary confinement. It drives inmates mad, Graves says, and gradually strips them of their humanity over time. He says that solitary confinement makes the "criminal justice system the criminal," and calls conditions in solitary cells "inhumane." Graves closes by talking about the lasting psychological impact living in solitary confinement has had on him.

My name is Anthony Graves and I am death row exoneree number 138. I was wrongfully convicted and sentenced to death in Texas back in 1992, where my nightmare began. Like all death row inmates, I was kept in solitary confinement. I lived under some of the worst conditions imaginable with the filth, the food, the total disrespect of human dignity. I lived under the rules of a system that is literally driving men out of their minds. I was one week away from my 27th birthday when I was arrested, and this emotional torture took place for the next 18.5 years. I survived the torture by believing in my innocence and hoping that they would make it right. My life was saved, but those 18.5 years were no way to live.

I lived in a small 8 by 12 foot cage. I had a steel bunk bed, with a very thin plastic mattress and pillow that you could only trade out once a year. By the time a year comes around, you've been virtually sleeping on the steel itself. I have back problems as a result. I had a steel toilet and sink that were connected together, and it was positioned in the sight of male and female officers. They would walk the runs and I would be in plain view while using the toilet.

I had a small shelf that I was able to use as a desk to write on. This was the same shelf that I ate at. There was a very small window up at the top of the back wall. In order to see the sky or the back of the building you would have to roll your plastic mattress up to stand on. I had concrete walls that were always

---

Delivered June 19, 2012, at the US Senate Judiciary Committee Hearing, Washington, DC, by Anthony Graves.

7

> *Solitary confinement does one thing: it breaks a man's will to live and he ends up deteriorating. He's never the same person again.*

peeling with old dull paint. It's the image of an old abandoned one room project apartment.

I lived behind a steel door that had two small slits in it, the space replaced with iron mesh wire, which was dirty and filthy. Those slits were cut out to communicate with the officers that were right outside your door. There was a slot that's called a pan hole and that's how you would receive your food. I had to sit on my steel bunk like a trained dog while the officer delivered my food tray. He would take a steel crow bar and stick it into the metal lock on the pan hole, it would fall open, which then allowed the officer to place your tray in the slot. Afterward, he then steps back, which was the signal for me to get off the bunk and retrieve my food. This is no different from the way we train our pets.

The food lacks the proper nutrition, because it is either dehydrated when served to you or perhaps you'll find things like rat feces or a small piece of broken glass. When escorted to the infirmary I would walk by the kitchen and see an inmate cooking the food and sweating into it. The inmates who do have a little support from the outside usually try to only eat the food they can purchase from the prison commissary. There is no real medical care. After I was exonerated and able to go to a doctor, I was told that the food I had been eating caused me to have over 13 percent plaque in my veins, which can cause strokes, heart attacks, and aneurysms. I had no television, no telephone, and most importantly, I had no physical contact with another human being for at least 10 of the 18 years I was incarcerated. Today I have a hard time being around a group of people for long periods of time without feeling too crowded. No one can begin to imagine the psychological effects isolation has on another human being.

I was subjected to sleep deprivation. I would hear the clanging of metal doors throughout the night, an officer walking the runs and shining his flash light in your eyes, or an inmate kicking and screaming because he's losing his mind. Guys become paranoid, schizophrenic, and can't sleep because they are hearing voices. I was there when guys would attempt suicide by cutting themselves, trying to tie a sheet around their neck or overdosing on their medication. Then there were the guys that actually committed suicide.

I will have to live with these vivid memories for the rest of my life. I would watch guys come to prison totally sane and in three years they don't live in the real world anymore. I know a guy who would sit in the middle of the floor, rip his sheet up, wrap it around himself and light it on fire. Another guy would go out in the recreation yard, get naked, lie down and urinate all over himself. He would take his feces and smear it all over his face as though he was in military combat. This same man was executed; on the gurney and he was babbling incoherently to the officers, "I demand that you release me soldier, this is your captain speaking." These were the words coming out of a man's mouth, who was driven insane by the prison conditions, as the poison was being pumped into his arms. He was ruled competent to be executed.

I knew guys who dropped their appeals; not because they gave up hope on their legal claims but because of the intolerable conditions. I was able to visit another inmate before he was executed. I went there to lift his spirits and he ended up telling me that he was ready to go, and that I am the one who is going to have to keep dealing with this madness. He would rather die than continue existing under such inhumane conditions.

Solitary confinement does one thing: it breaks a man's will to live and he ends up deteriorating. He's never the same person again. Then his mother comes to see her son sitting behind plexiglass, whom she hasn't been able to touch in years, and she has to watch as her child deteriorates right in front of her eyes. This madness has a ripple effect. It doesn't just affect the inmate; it also affects his family, his children, his siblings and most importantly his mother. I have been free for almost two years and I still cry at night, because no one out here can relate to what I have gone through. I battle with feelings of loneliness. I've tried therapy but it didn't work. The therapist was crying more than me. She couldn't believe that our system was putting men through this sort of inhumane treatment.

I haven't had a good night sleep since my release. My mind and body are having a hard time making the adjustment. I have mood swings that cause emotional breakdowns. Solitary confinement makes our criminal justice system the criminal.

It is inhumane and by its design it is driving men insane. I am living amongst millions of people in the world today, but most of the time I feel alone. I cry at night because of this feeling. I just want to stop feeling this way, but I haven't been able to.

[End of Testimony.]

About Anthony Graves

Anthony Graves is a former death row inmate from Texas who was exonerated in October 2010. He has since worked as an investigator for the Texas Defender Service, a nonprofit organization aimed at improving representation for defendants facing the death penalty. In August 1992, Graves was arrested after Robert Carter of Brenham, Texas, named him as Carter's accomplice in the murder of Bobbie Davis, Davis's daughter, and her four grandchildren. In the time between Graves's arrest and trial, Carter made several recantations regarding Graves's involvement. However, he implicated Graves in his trial testimony nonetheless. Graves was convicted and sentenced to death in November 1994. While incarcerated, Graves maintained his innocence and made repeated attempts to secure a post-conviction hearing. When Carter was executed in May 2000, his last words asserted Graves's innocence. In March 2006, the US Court of Appeals for the Fifth Circuit voided Graves's conviction and sentence. His case was reinvestigated and retried, and all charges against Graves were dismissed on October 27, 2010.

Human Trafficking and Forced Labor

By Mohamed Matter

In a speech delivered before the Tom Lantos Human Rights Commission in the House of Representatives, Dr. Mohamed Mattar, executive director of the Protection Project at Johns Hopkins University, discusses the status of human trafficking in the Arab world. Mattar first describes some of the work the Protection Project has done, including the training of judges and prosecutors on the rights of trafficking victims, the implementation of a national action plan to fight human trafficking in Egypt, and the establishment of law school clinics to draw up legislation protecting the rights of domestic workers. Human trafficking manifests in many forms, according to Mattar, with marginalized populations like immigrants, women, and children at particular risk. Foreign laborers—who comprise nearly 67 percent of the labor force in Persian Gulf countries—are especially vulnerable to exploitation, says Mattar. In many Arab countries, he explains, existing labor laws don't cover domestic workers, who represent 5.6 percent of total employment in the region. Mattar goes on to detail the challenges faced by those combatting human trafficking. Political instability, he says, perpetuates a favorable environment for traffickers. He gives ten recommendations for contributing to and improving the efficacy of existing systems to fight human trafficking in the Arab region, and closes by urging US officials to continue to work with Arab governments in their efforts to battle human trafficking.

Distinguished members of the Commission, thank you for allowing me the honor of testifying before you today on behalf of The Protection Project at The Johns Hopkins University School of Advanced International Studies on the status of human trafficking in the Arab region.

I am proud of the work of The Protection Project in combating human trafficking in different Arab countries, training prosecutors and judges in Saudi Arabia on the rights of victims of trafficking, implementing the national action plan to combat human trafficking in Egypt, educating religious leaders in Lebanon on human trafficking as a form of exploitation, establishing law clinics in law schools in Qatar, Oman, and Kuwait to draft laws on the rights of domestic workers, working with civil society in Jordan to adopt model laws on the establishment and operation of NGOs and cooperating with academic institutions in Iraq on the rights of the vulnerable people including victims of human trafficking.

Human trafficking, or trafficking in persons, takes many forms in the Arab World, including slavery, begging, domestic servitude, forced labor, temporary

---

Delivered November 28, 2012, at the Rayburn House Office Building, Washington, DC, by Mohamed Matter.

marriage, child marriage, sale of children for the purpose of adoption, prostitution, recruitment into armed forces, and trafficking of organs. In Egypt, an estimated two hundred thousand to one million street children are recruited into forced begging. Foreign laborers represent 66.9 percent of the total labor force in Gulf countries and they may be subject to exploitation. In Kuwait, Bahrain, Qatar, and the United Arab Emirates, foreign workers constitute over 75 percent of the labor force. Their inability to attain access to justice or seek adequate restitution is an egregious flaw within the *kafala* or "sponsorship system," and one which is inconsistent with international human rights standards. Domestic workers represent 5.6 percent of total employment in the Arab region. In Lebanon, there are currently 1.2 million foreign workers, mostly from Southeast Asia. Of those, 400,000 are employed as domestic workers who are typically not covered by existing labor laws, making them vulnerable to abuse and forced labor. The often indistinct identification of trafficking as smuggling further compounds the challenge in both correct identification of the issue and in utilizing an appropriate legal and social response.

I am encouraged by the many steps that have been taken to combat the problem since the passage of the United Nations Protocol to Prevent, Suppress, and Punish Trafficking in Persons, Especially Women and Children of 2000. The Qatar Foundation to Combat Human Trafficking is implementing a three-year Arab initiative to enhance the capacity of Arab parliamentarians, law enforcement officials and members of civil society to combat human trafficking. The Human Rights Commission in Saudi Arabia is chairing a unit to raise awareness about human trafficking in accordance with the principles of Islam and international legal standards. The National Coordinating Committee to Prevent and Combat Human Trafficking in Egypt is implementing a comprehensive action plan that focuses on the rights of the victims of trafficking.

Many Arab states are creating specific human trafficking units within their national police or organizing human rights commissions that tackle human trafficking through a multi-faceted approach. In the United Arab Emirates, the government's inter-ministerial National Committee to Combat Human Trafficking trains judges, law enforcement officials, and staff of the government's social services agency on human trafficking issues.

In Saudi Arabia, the Ministry of Labour has established an Expatriate Workers' Welfare Department, a decision by the Council of Ministers to restructure the relationship between workers and employers by prohibiting sequestration of a worker's passport and removing the term "sponsor" from the Residence Regulation. In addition to the Human Rights Commission, the National Anti- Corruption Commission was established to combat crimes of corruption, including crimes committed by public officials and involving trafficking in persons.

Despite the many steps forward, the challenges remain great as the result of conflicts which aggravate political instability and perpetuate infrastructure that is conducive to human trafficking. The War in Iraq, the conflict in Syria and regional instability following the Arab Spring in Egypt, Tunisia, Libya, Syria, and Yemen have exacerbated human rights challenges as both a result of the conflict itself and lapses in existing domestic legal frameworks.

Of the large numbers of Iraqi refugees, women in particular may be forced into prostitution by their families through so-called temporary marriages. Family members have coerced girls and women into prostitution to escape desperate economic circumstances, to pay debts, or to resolve disputes between families. Traffickers are increasingly targeting the Iraqi refugee population, with some Iraqi women and girls exploited by their families.

Increased instability and a void of effective control in Syria deepen Iraqi women's and girls' vulnerability to trafficking. As the conflict in Syria continues, I am concerned by increasing reports of Syrian children being used as child soldiers and the growing exploitation of children in organized street begging rings. I am also concerned that with the political unrest in Egypt, less attention will be devoted to the problem of human trafficking. This is particularly relevant in the Sinai. Since the revolution, police have largely been unable to control the Sinai, leaving refugees and migrants vulnerable to exploitation and trafficking by Bedouin gangs. The new Egyptian government must understand that an uncontrolled Sinai undermines Egyptian stability, is at odds with international legal obligations, and violates protected international human rights.

Existing domestic frameworks exhibit many gaps in adequately preventing trafficking, protecting victims, and prosecuting offenders. Many Arab governments have not developed a systematic approach to identifying victims or those who may be vulnerable, including those arrested for prostitution or foreign workers. Victims who are arrested for prostitution are not often recognized as victims of trafficking. In some Arab states, foreign trafficking victims are not offered legal alternatives to removal to countries in which they face hardship or retribution nor are victims actively encouraged to assist law enforcement in investigations against traffickers.

Improved data collection by the government agencies or nongovernmental organizations within Arab states can significantly improve the response to violations of human trafficking in the region. At present, few countries provide accurate data on migrant flows, most available data is outdated, and cases of human trafficking and smuggling are resoundingly conflated, delivering misleading representations of each issue in the country.

Consequently, the path is difficult.

I am proposing ten recommendations that I believe will contribute to the existing mechanisms that have already been created to ensure their effective implementation and to mobilize the various stakeholders who are engaged in combating human trafficking in the region.

First, expand the role of civil society in combating human trafficking in the Arab region, including academic institutions, corporations, media, nongovernmental organizations, and religious institutions, which must function freely and properly without restrictions or limitations. Following the approval of a new constitution in 2011, Morocco's legal environment enables civil society organizations and provides no outright restrictions on operations, while still maintaining the religious integrity of the State. However, NGOs in other parts of the Arab world may be restricted in obtaining a license to engage in advocacy for human rights including the rights of victims of trafficking. They may also be subject to termination without any judicial oversight. Many NGOs operating in the Arab world are not allowed to receive foreign funding, which further restricts their capability to carry out any programs or initiatives to enhance human rights in the region. Using the Moroccan model, we should encourage Arab states to recognize the potential for partnerships with civil society and the necessity of a supportive domestic framework that will allow them to flourish.

Second, utilize the good principles of Islam, Judaism and Christianity that play an important role in the lives of all Arabs. Islamic scholarly opinions, or *Fatwas,* have been issued on topics related to trafficking and forced labor, and have had important implications for cultural attitude and social response. In a *Fatwa* issued on September 3, 2001, by the Saudi Arabian Grand Mufti regarding the Abuse of Foreign Labor by Saudi employers, it was stated, "Blackmailing and threatening [foreign] laborers with deportation if they refuse the employers' terms, which breach the contract, is not allowed." In a *Fatwa* issued by Sheik Youssef el Qaradawi, in March 2008 on the sponsorship rule: "The [s]sponsorship system nowadays produced visas market[s], leaving tens [sic] of workers living in subhuman conditions, as a large number of laborers are accommodated in small areas. It is really a shame and also it is against the Islamic principles which call for respecting human rights." Most recently, in a *Fatwa* issued on July 5, 2011, by Abdul Nasser Abu Basal, President of the World Islamic Sciences and Education University: "When trafficking occurs in an organized manner and on a large scale, the punishment should be the same as the punishment for highway robbery." Similar *Fatwas* should be encouraged to influence human behavior and emphasize the call of religion to condemn human exploitation.

Third, move beyond specific anti-trafficking legislation to trafficking-related laws including child protection laws, laws on violence against women, laws that enhance access to justice, laws that guarantee access to information, and labor laws that do not discriminate against foreign labor and provide protection to all forms of labor, including domestic work. As I always argue, only when human rights are enhanced and fully guaranteed for the people of the Middle East will human trafficking be successfully confronted and eliminated.

Fourth, fill the gaps in the domestic legislative framework. Currently, the following Arab states have human trafficking legislation: Syria, United Arab Emirates, Algeria, Bahrain, Djibouti, Egypt, Jordan, Mauritania, Oman, Saudi Arabia, Qatar, Iraq, and Lebanon. We should provide technical assistance to Tunisia, Yemen, Sudan, Palestine, Morocco, Libya and Kuwait, who are currently drafting anti-trafficking legislation. States should also consider enhancing the penalty in cases of aggravated circumstances, such as when the perpetrator of the crime is taking advantage of a vulnerable victim who has no alternative but to submit to exploitation.

Fifth, ratify International Labour Convention No. 189 on Decent Work for Domestic Workers, which has entered into force after Uruguay and the Philippines deposited the two needed instruments for ratification. We should also advise Arab states to ratify the Optional Protocol to the Convention on the Elimination of All Forms of Discrimination against Women. In addition, we should urge countries that still did not ratify the International Covenant on Civil and Political Rights and the International Covenant on Economic, Social and Cultural Rights to ratify these international conventions.

Sixth, cooperate with the League of Arab States, which provides the collective platform of human rights for all Arab states. Recently, the Arab League adopted the Strategy to Combat Human Trafficking, a model law on combating human trafficking, and established a specific unit that will receive reports from the Arab countries on the status of human trafficking. We should work with the Arab League to enhance these enforcement mechanisms.

Seventh, implement the Arab Charter on Human Rights.

Article 9 of the Arab Charter states:

No one shall be subjected to medical or scientific experimentation or to the use of his organs without his free consent and full awareness of the consequences and provided that ethical, humanitarian and professional rules are followed and medical procedures are observed to ensure his personal safety pursuant to the relevant domestic laws in force in each state party. Trafficking in human organs is prohibited in all circumstances.

Article 10 of the Arab Charter states:

All forms of slavery and trafficking in human beings are prohibited and are punishable by law. No one shall be held in slavery and servitude under any circumstances.

Forced labor, trafficking in human beings for the purpose of prostitution or sexual exploitation, the exploitation of the prostitution of others or any other form of exploitation or the exploitation of children in armed conflict are prohibited.

These articles must be read in accordance with Article 43 of the Arab Charter, which provides that:

Nothing in this Charter may be construed or interpreted as impairing the rights and freedoms protected by the domestic laws of the States parties or those set forth in the international and regional human rights instruments which the States parties have adopted or ratified, including the rights of women, the rights of the child and the rights of persons belonging to minorities.

Consequently, Articles 9 and 10 of the Arab Charter should be interpreted in accordance with the United Nations Protocol on Trafficking.

Eighth, work with human rights institutions to maintain combating human trafficking as a priority. We should be providing the necessary training to the Saudi Arabian Human Rights Commission, the Qatar National Human Rights Commission, and similar human rights organizations in the various Arab states. This is imperative in light of the recent developments in the region that may otherwise challenge government resources. I am encouraged by the new draft of the Egyptian Constitution. In Article 71, human trafficking is explicitly prohibited, especially forced labor and sexual exploitation. We should encourage other Arab countries that are in the process of drafting a new constitution to incorporate anti-trafficking provisions in new legislative frameworks.

> *In some Arab states, foreign trafficking victims are not offered legal alternatives to removal to countries in which they face hardship or retribution nor are victims actively encouraged to assist law enforcement in investigations against traffickers.*

Ninth, enhance the capacity of anti-trafficking units that have been established by the government to combat human trafficking. These units must receive training especially on investigating and prosecuting cases of human trafficking. This training should include judges, police, lawyers, and law enforcement officials. It is noted that few prosecutions have been reported. Our prosecutors in the United States can serve as a valuable asset in providing technical support for such training in the Arab region.

And finally, educate law enforcement and service providers on the rights of victims to ensure that they are not penalized for unlawful acts committed as a direct result of being trafficked. Victims' rights can be protected further by increasing efforts to consistently and correctly identify victims of trafficking. The ultimate goal of any strategy to combat human trafficking is to protect our victims and to ensure that they are receiving the proper assistance and care. Only when we rescue victims of human trafficking and provide them with full and adequate protection, can we make the claim that we are succeeding in combating human trafficking.

The United States, through the Office to Monitor and Combat Trafficking in Persons, and through the mechanisms embodied in the Trafficking in Persons Report, has been instrumental in engaging the Arab governments in their efforts to combat human trafficking. This US engagement should continue, especially in light of the recent political developments in the region.

About Mohamed Mattar

Mohamed Mattar has been the executive director since 2005 of the Protection Project, a not-for-profit human rights institute at the Johns Hopkins University School of Advanced International Studies (SAIS). There, he leads efforts to combat human trafficking and to promote global compliance with human rights standards. In addition to his work with the Protection Project, Mattar teaches international and comparative law as well as a variety of other law courses at American University, Indiana University, Johns Hopkins SAIS, and Georgetown University. He is also a visiting professor at the Arab

University of Beirut in Lebanon. Mattar was born on January 19, 1957, in Alexandria, Egypt. As an undergraduate, Mattar attended Alexandria University Faculty of Law, earning a bachelor of law degree in 1978. He received his master of comparative laws and master of law degrees from the University of Miami and Tulane University, respectively, before earning his doctor of juridical sciences degree from Tulane in 1986.

Why We Need to Close Guantanamo

By Elisa Massimino

In an address to the United States Senate Subcommittee on the Constitution, Civil Rights, and Human Rights, the president and CEO of Human Rights First, Elisa Massimino, explains how abuses at the Guantanamo Bay Detention Center in Cuba, established in the wake of the terrorist attacks of September 11, 2001, contradict the humanitarian values of the United States. She illustrates the human rights abuses occurring at Guantanamo by reading letters written by relatives of prisoners, collected by Reprieve, a human rights organization that represents fifteen prisoners in Guantanamo Bay. One of the letters concerns a man who has been a prisoner at Guantanamo for more than a decade without charge or trial. Massimino outlines logical reasons for closing Guantanamo, including the impending end of US combat operations in Afghanistan in 2014.

Chairman Durbin, Ranking Member Cruz and Members of the Subcommittee, thank you for inviting me to be here today to share my perspective on the national security, fiscal and human rights implications of our policies at the Guantanamo Bay Detention Center. We are deeply grateful to this subcommittee and to you, Mr. Chairman, for your leadership on this and so many other human rights issues. Your tireless commitment to keeping human rights on the agenda of the United States Congress helps to ensure that our nation lives up to its ideals, and can lead the world by example.

My name is Elisa Massimino. I am the President and Chief Executive Officer of Human Rights First. Human Rights First is one of the nation's leading advocacy and action organizations, and the only group whose central mission is to advance American global leadership on human rights. We believe that upholding human rights is not only a moral obligation; it is a vital national interest. America is strongest when our policies and actions match our values. For 35 years, Human Rights First has worked to ensure that our country is a beacon on human rights in a world that sorely needs American leadership.

In a world that for many is characterized by tyranny, war, and injustice, the United States stands as a beacon. Despite our many failings, the United States has a long history of advancing human rights, having played a leading role in developing the international laws and standards that define and enforce them, and continuing today by protecting refugees and supporting human rights defenders on the frontlines of the struggle for freedom in many countries around the world. Domestically,

Delivered July 24, 2013, at the hearing on closing Guantanamo before the United States Senate Subcommittee on the Constitution, Civil Rights, and Human Rights, Washington, DC, by Elisa Massimino.

respect for freedom, democracy, and the rule of law defines our political culture and constitutional system, setting an example for people around the world who seek to advance democracy and human rights in their own societies.

A glaring exception to this narrative is the post-9/11 abuses committed by our government, defined largely by Guantanamo and the torture of detainees in US custody. It's hard to overstate how much this has undermined our country's moral standing and credibility. In my role as the head of an international human rights organization, the scenarios in which I most often hear about Guantanamo are not in our domestic political debates here at home or in our courts. I hear Guantanamo raised by officials of repressive governments who use it to deflect criticism of their own policies by charging hypocrisy. And I hear about Guantanamo from human rights defenders around the world who tell me that the best thing the United States can do to support their bids for freedom and democracy is to make sure that our country can lead by example, including closing Guantanamo. Three years ago, I brought two dozen human rights and democracy activists from around the world to the White House to meet with President Obama, and that's exactly what they told him.

The ability of the United States to credibly push other governments to respect human rights is seriously compromised when we have failed to correct the post-9/11 abuses that have cast a shadow on America's foreign policy over the last decade. And that shadow will continue to loom large until Guantanamo is closed, and the policies of indefinite detention and military commission trials are ended.

There have been instances in the life of our relatively young country when we have pursued policies out of fear that we later realize are inconsistent with our values. Sometimes it takes hearing the perspective of those outside our national community, who know the values for which we hold ourselves out, to remind us of who we are. Consider the perspective of some family members of Guantanamo detainees. Several have written letters to you in advance of this hearing, and I want to read a few excerpts from them. Nabil Hadjarab is an Algerian man who has been detained at Guantanamo for over a decade without charge or trial. He has been unanimously cleared for transfer by our government's security and intelligence agencies. Here's what his uncle Ahmed Hadjarab wrote:

> I must admit that my perception of the United States of America has been severely tarnished by this issue. When in 2002, I was told that Nabil was detained by the Americans, I thought that at least he would have a right to a fair trial. I thought his rights would be respected and that justice would prevail. What I feel today is mostly incomprehension. How can this nation, one that prides itself of defending Human Rights, close its eyes to these violations of its founding principles?

Hisham Sliti from Tunisia has been held in Guantanamo for more than a decade without charge or trial. He has also been cleared for transfer. His mother, Maherzia Sliti, wrote:

> One of the worst things is the uncertainty, and the false hope that things are about to change. Sometimes I hear rumors that men have been released from Guantanamo

and that Hisham is one of them. I miss and love my son so much that although my mind knows the rumors are probably false, my heart believes them every time. And every time I am devastated when I realize he is not coming home. I do not understand why my son is still in Guantanamo after all these years, when we know he has been cleared. We never thought the United States was the kind of place where people could be held like this.

Ahmed Belbacha, an Algerian, has been held since 2002 without charge or trial. He has been cleared for transfer. His brother Mohammed Belbacha wrote:

> My family is horrified at how Ahmed and others in Guantanamo have been treated. Algerian youth has long looked up to America for its democracy and respect for human rights. We always associated a lot of good with it. But now, America has lost its standing not just with our family, but with Algerian youth as a whole. Arbitrary arrest, detention without trial, renditions and torturous interrogation methods have cast a dark stain upon America's reputation.

These excerpts come from letters collected by Reprieve, a human rights organization that currently represents fifteen prisoners in Guantanamo Bay and has provided assistance for many more. Attorneys and family members of Guantanamo detainees submitted the full versions of these and other letters to the hearing record. I encourage you to read them. I raise these issues of justice and America's moral standing in the world because I want to be clear that what's at stake in figuring out a way to close Guantanamo is our ability to lead by example, and our reputation for upholding justice and the rule of law.

There are some who say that we need Guantanamo to hold and interrogate detainees that can't be tried in civilian court because they were captured by our military on the battlefield. But the military has never needed Guantanamo for battlefield captures; those detainees have typically been held in detention facilities in theater. Moreover, the vast majority of terrorism suspects captured abroad are dealt with by the security and law enforcement services of our foreign counterparts, and that's how it should be. Since 9/11, more than 120,000 suspected terrorists have been arrested around the world, and more than 35,000 have been convicted.[1] Our military cannot—and should not—be the world's police force or jailor.

In cases in which we have needed to detain, interrogate, and jail terrorism suspects, our civilian system has handled these cases remarkably well. Since 9/11, civilian federal courts have handled nearly 500 cases related to international terrorism, including at least 67 where suspects were captured abroad,[2] often in inhospitable environments. Despite claims to the contrary, there is no credible evidence that trying these cases in civilian courts has caused breaches of sensitive national security information, or invited attacks on US soil.

Nor does the civilian process preclude us from obtaining actionable intelligence to disrupt terrorism plots. The administration has established a High-Value Interrogation Group (HIG) that has been deployed in a number of cases to interrogate terrorism suspects using lawful and effective methods. Even in more routine

Since 9/11, more than 120,000 suspected terrorists have been arrested around the world, and more than 35,000 have been convicted. Our military cannot—and should not—be the world's police force or jailor.

terrorism cases, and in situations where Miranda rights and other due process protections are respected, offering plea deals and working with the defendant's family and lawyers, in addition to lawful interrogations, have produced a wealth of actionable intelligence information, including: telephone numbers and email addresses used by al Qaeda and other terrorist groups; information about al Qaeda communications methods and security protocols; information about their recruiting and financing methods; the location of al Qaeda training camps and safe houses; information on al Qaeda weapons programs; the identities of operatives involved in past attacks; and information about future plots to attack US interests.[3] By contrast, detention and trial at Guantanamo has proven highly problematic on several levels. Since 9/11, only 7 detainees have been convicted by military commission. Two of those convictions were recently overturned by a federal appeals court because the crimes with which the detainees were charged were not war crimes—the only acts over which military commissions have jurisdiction—at the time the offenses were committed. More broadly, in contrast to the civilian system, in Guantanamo—where detention is indefinite and Congress has made it difficult to effect transfers out of the prison—there is not the same kind of leverage (e.g., offering release or shorter detention in exchange for cooperation) to exploit with detainees.

There are other pragmatic reasons to move forward with closing Guantanamo. The impending end of combat operations in Afghanistan in 2014 increases the urgency for Congress and the administration to determine the disposition of all law-of-war detainees. The detainees at Guantanamo were apprehended and detained pursuant to the 2001 Authorization for Use of Military Force. As hostilities come to an end, Guantanamo detainees will have a legitimate claim before the courts that they should be released. Congress and the administration should proactively determine the lawful disposition of detainees now, or the courts could force those dispositions later.

There has long been a national security consensus that Guantanamo should be closed. More than 50 retired generals and admirals, along with three Secretaries of Defense—Gates, Panetta and Hagel—have called for Guantanamo to be closed. Today's witnesses underscore that many senior military leaders believe that closing Guantanamo is a national security imperative.

As a national security issue, closing Guantanamo should be beyond politics. And it has been in the past. In 2008, there was significant bipartisan consensus that Guantanamo should be closed. Then-President Bush said he wanted to close Guantanamo,[4] as did then-candidates Obama and McCain.[5] That consensus has started to re-emerge, with Senator McCain recently stating that Guantanamo should be closed, and emphasizing that it would be an "act of courage" to transfer detainees out of Guantanamo and into the United States as part of a plan to close the facility.

And Guantanamo can be closed—safely and securely. This is not to say that closing Guantanamo will be easy—if were, Guantanamo would already be closed. There are difficult legal, practical, and political problems that must be addressed to move forward.

But there is a pragmatic path forward to close Guantanamo, if the administration and Congress demonstrate sustained and focused leadership to get the job done.

I want to spend a few minutes outlining this path forward.

In 2009, President Obama signed an executive order establishing an interagency taskforce to conduct a review and recommend lawful dispositions of the detainees being held at Guantanamo.[6] Since then, 72 prisoners have been transferred, repatriated or resettled, and a number of other detainees have died—either by suicide or other causes—bringing the current detainee population down to 166.[7] Transfers have stalled in part because of restrictions imposed by Congress in 2010, 2011 and 2012, and because the administration has failed to exercise the authority Congress gave it in 2012 under the National Defense Authorization Act to waive the transfer restrictions by invoking, among other requirements, national security interests.

Concerns about recidivism—the possibility that a released detainee may "return to the fight"[8]—are understandable, as they are in the criminal context. But, as many analysts have detailed, the claims about recidivism of detainees who have already been released are inflated. The claim by members of Congress and some in the media that 28 percent of former Guantanamo detainees have "rejoined the fight" or "returned to the battlefield"[9] is highly misleading. It appears to be based on unreliable or unconfirmed reports of suspected activities, and in any event includes detainees that may not have participated in any terrorist plots or attacks. The process to evaluate potential transfers has changed since the prior administration to more accurately capture post-transfer risk, leading to fewer cases of recidivism for detainees transferred by the Obama administration. The Director of National Intelligence's recidivism assessment should be revised to more accurately reflect the circumstances in which former detainees that have engaged in terrorist plots or attacks against the United States so that evaluation—and mitigation—of this risk is grounded in reality, not hyperbole.

Nonetheless, as senior military commanders have told me, transfers of detainees from Guantanamo—just as transfers of detainees out of detention facilities in Iraq and Afghanistan—have always been about risk management, not risk elimination. Some detainees pose little risk; others will pose more. Establishing a "zero tolerance for risk" policy with respect to individual detainees is neither wise nor necessary. Our military, intelligence, law enforcement, and diplomatic agencies, along with those of our foreign counterparts, can significantly mitigate the risks of transferring detainees out of Guantanamo through security assurances, monitoring, rehabilitation and other reasonable measures. The risks associated with keeping Guantanamo open are harder to mitigate, and the harm is potentially far more lasting.

Notes

1. Martha Mendoza, Global Terrorism: 35,000 Worldwide Convicted For Terror Offenses Since September 11 Attacks, AP, September 3, 2011, available at: http://www.huffingtonpost.com/2011/09/03/terrorismconvictions- since-sept-11_n_947865.html.
2. Deborah Pearlstein, Counterterrorism in Court, *OPINIO JURIS*, March 25, 2013, available at: http://opiniojuris.org/2013/03/25/counterterrorism-in-court/.
3. David Kris, Law Enforcement as a Counterterrorism Tool, *JOURNAL OF NATIONAL SECURITY LAW AND POLICY*, June 2011, at 85, available at: http://jnslp.com/wpcontent/ uploads/2011/06/01_David-Kris.pdf.
4. Bush Says He Wants To Close Guantanamo, *CBS NEWS/AP*, February 11, 2009, available at: http://www.cbsnews.com/2100-250_162-1596464.html.
5. The Candidates on Military Tribunals and Guantanamo Bay, *COUNCIL ON FOREIGN RELATIONS*, August 24, 2008, available at: http://www.cfr.org/world/candidates-military-tribunals-guantanamo-bay/p14751.
6. Guantanamo Review Task Force, Final Report, January 22, 2010, available at: http://www.justice.gov/ag/guantanamo-review-final-report.pdf.
7. Sarah Childress, Four Obama Policies That Help Keep Guantanamo Open, *PBS/FRONTLINE*, May 1, 2013, available at: http://www.pbs.org/wgbh/pages/frontline/foreign-affairs-defense/four-obama-policiesthat-help-keep-guantanamo-open/.
8. The term *recidivism* is used in this testimony solely because of its widespread use in the detainee transfer context. However, the term is inaccurate here for two reasons. First, many detainees did not commit any crimes or acts of terrorism prior to being detained at Guantanamo and therefore any future act of terrorism would not constitute "recidivism." Second, as is noted in the testimony, much of the conduct that is counted as recidivist does not actually entail criminal or terrorist activity.
9. Senator Kelly Ayotte, Floor Speech on Counterterrorism Policy (November 29, 2012), available at: http://www.c-spanvideo.org/clip/4179700.

About Elisa Massimino

Elisa Massimino is currently the CEO and Executive Director of Human Rights First, a leading human rights advocacy organization. She was appointed in September 2008. Prior to this position, Massimino served as an attorney for Human Rights First and as the organization's Washington director from 1997 to 2008. Massimino earned her bachelor's degree in philosophy from Trinity University in 1982 and her master's in philosophy from Johns Hopkins University in 1984. She also holds a law degree from the University of Michigan Law School. Massimino is an adjunct law professor at Georgetown University where she teaches human rights advocacy. In addition she teaches refugee and asylum law at George Washington University and law courses on terrorism and human rights at American University. She has also taught international human rights law at the University of Virginia. Previously, she worked as an attorney in the Washington-based law firm Hogan & Hartson. Massimino frequently testifies before Congress on issues concerning human rights and policy law, and she has appeared on a number of media outlets, including ABC News, MSNBC, National Public Radio, and the BBC.

Ending Gender Inequality Leads to a More Perfect Union

By Bill Clinton

In his acceptance speech at the 2013 GLAAD Media Awards in Los Angeles, California, former US president Bill Clinton speaks about the importance of equality in creating a more perfect union. He encourages the American people to keep moving forward in the fight to defeat the Defense of Marriage Act (DOMA) and achieve marriage equality, and he commends Edith Windsor, plaintiff in the 2013 Supreme Court case United States v. Windsor, *for her efforts. Decided in June 2013,* United States v. Windsor *struck down the portion of DOMA that prohibited federal recognition of same-sex marriage, although the law's provisions allowing states to refuse to recognize such unions still stands. Clinton also asserts the need to pass the Employment Non-Discrimination Act (ENDA), which would prevent discrimination on the bases of sexual orientation or gender identity in hiring and employment. Clinton thanks his daughter, Chelsea, for her impact on his acceptance of gay people; he tells of her gay friends that he now considers a part of his extended family. He asserts that people who oppose equal rights for homosexuals are acting out of concern for their own identity, rather than any real concern about anyone else.*

I want to thank GLADD for the award and congratulate the other honorees. I was very impressed by the speech of my predecessor up here, and I cannot hope to equal it. But I would like to say amen to it, it was quite wonderful. Steve Warren and Dean Hansell really deserve their awards.

I think that the staff, board of directors, and the most active supporters of GLADD deserve the award I'm getting, because they are the real agents of change. They had this idea, a long time ago. There'd be a lot of people lobbying Congress, but somebody ought to be personalizing and humanizing these issues for the LGBT community. They actually believed you could reach the human heart; they actually believed that people could think and feel differently, because we are after all a country founded on the principle that all of us were created equal, and therefore endowed with certain rights. A country with the Constitution guaranteed us equal rights under the law; a country with founders who understood that we were nowhere near living up to our ideals when we got started. When we got started, only white, male property owners could vote. And the whole, long history of America is just what the founders pledged their lives, fortunes, and sacred honor to, a journey toward a more perfect union. Now, when that phrase was used in the eighteenth

---

Delivered April 22, 2013, at the GLAAD Media Awards, Los Angeles, California, by Bill Clinton.

century, it had a very distinct meaning at that time. Lives, fortunes, and sacred honor were pledged to the proposition that the Enlightenment was real. It simply meant that a more perfect union meant that we are not now perfect, we will never be perfect, but we can always be more perfect or better than we are.

And this whole history of our country has been a history sometimes racing but usually stumbling in the right direction. All of you have helped us to be more worthy of what we said we were about in the beginning. I am very honored to join with Edie Windsor, who called and told me she couldn't be here tonight, and we are all pulling for her health. I want her to be around to celebrate her victory. And, with so many others, including President Obama, Vice-President Biden, the whole Obama administration, urging the Supreme Court to overturn the Defense of Marriage Act. I want to keep working on this until not only DOMA is no longer the law of the land but until all people, no matter where they live, can marry the people they love.

For example, when I flew here from New York, I knew I'd still be married when I got here. Heck, I'm going to Texas next week to the George W. Bush's Library dedication, and I'll still be married when I get there. You have helped me come to the place where I am tonight. That's why you are the true agents of change. But we have all learned in our interdependent society, and in our increasingly interdependent world, that whenever any people anywhere are denied any rights, it diminishes us all. That's why we were so gripped to our televisions after those bombs exploded at the Boston Marathon. That little child, that eight-year-old child, was our child. And the same is true here. I believe you will win the DOMA fight, and I think you will win the constitutional right to marry—if not tomorrow, then the next day, or the next day.

I think it's important that GLADD still has a full agenda. I supported and tried to pass ENDA without success—we still need to pass that. From what you've seen tonight, you know we still need to fight bullying, and we still need the right kind of immigration reform that does not discriminate against anybody. I thank you, by the way, for the work you've done on the scouting issue; it looks like we are half way home on that. But we are stumbling toward our more perfect union.

There is one other person I'd like to thank for this award, who I did not know was even in town until late this afternoon—that's my daughter Chelsea. She had a profound impact, in many ways, in the way I see the world. It's sort of humbling when you get to be my age and your child knows more than you do about everything. But Chelsea and her gay friends, and her wonderful husband, have modeled to me the way we all should treat each other without regard to our sexual orientation, or any other artificial difference that divides us. Many of them come and join us every Thanksgiving for a meal. I have grown quite

> *Don't you let anybody tell you otherwise—you have made this a better, a more interesting, and a more well-prepared country for the future. We need you, fully armed, for the continued struggle for equality.*

attached to them. And over the years, I was forced to confront the fact that people who oppose equal rights for gays in the marriage sphere are basically acting out of concerns for their own identity, not out of respect for anyone else. All of us see ourselves when we wake up in the morning with a complex of positive and negative feelings. Did you ever feel like you have a scale inside; some days you wake up and your afraid it's not going to be a very good day because the negative scales way more than the positive ones. And there's some days when you wake up and feel like a world-beater, and you even forget there's a negative scale inside.

This whole question of identity is going to dominate a lot of the next thirty years. We are less racist, less sexist, for all the problems we are far less homophobic than we used to be, but we have a new bigotry in America—apparently we don't want to be around anybody that disagrees with us about anything. And, all these people around the world that have chosen a clenched fist over an open hand, constant conflict over caring and creative cooperation; that's about them, that's not about the issue at hand or about other people. Whenever we turn away from treating someone else with the dignity and honor and respect we would like accorded to ourselves, we have to face that fact that it's about us. And we are afraid we wouldn't be us if we couldn't hold on to just this, that, or the other little box that no longer makes any sense, in a world where we are all crashing together. I learned that from watching my daughter, my terrific son-in-law, and their friends, and the way they have graced Hillary's life and mine, and become our friends.

So, I urge you to stay on your strategy, speak to people's minds and hearts, keep the specific agenda. When you have won DOMA, when you have won marriage equality everywhere, ask yourself—how in the world did we ever win a great cultural battle and we still can't even pass ENDA? What is wrong with this picture? Make sure this immigration law passes, but that it is fair to everybody.

The whole story in the life of our country, of a more perfect union, is to widen the circle of opportunity, to strengthen and enhance the reach of freedom, and to cement deeper bonds of community as it gets even more diverse. Don't you let anybody tell you otherwise—you have made this a better, a more interesting, and a more well-prepared country for the future. We need you, fully armed, for the continued struggle for equality. You are the agents of change. I am getting this award tonight because I was the object of your affection; or not, as the case may be. My daughter led me to support the marriage equality law in New York, when we were debating it, to oppose North Carolina's denial of marriage equality, to do all these other things. So, I want to thank her, too. Thank you GLADD, thank you Chelsea, god bless you all. Stay at the task. Thank you.

About Bill Clinton

Bill Clinton was the forty-second president of the United States, serving two terms, from 1992 to 2001. Prior to assuming the presidency, Clinton was governor of Arkansas, serving five nonconsecutive terms, from 1979 to 1981 and from 1983 to 1992, and

Arkansas attorney general from 1977 to 1979. He was born on August 19, 1946, in Hope, Arkansas, and graduated from Georgetown University in 1968. Clinton studied at Oxford University on a Rhodes Scholarship. In 1973, he received his law degree from Yale University. In 1974, he unsuccessfully campaigned to represent Arkansas's Third District in Congress. The following year, he married Hillary Rodham, who would go on to be the First Lady, a US senator from New York, and the secretary of state. Clinton's second term was rocked by scandal following the revelation of his affair with a White House intern. He was impeached in 1998 on charges related to the incident, but was found not guilty by the Senate. Since leaving the presidency he has remained active in politics and public affairs, supporting both his wife and President Barack Obama, and engaging in charitable and philanthropic initiatives in the United States and around the world.

UN Resolution on Human Rights, Sexual Orientation and Gender Identity

By Ban Ki-moon

Delivered at a United Nations special event in New York entitled Leadership in the Fight against Homophobia, UN Secretary General Ban Ki-moon outlines the many ways lesbian, gay, bisexual, and transgender (LGBT) people are discriminated against around the globe and discusses effective actions that are helping fight homophobia. Ban highlights recent improvements in government policies concerning sexual orientation and gay marriage, including Argentina's same-sex marriage legislation. He also highlights efforts to stop pending legislation that would criminalize aspects of homosexuality in countries such as Ukraine. He welcomes some of the guests at the event, including Puerto Rican pop star Ricky Martin, Ukrainian activist Olena Shevchenko, and South African singer Yvonne Chaka Chaka, thanking them for their support for LGBT rights. He calls for replacing nineteenth-century laws that he describes as a legacy of colonialism with modern, progressive laws that protect all people regardless of their sexual orientation. He further asserts that even in countries where the majority favors laws discriminating against LGBT people, the state has a responsibility to protect the basic rights of vulnerable minorities against that majority.

Thank you all for coming to this remarkable meeting. What a meaningful way to commemorate Human Rights Day. I welcome all of the activists, supporters and others here today.

The very first article of the Universal Declaration of Human Rights proclaims, "All human beings are born free and equal in dignity and rights."

All human beings—not some, not most, but all.

No one gets to decide who is entitled to human rights and who is not.

The United Nations has a proud record of combating racism, promoting gender equality, protecting children and breaking down barriers facing persons with disabilities.

We have a long way to go in all of these areas. But we are turning the tide on discrimination in both law and practice. Slowly, some old prejudices have started to dissolve.

Yet others remain in place, with horrendous consequences.

Around the world, lesbian, gay, bisexual and transgender people are targeted, assaulted and sometimes killed. Children and teens are taunted by their peers, beaten

Delivered December 11, 2012, at the United Nations special event on "Leadership in the Fight against Homophobia," New York, New York, by Ban Ki-moon.

> *It is an outrage that in our modern world, so many countries continue to criminalize people simply for loving another human being of the same sex. In many cases, these laws are not home-grown. They were inherited from former colonial powers.*

and bullied, pushed out of school, disowned by their own families, forced into marriage, and, in the worst cases, driven to suicide.

LGBT people suffer discrimination because of their sexual orientation and gender identity at work, at clinics and hospitals, and in schools—the very places that should protect them.

More than 76 countries still criminalize homosexuality.

I am pained by this injustice. I am here to again denounce violence and demand action for true equality.

Let me say this loud and clear: lesbian, gay, bisexual and transgender people are entitled to the same rights as everyone else. They, too, are born free and equal. I stand shoulder-to-shoulder with them in their struggle for human rights.

I am proud that as Secretary-General I have a global platform to highlight the need to end violence and discrimination based on sexual orientation and gender identity.

The United Nations should lead by example. I recently reiterated to all senior managers that discrimination against staff on the basis of sexual orientation will not be tolerated. I have also asked that the UN's rules and policies be examined to ensure that the rights of our LGBT staff are protected.

More and more governments are working to tackle homophobia. Last year, the Human Rights Council adopted the first UN resolution on human rights, sexual orientation and gender identity, which expressed "grave concern" at violence and discrimination against LGBT people.

The High Commissioner for Human Rights published the first UN report dedicated to the problem, which was then debated at the Human Rights Council, marking another UN first.

The past decade has seen far-reaching reforms in Europe, the Americas and a number of Asian and African countries, and extraordinary shifts in social attitudes in many parts of the world.

I applaud Argentina for introducing some of the most progressive legislation in the world on same-sex partnerships and gender recognition. I am pleased that we are joined today by Blas Radi, from Argentina, who helped drive the gender identity law adopted there earlier this year.

I also welcome Olena Shevchenko who leads an important human rights effort in Ukraine.

In a number of countries, including Ukraine, draft laws have been proposed that would criminalize public discussion of homosexuality—potentially making meetings such as this one illegal. I deplore these kinds of measures wherever they are introduced. They threaten basic rights, feed stigma and lead to more abuse.

We are also pleased to have Gift Trapence, a prominent human rights defender from Malawi. When I visited Malawi in 2010, two young men had just been sentenced to 14 years of hard labor for the so-called "crime" of celebrating their wedding. At my request, the then President Bingu wa Mutharika pardoned them, on the very day when I asked him, but he defended criminal sanctions. Now under the new leadership of Her Excellency President Joyce Banda, Malawi is weighing possible changes in the law. I hope Malawians take the opportunity to turn a page.

Distinguished friends,

We must all speak out against homophobia, especially those who are considered leaders in society as well as others in the public eye.

Let me say a big Bienvenido to pop sensation Ricky Martin. Muchas Gracias! You are a wonderful role model for LGBT youth and for all people. Thank you.

I am again honored to share the stage with Yvonne Chaka Chaka—a global superstar and a champion of development, including as a Goodwill Ambassador for UNICEF and Roll Back Malaria. Thank you very much.

Yvonne, you are known as the Princess of Africa. Today, you are our Queen of Equality.

Our guests—and you here today—have helped to open a door. We cannot let it close.

It is an outrage that in our modern world, so many countries continue to criminalize people simply for loving another human being of the same sex. In many cases, these laws are not home-grown. They were inherited from former colonial powers.

Laws rooted in 19th century prejudices are fueling 21st century hate. In other cases new discriminatory laws are being introduced.

These laws must go. We must replace them with laws that provide adequate protection against discrimination, including on the basis of sexual orientation and gender identity.

This is not optional. It is a State obligation, based on the principle of non-discrimination—a fundamental tenet of international human rights law.

We also need a broad public education effort to spread understanding and counter fear.

When I meet with leaders from around the world I raise my voice for equality for LGBT people.

Many leaders say they wish they could do more. But they point to public opinion as a barrier to progress.

I understand it can be difficult to stand up to public opinion. But just because a majority might disapprove of certain individuals does not entitle the State to withhold their basic rights.

Democracy is more than majority rule. It requires defending vulnerable minorities from hostile majorities. It thrives on diversity. Governments have a duty to fight prejudice, not fuel it.

I am deeply grateful to the cross-regional LGBT core group of Member States for bringing us together. I hope many other countries will join you.

You and I and people of conscience everywhere must keep pushing until we realize the promise of the Universal Declaration of Human Rights for all people. The freedom, dignity and equal rights that all people are born with—must be a living reality each and every day of their lives.

Thank you very much.

About Ban Ki-moon

Ban Ki-moon has been the eighth secretary-general of the United Nations since January 1, 2007. Prior to his election as secretary-general, Ban spent thirty-seven years at South Korea's foreign ministry and held a number of high-ranking positions, including the minister of Foreign Affairs and Trade (2004–2006). Ban was born in Eumseong County, North Chungcheong Province, Japanese Korea (now South Korea), on June 13, 1944. He earned his bachelor's degree in international relations from Seoul National University in 1970. He also holds a master's degree in public administration from Harvard University's Kennedy School of Government. Ban received his first posting to the United Nations in 1975 as a member of the South Korean Foreign Ministry's United Nations Division. He has also been involved with inter-Korean relations, including in 1992 when, following the adoption of the Joint Declaration on the Denuclearization of the Korean Peninsula, he served as the vice-chair of the South-North Joint Nuclear Control Commission. In 1999, he was the chairman of the Preparatory Commission for the Comprehensive Nuclear Test Ban Treaty Organization. Ban also served as the chef de cabinet during the Republic of Korea's 2001–2002 presidency of the UN General Assembly. On June 21, 2011, he was unanimously re-elected as secretary general of the United Nations by the General Assembly.

Revisiting the Success and Continued Challenges of the Vienna Declaration

By Navi Pillay

Delivered in Vienna, Austria, on the twentieth anniversary of the World Conference on Human Rights, Navi Pillay, the UN High Commissioner for Human Rights, celebrates the progress made during the two decades since the passage of the Vienna Declaration and Programme of Action (VDPA) at the 1993 World Conference on Human Rights. Despite improvements such as the establishment of a permanent International Criminal Court, Pillay asserts that the world has failed to honor many aspects of the Vienna Declaration, including protecting civilians from slaughter in places such as Syria and Rwanda. According to Pillay, the anniversary of the World Conference on Human Rights provides an opportunity to reconsider the goals established twenty years ago and to revitalize the Vienna Declaration.

Excellencies, dear colleagues, ladies and gentlemen,

It is moving to be among so many friends today, in order to commemorate an occasion of such significance to me and to my Office.

Twenty years ago, more than 7,000 participants gathered for the World Conference on Human Rights. Many of you were here, as was I—representing a women's activist group. All of us were anxious to achieve a good outcome.

Western countries favored civil and political rights; the Eastern bloc, and many developing nations, argued that economic, social and cultural rights, and the right to development, had priority. In addition, a sizeable group of countries were vigorously arguing that the Universal Declaration of Human Rights was the product of a specifically Western culture, and that in reality human rights should be considered relative to the characteristics and traditions of different cultures.

Moreover, the world was in the midst of a series of dramatic upheavals. Some of these—like the fall of the Berlin Wall—were very positive; and some—like the sudden rash of deeply destructive internal conflicts—extremely negative. It was the best of times and worst of times, forming the backdrop to the Vienna conference.

The end of the Cold War had made it seem the right moment for a new world to review its agenda for human rights. But by the time the Conference took place, a terrible armed conflict was raging close by in the former Yugoslavia. Indeed, there were mass killings and other atrocities taking place less than a day's drive from the conference rooms where the World Conference was taking place, and from where we are today.

Delivered June 17, 2013, at the Vienna + 20 Conference, Vienna, Austria, by Navi Pillay.

The Vienna Consensus

And yet, as discussions unfurled, a consensus emerged. The key to this was the notion of universality, indivisibility and interrelatedness of all human rights. You see, a number of States had been resisting the entire concept of economic and social rights—because they saw them as aspirations, rather than rights intrinsic to human dignity and freedom. The vision of an interrelated and interdependant constellation of human rights allowed for economic and social rights to be on board, as well as the right to development.

The debate regarding the alleged cultural specificities of human rights was resolved with an equally deft and inclusive approach. Of course, all countries are indeed not the same, and all voices must, naturally, be heard. But these cultural specificities in no way erode the universality of human rights.

The formula that ultimately created consensus on this point was the following: you choose your path, but the goal is something we hold in common. Your specificity will influence the way you move forward. But that goal—of human dignity and human freedom, via implementation of the human rights elucidated in the International Bill of Rights—is something that we all share.

And so the assembled delegates overcame major differences on contentious issues such as universality, sovereignty, impunity, and how to give a voice to victims. The result was a powerful outcome document: the Vienna Declaration and Programme of Action (VDPA).

The VDPA is the most significant human rights document produced in the last quarter of a century and one of the strongest human rights documents of the past hundred years. We owe it to the goodwill and hard work of many dedicated and experienced professionals led by Ibrahima Fall. It crystalized the principle that human rights are universal, indivisible, interdependent and interrelated, and firmly entrenched the notion of universality by committing States to the promotion and protection of all human rights for all people "regardless of their political, economic, and cultural systems."

The Vienna Conference led to historic advances in many vital areas, among them women's rights; the fight against impunity; the rights of minorities and migrants; the rights of children.

Much progress has occurred during the past two decades, thanks to the path laid down in Vienna. We can justly celebrate a number of important landmark agreements, including on the world's first permanent International Criminal Court—the creation of which received a significant boost at Vienna—as well as new mechanisms to promote and protect the human rights of women, minorities, migrant workers and their families and other groups. Vienna opened the door to stronger UN

> *[E]ven as I speak to you now, women are being abducted and raped, hospitals are being targeted, and indiscriminate shelling and deliberate massacres stain the earth with the blood of innocents.*

human rights mechanisms, including an expansion—that still continues today—in the number of Special Procedures. Until Vienna, they had all been focused on civil and political rights. Today, the 48 Special Procedures cover the entire spectrum of human rights.

Vienna also provided a significant boost to the Treaty Bodies—which are also continuing to expand, as more States ratify more human rights treaties—and to the important system of National Human Rights Institutions which are now to be found in 103 countries. Of these, sixty-nine are currently accredited with "A" status.

But we must recognize that in many areas, we have failed to build on the foundations of the VDPA. The inspiring opening promise of the Universal Declaration—that all human beings are born equal in dignity and in rights, and that these will be respected as such—is still only a dream for far too many people.

Failure to Protect

This week twenty years ago, snipers were gunning down children in the streets of Sarajevo, and the carnage of that hideous conflict darkened the horizon of Europe.

Today, only a little further away, the children, women and men of Syria cry out in pain and beg for our aid. And once again, we are failing them—as we have done in a succession of other horrific conflicts, including Afghanistan, Somalia, Rwanda, the Democratic Republic of Congo and Iraq—to name just a few.

Time and again, the international community has promised to protect civilians from slaughter and gross violations of rights. And yet even as I speak to you now, women are being abducted and raped, hospitals are being targeted, and indiscriminate shelling and deliberate massacres stain the earth with the blood of innocents.

All this is intolerable. And yet it continues to happen. Our progress along the path that we laid down in Vienna 20 years ago has been marked by constant setbacks as well as the many achievements I listed earlier. Some promises have been half fulfilled—for example in the area of international justice, where we have an international court, to which some deserving situations are referred and others—including Syria—are not. But twenty years ago we had had no international courts at all since Nuremberg, despite the commission of international crimes.

In 2005, the World Summit—in a logical extension of all that had been agreed in Vienna—adopted by consensus the concept of the Responsibility to Protect. But Syria is just the latest example of a situation where we have failed dismally to live up to that responsibility—at the cost, so far, of more than 93,000 lives.

When we come here, we are not celebrating history. We are talking about a blueprint for a magnificent construction that is still only half built. It is essential that we view the VDPA as a living document that can and should continue to guide our actions and goals. Human rights are still not universally available, or viewed as indivisible and interrelated, despite our promise to make them so. States still continue to make arguments about cultural relativity. Women, minorities and migrants are still discriminated against and abused. The right to development is still not accepted by everybody. Power still corrupts, and leaders are still prepared to sacrifice their people in order to retain it.

The Way Forward

I believe this 20th anniversary provides us with a very important opportunity to go back to Vienna in order to rediscover the way forward.

It was in Vienna, twenty years ago, that non-governmental organizations spearheaded a drive for the creation of the post of High Commissioner for Human Rights. This was to ensure that an independent, authoritative voice would speak out against human rights violations wherever they occur; to coordinate and support the work of a range of different bodies; and to utilize the weight of the United Nations to support human rights for all.

It is my honor to occupy that post today, and I believe my Office has come a long way in the first two decades of its existence. But it, like so much else, is not a finished product. We have a huge task—to promote and protect the human rights of everyone everywhere—and clearly insufficient resources to carry it out. But I do believe the Office has filled a major vacuum in the UN system and become an increasingly strong and authoritative advocate for victims across the globe, a voice for the voiceless. And a voice, created by States, that is in a position to remind States of the laws and promises they have made which they are failing to live up to.

Another key achievement of Vienna was to provide a major boost to civil society organizations and other human rights defenders. They have expanded to a degree that was unimaginable at the time, especially at the national level. But they are also, today in 2013, facing unprecedented challenges, including restrictive laws and reprisals—even reprisals for taking part in UN proceedings on UN premises. In one way, perhaps, this is a measure of their impact. But it is also a deeply disturbing sign of regression.

We need to do our utmost to revive the spirit of the Vienna Declaration, and relearn its messages. We must refocus on its startling clarity of purpose which, at the time, we had scarcely dared hope to achieve. It reaffirmed the dignity and rights of all, and showed us how to achieve them. It crystallized the concepts of universality, and impartiality with regard to justice. It showed us the way forward, and to some extent we have followed that path. But, sadly, reprehensibly, we also continue all too often to deviate from it.

Thank you.

About Navi Pillay

Navi Pillay is currently the UN High Commissioner for Human Rights. Prior to this position, Pillay served as a judge on the International Criminal Tribunal for Rwanda (1995–2003) and the International Criminal Court in the Hague (2003–2008), where she saw cases dealing with war crimes, genocide, and crimes against humanity. Pillay was born on September 23, 1941, in Durban, Natal Province, South Africa. She received her bachelor's degree from the University of Natal in 1963 and her LLB (bachelor of laws) in 1965. She then earned her LLM (masters of laws) in 1982 and her doctorate in law in 1988 from Harvard University. In 1967, Pillay became the first non-white woman to open a law firm in Natal, South Africa. For more than twenty-five years, she acted as a defense attorney for antiapartheid campaigners and trade unionists in South Africa. Pillay cofounded the internal nongovernmental organization Equality Now, an organization that promotes women's rights, in 1992. In 1995 President Nelson Mandela appointed Pillay to be a judge on the High Court of South Africa. She was approved by the General Assembly on July 28, 2008, for a four-year term as the UN High Commissioner for Human Rights. Pillay was approved for a two-year term in 2012.

Expansion of War Crimes Reward Program: A Discussion

By Stephen J. Rapp, Sarah Pray, Fatou Bensouda,
Mark Quarterman, and Lisa Dougan

Hosted by the Office of Global Criminal Justice in the US State Department, a four-person expert panel discusses issues relating to war crimes, including the importance of arrest warrants in bringing war criminals to justice. Stephen Rapp, the US ambassador-at-large for war crimes, contends that it is difficult to bring war criminals before the International Criminal Court (ICC) because the court does not have its own police force. The ICC, therefore, relies on the cooperation of national governments to apprehend criminals. The panel discusses two war criminals with active arrest warrants: Sylvestre Mudacumura, the alleged leader of a Hutu rebel group in Rwanda, and Joseph Kony, the leader of the Lord's Resistance Army in Uganda. The international criminal justice system is still in the early stages of operation, and the panel contends that one area in need of improvement is the cooperation of national governments in complying with arrest warrants and not allowing fugitives to cross their borders.

Sarah Pray: Good morning everyone, and welcome to this Google+ Hangout, hosted by the Office of Global Criminal Justice. My name is Sarah Pray from the Open Society Foundation and we have four distinguished, fantastic panelists for you this morning. We're going to start with Ambassador Stephen Rapp. We also are very privileged to have the ICC Chief Prosecutor Madame Fatou Bensouda with us and two of my colleagues from civil society: Mark Quarterman who is the Director of Research for the Enough Project and Lisa Dougan who is the Director of Civic Engagement for Invisible Children. As many of you are likely aware, on January 15th of this year the War Crimes Rewards Program was expanded and I think we're going to kick off the conversation with Ambassador Rapp telling us a little about this expansion and what it means for the global fight to end impunity. So Ambassador Rapp, turn it to you?

Ambassador Stephen Rapp: Yes, good to be on today, Sarah. As you said, in January we had a new law signed by President Obama, legislation that had cleared Congress supported by Senator Kerry, now Secretary Kerry, now my boss, and also by Republicans such as Congressman Royce, the Chairman of the House Foreign Affairs Committee. That legislation permitted us to add to those on whom we offer rewards—we've been, since 1998, able to offer rewards of up to $5 million for

Delivered April 10, 2013, at Google+ Hangout, hosted by the Office of Global Criminal Justice, Washington, DC, by Stephen J. Rapp, Sarah Pray, Fatou Bensouda, Mark Quarterman, and Lisa Dougan.

information leading to the arrest, the transfer, or the conviction of individuals that are charged at the International Criminal Tribunals for Rwanda, or Yugoslavia, or the special court for Sierra Leone. This law allowed us to add to that list persons who were indicted by other international courts or by hybrid or mixed courts, and it was specifically intended that we would be able to do that with people that are sought by the ICC. And of course, the ICC for more than the last six years has sought the arrest of Joseph Kony, and Okot Odhiambo, and Dominic Ongwen of the Lord's Resistance Army, alleged to be responsible for mass atrocities in Uganda, DRC, in the Central African Republic, and elsewhere in Central Africa. And we've now gone through the process of adding those three individuals to our list and publicizing rewards. We've also intended to add Bosco Ntaganda and Sylvestre Mudacumura, who've both been charged by the ICC for crimes in the Democratic Republic of Congo. Of course, Bosco turned himself in at our embassy in Kigali, Rwanda, on the 18th of March and surrendered to the Hague on the 22nd, and is now awaiting confirmation in some detention at the ICC.

Sylvestre Mudacumura is alleged to be the leader of a militia group, the FDLR, associated with those responsible for the Rwandan genocide in 1994, who went into the Congo thereafter. He's charged by the ICC. We've added him to the list as well. We have this program where people can contact us confidentially; they can communicate with our embassies and a way to talk with them can be set up where their identities won't be endangered. They can also contact us through the website of the State Department, www.state.gov/warcrimesrewards. If you do that, we'll look at that information and be in touch, and then develop that with other intelligence in ways that can help bring these individuals to justice. It's important to note this is not a bounty; it's not a dead or alive kind of Old West reward. This is information leading to the arrest, the transfer, or the conviction of these individuals that have been charged by these international or internationalized courts. And no money is paid before one of those things has happened. And so, if the information is provided today and it helps make possible an arrest next year, then we'll look back at the information and how it was used to build that operation and consider and provide for a reward that would be then delivered to the individual confidentially. Nothing in advance and only if in fact we've been able to bring this individual in. We see this as something that can particularly aid our efforts to bring Joseph Kony and his group, the commanders of the Lord's Resistance Army, to justice.

People are familiar with the fact that the US is strongly engaged with regional militaries in the countries that are threatened to chase Kony and bring him in and to neutralize the Lord's Resistance Army that continues to plague this region. But that operation needs intelligence. It needs people close to Kony that are prepared to get the information out in a very timely way to those that can act on it. We've had a lot of people that have come out as defectors, and one of the good parts of the operation to date has been the way that materials, leaflets are distributed and people are encouraged to come to safe places where they can defect and the message is clear that for those lower and mid-level people there's not going to be any risk of prosecution.

But we also want others to realize it's not just a matter of getting out and being safe, which, of course, is critically important in diminishing the force that Kony has; it's also bringing out the information and finding ways to communicate it very, very quickly so that it can be used by those with whom we're working and advising in the region to actually effect the arrest and transfer of these individuals so that they can face their accusers in a court of law, before the ICC and The Hague. Great to be on with everybody today and I look forward to answering questions and look forward to the comments, and it's great to see Fatou Bensouda who was here in Washington last week and was personally present. I was proud to see her in the State Department, present when we announced this expansion of our rewards program and the designation of these additional individuals.

Sarah Pray: Thank you Ambassador Rapp and you've provided the perfect segue to the question of how this will impact Madame Prosecutor's work in the International Criminal Court. So I'm hoping Madame Prosecutor that you would be willing to discuss how this expansion will affect your work seeking accountability in Congo and any future work there and with the Lord's Resistance Army.

Fatou Bensouda: Well thank you very much. Good afternoon, everyone; Ambassador Rapp, good afternoon. I'm very glad to be participating in this Google Hangout and also equally glad that I was there with you last week in Washington to participate when you launched this program, especially now extended to the ICC fugitives. Trials can only start if you have persons who are wanted by the court, before the court. And for people like Joseph Kony, Okot Odhiambo, Dominic Ongwen, and the two that we've lost in the Lord's Resistance Army, as well as in the Democratic Republic of Congo, Sylvestre Mudacumura. Arrest warrants have been out for Joseph Kony and his group since 2004. And for Mudacumura it is only recent, but it all comes down to the same thing that we need these people before the court for the court to be able to effectively carry out its mandate. So this is a development that we welcome greatly. The fact that it is now extended to our fugitives and that it is up to $5 million for information leading to their arrests. And I am emphasizing information leading to their arrests or to their conviction because that means that they have to be brought to the court alive, and this is very important.

I am glad that you emphasized that it is not a bounty, that it is actually a reward for information. And that it is not looking to just finding them to kill them, but actually to get them arrested and brought before the International Criminal Court in the case of those fugitives that we want. This is absolutely crucial. This is absolutely important for the role of the Court and last week when I was in Washington I expressed the appreciation of the International Criminal Court, but especially of my office, for this development—the fact that ICC fugitives can now be part of this reward program. We welcome it very much and we know that it is going to definitely provide incentives for information and that this is going to lead to the arrest of people who have allegedly committed very grave crimes. We also welcome the fact that the alleged victims of these crimes will finally see that those who are going to be held responsible for these crimes will be brought to justice. So this is a very welcome development indeed.

Sarah Pray: Thank you, Madame Prosecutor. The Enough Project and Invisible Children are both well known for their efforts to elevate the issue of Joseph Kony and the Lord's Resistance Army, so I'm hoping we can turn to Mark and Lisa to get your reactions. Mark, perhaps we'll start with you? Any comments you have on the expansion of the rewards program?

Mark Quarterman: I think it's a very welcome development. I'd like to echo Prosecutor Bensouda's statement about it, saying that this is one more step to bringing about justice, to bringing these people who have had arrest warrants against them for some time to justice. I welcome the step by the United States and think it's an important contribution to international justice and to ending impunity. I'd just like to thank you, Sarah, though, for hosting us, to Ambassador Rapp in the State Department for providing this opportunity. It's wonderful to see Prosecutor Bensouda again and, of course, to be with our close partners Invisible Children as well. But no, we see this as a very useful step and look forward to it bearing fruit.

Sarah Pray: Great. Lisa, anything you would like to say, anything to add?

Lisa Dougan: Yeah, thank you so much and first I want to say thank you to the State Department, Ambassador Rapp, Madame Prosecutor. It's really a pleasure to be with you all and to be with our colleagues at the Enough Project. We also welcome this expansion and we're very celebratory when we were able to hear the announcement that top LRA commanders were added to the War Crimes Rewards Program. For most of last year in 2012, as part of our Kony 2012 campaign, we actually had thousands of activists across the United States that were lobbying their members of Congress to see the passage of legislation that enabled this expansion. They lobbied both in-district and came to Washington, D.C., and lobbied on the Hill. So we were very excited and encouraged by last week's announcement and we see it as another encouraging sign that the administration is committed to seeing an end to LRA violence and that voices of people who want to see this conflict come to an end are being heard in Washington. I would say that while we very much see this new tool as having a lot of potential to bring information about Kony's location and top LRA commanders' location to lead to their arrest, as well as potentially encouraging the defection of lower-level commanders and combatants. And we do see it as one tool within a comprehensive effort that is all needed. And Ambassador, you alluded to the fact that the US has been engaged in a comprehensive counter-LRA effort that is really reaping positive results: 93 percent reduction in LRA killings since 2010, huge reductions in the abductions of civilians as well as an increase in defections, so the comprehensive

We need arrest strategies to ensure perpetrators face justice and that victims will find redress. It will also impact the credibility and legitimacy of the International Criminal Court and the systems of justice that has been set up by 120 states in Rome. I believe all actors have a role to play.

strategy of the US to address this in collaboration with the African Union and regional governments is really working.

We'd really love to see the implementation of this War Crimes Reward Program in tandem with a sustained, committed comprehensive effort and we think that all those things together could mean that an end to LRA violence is very near, bringing Joseph Kony to justice is very near, and that could be a victory first for communities on the ground, but also for the United States and for international justice as a whole and could be part of the legacy of the Obama administration. So I'll just end by saying that last year 3.7 million people signed the Kony 2012 pledge, committing to keep their leaders accountable to seeing an end to LRA violence and bringing Joseph Kony to justice. At the end of last year 10,000 people gathered in Washington to turn the volume up on that message and to renew their commitment and call on leaders to stay engaged. And so I just want to say on behalf of those 3.7 million and the 10 million that came to Washington that we're very grateful for these new developments and we urge the administration to stay committed and ensure that the LRA doesn't receive safe haven in areas like Central African Republic, Democratic Republic of Congo and to stay in the effort, keep the mission going until LRA violence finally ends. Thank you very much for allowing us to be here.

Sarah Pray: Thanks, Lisa. So Ambassador Rapp, the first question to you. Lisa just alluded to the suspected location of Joseph Kony in the Central African Republic. I'm wondering if you could comment on how this program will potentially improve the chances of finding him considering not only the remoteness of where he is suspected to be, but also the current political developments in the C.A.R.

Ambassador Rapp: Well on the first point, we want to get the news about it, and we'll be distributing information in the affected areas in the same way that we earlier distributed information to encourage defections, which we certainly will also continue to do. And looking for people to provide us, in whatever way is possible, information that can really help develop operations that will make an arrest possible. So we see this as essential and we've already seen that this kind of information, in the Bosco Ntaganda case, the fact that it was at least out there that we were going to make that designation, led to a situation where an individual didn't know who he could trust anymore. It became a situation that ended up that an individual coming and standing up to the charges against him. But now on the question of the Central African Republic, and everyone that's followed this has seen how there has been an illegal change of government in the Central African Republic. This armed movement, a coalition of various armed forces, has taken control of Bangui. That does create challenges. On one hand, that group has signaled it doesn't want to see foreign forces operating within the country, but on the other hand, it's signaled that it wants to see the end of Joseph Kony, that its members recognize this causes problems for their fellow citizens, particularly in the eastern part of the country.

At this time, we are working with our allies in the region, who are taking the lead in this area. There's the community, the economic community of Central African States, that's had meetings in N'Djamena in Chad. The African Union, which, of course, supported the effort on Kony and pushed the establishment of a regional task force also taking a hand to ensure the constitutional and legal government is restored in the C.A.R. And that's a condition for engagement of various countries with the military and other forces there. This is ongoing but certainly it involves making sure that there is promises of early elections, and then in the period between now and elections, that there is a broad based government that follows the patterns set by the Libreville Accords that were implemented prior to the change of control in Bangui, in which Nicholas Tiangaye was appointed as Prime Minister by President Bozize under that agreement. We look for a similar government, most likely under his leadership, to be appointed as well that would be constitutional and legal and that we could work with to continue the Kony efforts. We're convinced that there is common ground on this issue and no one in the C.A.R. wants to see the continued threat of Joseph Kony.

So we're hopeful that within a brief period of time, active operations can continue. As it stands right now, the Ugandan forces that have been present in the C.A.R. as part of this operation, in collaboration with the government of the C.A.R., remain there but have stood down from active operations, and we've continued our presence in an advisory capacity but not in terms of active operations. We hope that it will soon be possible to recommence those operations in collaboration with a constitutional and legal government in the C.A.R., because this is obviously a very important front in this fight and a place that everyone knows Kony and others have often found refuge and committed their acts against civilian populations.

Sarah Pray: Thank you, Ambassador. Recognizing that we only have a few minutes left, so perhaps one more question for Madame Prosecutor and then a last question for my civil society colleagues. Madame Prosecutor, you mentioned how many years it has been since the ICC work in Congo began. I'm wondering if you could talk a little about that. Why is the Congo context different? And how you see this rewards for justice program potentially changing the way that the ICC operates its Congo cases.

Fatou Bensouda: I think it is important to place this within the wider discussion on arrests. We need arrest strategies to ensure perpetrators face justice and that victims will find redress. It will also impact the credibility and legitimacy of the International Criminal Court and the systems of justice that has been set up by 120 states in Rome. I believe all actors have a role to play. States in devising strategies, executing arrest warrants, having nonessential contacts with ICC fugitives, and civil society also have a role in bringing awareness and pushing states to act.

Sarah Pray: Thank you. Mark and Lisa, I know that Ambassador Rapp's team is planning on putting out posters and matchbooks and getting the word out about this program. Are either of your groups going to publicize this and if so, how?

Mark Quarterman: Lisa, maybe I'll defer to you first because you have an extensive project aimed at defection, among other things, in Uganda and then I'll chip in after.

Lisa Dougan: Sure, and I can give maybe a quick answer to that. There are some of my colleagues at Invisible Children who spend significant amounts of time on the ground working with local civil society and could speak better to it. I think that one thing that we really value is ensuring that expectations are set appropriately amongst the local communities and that there is clear communication with civil society and it's something that I know we've been in touch with the State Department about before and so we think a lot of what we would like to try and do and ensure that there is appropriate and thorough communication with local communities about what this is and isn't, because I think a lot of times these communities are so hungry for security, so hungry for an end to this violence that they may jump on things assuming that it's more of a silver bullet than it might be. So I think with our work on the ground, the network of civil society we're in communication with regularly, our work with FM radio programs and "come home" messaging, I think those will certainly play a part in helping people understand what this is, how they might be able to contribute, getting the word out, but then also what it isn't so expectations are set appropriately.

Mark Quarterman: I'd just like to say that I think Invisible Children is doing great work on the ground and can play a useful role in this. I'd like to go back to what Madame Bensouda said, though, and say that this is part of a much larger context involving the credibility of international criminal justice and the credibility of the International Criminal Court. Of course, the court does not have a police force that it can send out to arrest fugitives, so it has to rely on national governments and their justice systems to carry this out. This is extremely difficult. We have to recognize we are at the early stages of the international criminal justice movement and we are seeing a number of hiccups, but rewards for justice can add more incentive for cooperation. And really top to bottom, it's partly having local communities cooperate but it's also having governments cooperate to prevent fugitives, high and low, in their countries from moving across borders, from finding refuge in places, from not being arrested when there are standing arrest warrants. This is a useful step; I applaud the US for taking this step, but there is—we're still climbing a very high mountain and at the very early stages of it. One last thing I'd like to say too is I welcome this especially because of this one more step of US cooperation with the International Criminal Court. I'd like to make a pitch for the US ratifying the Rome Statute and fully becoming a member of the International Criminal Court, but I really applaud this important step that the State Department, the US government, and Ambassador Rapp have made.

Sarah Pray: Thank you, Lisa and Mark. So we've come to the end of our time. I'm wondering if Madame Prosecutor or Ambassador Rapp, you have any final words they want to share with us? Madame Prosecutor?

Fatou Bensouda: It's just to really re-emphasize what has been said, and particularly the cooperation that we are receiving from the US government. I also want to thank you for applauding that, as I said at the beginning, we are very much appreciative of this. We are very much appreciative of the fact that ICC fugitives are part of this rewards program and we are really, as I said, very hopeful that this will quickly yield results for these people to be brought to—before the ICC and be brought to justice.

Sarah Pray: Hear! Hear! Ambassador Rapp, the final word is yours.

Ambassador Rapp: Well let me say—echo what Mark said earlier, that this is really part of sending a message that there will be accountability for mass atrocities, that there are consequences. There will be prosecutions and by sending that message, to deter these crimes and prevent others from falling victim to them. I do want to emphasize again that this is just one part of a comprehensive approach. As we heard—the approach we have taken to date has reduced the number of attacks against civilians, the number of killings. It has had positive effects to date but it will only really have permanent positive effects if we can eliminate this threat. I also want to note that in terms of the funds here, this is just one part of the ways in which the United States supports development and the populations in these areas. Of course, we recall that it was in May of 2010 that Congress passed legislation that called for effective action against the Lord's Resistance Army, but also the reconstruction of northern Uganda. So people say spend the money on something else; we're doing that as well, we're doing those things but if we're going to be able to have security, and people know that what they build will be safe and secure for the future and that they and their families are safe and secure from the kind of attacks and abductions that make people huddle at night at peril from falling victim to Kony. Unless we have that kind of security, it's very difficult to have development and a quality of life. And so, these things have to go hand in hand but now I think the key part of this is, let's bring Joseph Kony to justice and Odhiambo Ongwen, and Mudacumura as well.

Sarah Pray: Thank you, Ambassador Rapp. Well thank you all for joining us! Thanks to Enough and Invisible Children for your good work. Thank you, Madame Prosecutor for joining us. And, of course, Ambassador Rapp and to the Office of Global Criminal Justice, thank you very much for hosting this and for this new exciting development. I know all of us in civil society welcome it and can't wait to see what happens. So thank you all for joining and thanks to those of you off in the Internet land for participating in this.

Ambassador Rapp: For hanging out with us!

About the Panelists

Stephen J. Rapp is ambassador-at-large with the Office of Global Criminal Justice in the United States Department of State. He assumed office in September 2009. From 2007 to 2009, Rapp served as prosecutor of the Special Court for Sierra Leone, leading the prosecutions of former Liberian president Charles Taylor. From 2001 to 2007, he was senior trial attorney and chief of prosecutions at the International Criminal Tribunal for Rwanda.

Sarah Pray is the senior policy analyst for Africa with the Open Society Foundations. Prior to her work with Open Society, Pray worked as an attorney at the Robert F. Kennedy Center for Human Rights. She received her law degree from Boston College Law School.

Fatou Bensouda is the chief prosecutor of the International Criminal Court. She was sworn in on June 15, 2012, after having served as deputy prosecutor since 2004.

Mark Quarterman is the director of research and editorial at the Enough Project, a Washington, DC–based organization aimed at combating genocide and crimes against humanity.

Lisa Dougan is the director of civil engagement for Invisible Children, an activist organization that seeks to raise awareness of the use of child soldiers by militant groups in Uganda and the surrounding region.

2

Issues in Health Care
and Medicine

A man fills out an information card during an Affordable Care Act outreach event hosted by Planned Parenthood. Enrollment for the Affordable Care Act, sometimes referred to as Obamacare, began on October 1, 2013.

Achieving an Aids-Free Generation

By Hillary Rodham Clinton

In remarks delivered at the 2012 International AIDS Conference in Washington, DC, Secretary of State Hillary Rodham Clinton lauds the progress made in the field of HIV/ AIDS research and treatment. The 2012 conference was the first in the United States since 1990, when the event was held in San Francisco at a time when an AIDS diagnosis was what Clinton calls a death sentence. She discusses the President's Emergency Plan for AIDS Relief (PEPFAR)—launched during the administration of President George W. Bush—and how the administration of President Barak Obama is building and evolving the program. Clinton reaffirms America's commitment to creating an AIDS-free generation and defines what that means. She outlines progress made and steps taken by various US government agencies that contribute to HIV/AIDS prevention and treatment. Clinton announces an $80 million investment aimed at helping HIV-positive pregnant women get affordable, accessible treatment, and details three more funding initiatives designed to extend service to at-risk and marginalized populations. While international support and collaboration have accomplished much, Clinton says, the movement to fight AIDS the world over ought to strive for country ownership of treatment and prevention efforts. She closes with an anecdote recalling a 1996 visit to the AIDS Memorial Quilt with her husband, Bill Clinton, in which the two were shocked and saddened by the size of the memorial—a knitted quilt begun in 1987 composed of more than 48,000 individual panels memorializing those who have died of AIDS.

Good morning, and—(applause)—now, what would an AIDS conference be without a little protesting? We understand that. (Applause.) Part of the reason we've come as far as we have is because so many people all over the world have not been satisfied that we have done enough. And I am here to set a goal for a generation that is free of AIDS. (Applause.) But first, let me say five words we have not been able to say for too long: "Welcome to the United States." (Applause.) We are so pleased to have you all finally back here.

And I want to thank the leaders of the many countries who have joined us. I want to acknowledge my colleagues from the Administration and the Congress who have contributed so much to the fight against AIDS. But mostly, I want to salute all of the people who are here today who do the hard work that has given us the chance to stand here in 2012 and actually imagine a time when we will no longer be

Delivered July 23, 2012, at the International AIDS Conference, Washington, DC, by Hillary Rodham Clinton.

afflicted by this terrible epidemic and the great cost and suffering it has imposed for far too long. (Applause.) On behalf of all Americans, we thank you.

But I want to take a step back and think how far we have come since the last time this conference was held in the United States. It was in 1990 in San Francisco. Dr. Eric Goosby, who is now our Global AIDS Ambassador, ran a triage center there for all the HIV-positive people who became sick during the conference. They set up IV drug drips to rehydrate patients. They gave antibiotics to people with AIDS-related pneumonia. Many had to be hospitalized and a few died.

Even at a time when the world's response to the epidemic was sorely lacking, there were places and people of caring where people with AIDS found support. But tragically, there was so little that could be done medically. And thankfully, that has changed. Caring brought action, and action has made an impact.

The ability to prevent and treat the disease has advanced beyond what many might have reasonably hoped 22 years ago. Yes, AIDS is still incurable, but it no longer has to be a death sentence. That is a tribute to the work of countless people around the world—many of whom are here at this conference, others who are no longer with us but whose contributions live on. And for decades, the United States has played a key role. Starting in the 1990s under the Clinton Administration, we began slowly to make HIV treatment drugs more affordable, we began to face the epidemic in our own country. And then in 2003, President Bush launched PEPFAR with strong bipartisan support from Congress and this country began treating millions of people.

Today under President Obama, we are building on this legacy. PEPFAR is shifting out of emergency mode and starting to build sustainable health systems that will help us finally win this fight and deliver an AIDS-free generation. It's hard to overstate how sweeping or how crucial this change is. When President Obama took office, we knew that if we were going to win the fight against AIDS we could not keep treating it as an emergency. We had to fundamentally change the way we and our global partners did business.

So we've engaged diplomatically with ministers of finance and health, but also with presidents and prime ministers to listen and learn about their priorities and needs in order to chart the best way forward together. Now I will admit that has required difficult conversations about issues that some leaders don't want to face, like government corruption in the procurement and delivery of drugs or dealing with injecting drug users, but it has been an essential part of helping more countries manage more of their own response to the epidemic.

We've also focused on supporting high-impact interventions, making tough decisions driven by science about what we will and will not fund. And we are delivering more results for the American taxpayer's dollar by taking simple steps—switching to generic drugs, which saved more than $380 million in 2010 alone. (Applause.)

And crucially, we have vastly improved our coordination with the Global Fund. Where we used to work independently of each other, we now sit down together to decide, for example, which of us will fund AIDS treatment somewhere and which of us will fund the delivery of that treatment. That is a new way of working together for both of us, but I think it holds great results for all of us. (Applause.) Now all of these strategic shifts have required a lot of heavy lifting. But it only matters in the end if it means we are saving more lives—and we are.

Since 2009, we have more than doubled the number of people who get treatment that keeps them alive. (Applause.) We are also reaching far more people with prevention, testing, and counseling.

And I want publicly to thank, first and foremost, Dr. Eric Goosby, who has been on the front lines of all this work since the 1980s in San Francisco. (Applause.) He is somewhere in this vast hall, cringing with embarrassment, but more than anyone else, he had a vision for what PEPFAR needed to become and the tenacity to keep working to make it happen. And I want to thank his extraordinary partners here in this Administration, Dr. Tom Frieden at the Centers for Disease Control and Dr. Raj Shah at USAID. (Applause.)

Now, with the progress we are making together, we can look ahead to a historic goal: creating an AIDS-free generation. This is part of President Obama's call to make fighting global HIV/AIDS at home and abroad a priority for this administration. In July 2010, he launched the first comprehensive National HIV/AIDS Strategy, which has reinvigorated the domestic response to the epidemic—especially important here in Washington, D.C., which needs more attention, more resources, and smarter strategies to deal with the epidemic in our nation's capital.

And last November, at the National Institutes of Health, with my friend Dr. Tony Fauci there, I spoke in depth about the goal of an AIDS-free generation and laid out some of the ways we are advancing it through PEPFAR, USAID, and the CDC. And on World AIDS Day, President Obama announced an ambitious commitment for the United States to reach 6 million people globally with lifesaving treatment. (Applause.)

Now since that time I've heard a few voices from people raising questions about America's commitment to an AIDS-free generation, wondering whether we are really serious about achieving it. Well, I am here today to make it absolutely clear: The United States is committed and will remain committed to achieving an AIDS-free generation. We will not back off, we will not back down, we will fight for the resources necessary to achieve this historic milestone. (Applause.)

I know that many of you share my passion about achieving this goal. In fact, one could say I am preaching to the choir. But right now, I think we need a little preaching to the choir. And we need the choir and the congregation to keep singing, lifting up their voices, and spreading the message to everyone who is still standing outside.

So while I want to reaffirm my government's commitment, I'm also here to boost yours. This is a fight we can win. We have already come so far—too far to stop now.

I want to describe some of the progress we've made toward that goal and some of the work that lies ahead.

Let me begin by defining what we mean by an AIDS-free generation. It is a time when, first of all, virtually no child anywhere will be born with the virus. (Applause.) Secondly, as children and teenagers become adults, they will be at significantly lower risk of ever becoming infected than they would be today no matter where they are living. (Applause.) And third, if someone does acquire HIV, they will have access to treatment that helps prevent them from developing AIDS and passing the virus on to others.

So yes, HIV may be with us into the future until we finally achieve a cure, a vaccine, but the disease that HIV causes need not be with us. (Applause.)

As of last fall, every agency in the United States Government involved in this effort is working together to get us on that path to an AIDS-free generation. We're focusing on what we call combination prevention. Our strategy includes condoms, counseling and testing, and places special emphasis on three other interventions: treatment as prevention, voluntary medical male circumcision, and stopping the transmission of HIV from mothers to children.

Since November, we have elevated combination prevention in all our HIV/AIDS work—including right here in Washington, which still has the highest HIV rate of any large city in our country. And globally, we have supported our partner countries shifting their investments toward the specific mix of prevention tools that will have the greatest impact for their people. For example, Haiti is scaling up its efforts to prevent mother-to-child transmission, including full treatment for mothers with HIV, which will in turn, of course, prevent new infections. And for the first time, the Haitian Ministry of Health is committing its own funding to provide antiretroviral treatment. (Applause.)

We're also making notable progress on the three pillars of our combination-prevention strategy. On treatment as prevention, the United States has added funding for nearly 600,000 more people since September, which means we are reaching nearly 4.5 million people now and closing in on our national goal of 6 million by the end of next year. That is our contribution to the global effort to reach universal coverage.

On male circumcision, we've supported more than 400,000 procedures since last December alone. And I'm pleased to announce that PEPFAR will provide an additional $40 million to support South Africa's plans to provide voluntary medical circumcisions for almost half a million boys and men in the coming year. (Applause.) You know and we want the world to know that this procedure reduces the risk of female-to-male transmission by more than 60 percent and for the rest of the man's life, so the impact can be phenomenal.

In Kenya and Tanzania, mothers asked for circumcision campaigns during school vacations so their teenage sons could participate. In Zimbabwe, some male lawmakers wanted to show their constituents how safe and virtually painless the procedure is, so they went to a mobile clinic and got circumcised. That's the kind of leadership we welcome. And we are also seeing the development of new tools that would allow people to perform the procedure with less training and equipment than they need today without compromising safety. And when such a device is approved by the World Health Organization, PEPFAR is ready to support it right away. (Applause.)

And on mother-to-child transmission, we are committed to eliminating it by 2015, getting the number to zero. Over the years—(applause)—we've invested more than $1 billion for this effort. In the first half of this fiscal year, we reached more than 370,000 women globally, and we are on track to hit PEPFAR's target of reaching an additional 1.5 million women by next year. We are also setting out to overcome one of the biggest hurdles in getting to zero. When women are identified as HIV-positive and eligible for treatment, they are often referred to another clinic, one that may be too far away for them to reach. As a result too many women never start treatment.

Today, I am announcing that the United States will invest an additional $80 million to fill this gap. These funds—(applause)—will support innovative approaches to ensure that HIV-positive pregnant women get the treatment they need to protect themselves, their babies, and their partners. So let there be no mistake, the United States is accelerating its work on all three of these fronts in the effort to create an AIDS-free generation and look at how all these elements come together to make a historic impact.

In Zambia, we're supporting the government as they step up their efforts to prevent mother-to-child transmission. Between 2009 and 2011, the number of new infections went down by more than half. And we are just getting started. Together, we're going to keep up our momentum on mother-to-child transmission. In addition, we will help many more Zambians get on treatment and support a massive scale-up of male circumcision as well, two steps that, according to our models, will drive down the number of new sexually transmitted infections there by more than 25 percent over the next 5 years. So as the number of new infections in Zambia goes down, it will be possible to treat more people than are becoming infected each year. So we will, for the first time, get ahead of the pandemic there. And eventually, an AIDS-free generation of Zambians will be in sight.

Think of the lives we will touch in Zambia alone—all the mothers and fathers and children who will never have their lives ripped apart by this disease. And now, multiply that across the many other countries we are working with. In fact, if you're not getting excited about this, please raise your hand and I will send somebody to check your pulse. (Laughter and applause.)

But I know that creating an AIDS-free generation takes more than the right tools, as important as they are. Ultimately, it's about people—the people who have the most to contribute to this goal and the most to gain from it. That means embracing the essential role that communities play—especially people living with HIV—and the critical work of faith-based organizations. We need to make sure we're looking out for orphans and vulnerable children who are too often still overlooked in this epidemic. (Applause.)

And it will be no surprise to you to hear me say I want to highlight the particular role that women play. (Applause.) In Sub-Saharan Africa today, women account for 60 percent of those living with HIV. Women want to protect themselves from HIV and they want access to adequate health care. And we need to answer their call. PEPFAR is part of our comprehensive effort to meet the health needs of women and girls, working across United States Government and with our partners on HIV, maternal and child health, and reproductive health, including voluntary family planning and our newly launched Child Survival Call to Action.

Every woman should be able to decide when and whether to have children. This is true whether she is HIV-positive or not. (Applause.) And I agree with the strong message that came out of the London Summit on Family Planning earlier this month. There should be no controversy about this. None at all. (Applause.)

And across all of our health and development work, the United States is emphasizing gender equality because women need and deserve a voice in the decisions that affect their lives. (Applause.) And we are working to prevent and respond to gender-based violence, which puts women at higher risk for contracting the virus. And because women need more ways to protect themselves from HIV infection, last year we invested more than $90 million in research on microbicides. All these efforts will help close the health gap between women and men and lead to healthier families, communities, and nations as well.

If we're going to create an AIDS-free generation, we also must address the needs of the people who are at the highest risk of contracting HIV. One recent study of female sex workers and those trafficked into prostitution in low- and middle-income countries found that, on average, 12 percent of them were HIV-positive, far above the rates for women at large. And people who use injecting drugs account for about one third of all the people who acquire HIV outside of Sub-Saharan Africa. And in low- and middle-income countries, studies suggest that HIV prevalence among men who have sex with male partners could be up to 19 times higher than among the general population.

Now over the years, I have seen and experienced how difficult it can be to talk about a disease that is transmitted the way that AIDS is. But if we're going to beat AIDS, we can't afford to avoid sensitive conversations, and we can't fail to reach the people who are at the highest risk. (Applause.)

> **PEPFAR is part of our comprehensive effort to meet the health needs of women and girls, working across United States Government and with our partners on HIV, maternal and child health, and reproductive health, including voluntary family planning and our newly launched Child Survival Call to Action.**

Unfortunately, today very few countries monitor the quality of services delivered to these high-risk key populations. Fewer still rigorously assess whether the services provided actually prevent transmission or do anything to ensure that HIV-positive people in these groups get the care and treatment they need. Even worse, some take actions that, rather than discouraging risky behavior, actually drives more people into the shadows, where the epidemic is that much harder to fight.

And the consequences are devastating for the people themselves and for the fight against HIV because when key groups are marginalized, the virus spreads rapidly within those groups and then also into the lower-risk general population. We are seeing this happen right now in Eastern Europe and Southeast Asia. Humans might discriminate, but viruses do not.

And there is an old saying that goes: "Why rob banks? Because that's where the money is." If we want to save more lives, we need to go where the virus is and get there as quickly as possible. (Applause.)

And that means science should guide our efforts. So today I am announcing three new efforts by the United States Government to reach key populations. We will invest $15 million in implementation research to identify the specific interventions that are most effective for each key population. We are also launching a $20 million challenge fund that will support country-led plans to expand services for key populations. And finally, through the Robert Carr Civil Society Network Fund, we will invest $2 million to bolster the efforts of civil society groups to reach key populations. (Applause.)

Now Americans are rightly proud of the leading role that our country plays in the fight against HIV/AIDS. And the world has learned a great deal through PEPFAR about what works and why. And we've also learned a great deal about the needs that are not being met and how everyone can and must work together to meet those needs.

For our part, PEPFAR will remain at the center of America's commitment to an AIDS-free generation. I have asked Ambassador Dr. Goosby to take the lead on developing and sharing our blueprint of the goals and objectives for the next phase of our effort and to release this blueprint by World AIDS Day this year. We want the next Congress, the next Secretary of State, and all of our partners here at home and around the world to have a clear picture of everything we've learned and a roadmap that shows what we will contribute to achieving an AIDS-free generation.

Reaching this goal is a shared responsibility. It begins with what we can all do to help break the chain of mother-to-child transmission. And this takes leadership at every level—from investing in health care workers to removing the registration fees that discourage women from seeking care. And we need community and family leaders, from grandmothers to religious leaders, to encourage women to get tested and to demand treatment if they need it.

We also all have a shared responsibility to support multilateral institutions like the Global Fund. In recent months, as the United States has stepped up our commitment, so have Saudi Arabia, Japan, Germany, the Gates Foundation, and others. I encourage other donors, especially in emerging economies, to increase their contributions to this essential organization.

And then finally, we all have a shared responsibility to get serious about promoting country ownership—the end state where a nation's efforts are led, implemented, and eventually paid for by its government, its communities, its civil society, its private sector.

I spoke earlier about how the United States is supporting country ownership, but we also look to our partner countries and donors to do their part. They can follow the example of the last few years in South Africa, Namibia, Botswana, India, and other countries who are able to provide more and better care for their own people because they are committing more of their own resources to HIV/AIDS. (Applause.) And partner countries also need to take steps like fighting corruption and making sure their systems for approving drugs are as efficient as possible.

I began today by recalling the last time this conference was held here in the United States, and I want to close by recalling another symbol of our cause, the AIDS Memorial Quilt. For a quarter-century, this quilt has been a source of solace and comfort for people around the world, a visible way to honor and remember, to mourn husbands and wives, brothers and sisters, sons and daughters, partners and friends.

Some of you have seen the parts of the quilt that are on view in Washington this week. I well remember the moment in 1996 when Bill and I went to the National Mall to see the quilt for ourselves. I had sent word ahead that I wanted to know where the names of friends I had lost were placed so that I could be sure to find them. When we saw how enormous the quilt was, covering acres of ground, stretching from the Capitol building to the Washington Monument, it was devastating. And in the months and years that followed, the quilt kept growing. In fact, back in 1996 was the last time it could be displayed all at once. It just got too big. Too many people kept dying.

We are all here today because we want to bring about that moment when we stop adding names, when we can come to a gathering like this one and not talk about the fight against AIDS, but instead commemorate the birth of a generation that is free of AIDS.

Now, that moment is still in the distance, but we know what road we need to take. We are closer to that destination than we've ever been, and as we continue on this journey together, we should be encouraged and inspired by the knowledge of how far we've already come. So today and throughout this week let us restore our own faith and renew our own purpose so we may together reach that goal of an AIDS-free generation and truly honor all of those who have been lost.

Thank you all very much. (Applause.)

About Hillary Rodham Clinton

Hillary Rodham Clinton was the sixty-seventh US secretary of state from 2009 to 2013. She was elected to represent New York in the Senate in 2000, and was reelected in 2006. She campaigned for president in 2008, losing the Democratic primary to Barack Obama. Clinton is the wife of former president Bill Clinton. She was First Lady of the United States from 1992 to 2000. Clinton was born on October 26, 1947, in Chicago, Illinois. She graduated from Wellesley College in 1969, and received a law degree from Yale Law School in 1973. Clinton worked as an attorney in Arkansas in addition to holding an assistant professorship at the University of Arkansas School of Law. In 1977, President Jimmy Carter appointed Clinton to the Legal Services Corporation's board of directors. In 1978, she was appointed chair. She was nominated for the position of secretary of state in November 2008.

Let's Move!

By Michelle Obama

First Lady Michelle Obama delivers a speech at an event commemorating the second anniversary of the launch of Let's Move!, the First Lady's nationwide campaign to end childhood obesity. The event was sponsored by Let's Move Faith and Communities, a part of the initiative that works with neighborhood and faith-based organizations. Obama describes the progress made over the past two years and celebrates the members of Let's Move Faith and Communities, which has sponsored more than one thousand summer nutrition programs. She also thanks the more than three thousand professional chefs that have signed up to make the menus at local schools healthier. Obama compares the healthy eating and exercise habits of children when she was growing up with the more sedentary lifestyle of American children today and their unhealthy eating habits. She concludes that faith communities are vital to the effort of Let's Move! and serve as role models that inspire children to live healthier lives.

Mrs. Obama: Good morning! Oh, you rest yourselves. (Laughter.) I know you've been through a lot this morning—a little dancing, a little working out. So you need a little rest. (Laughter.)

But I want to thank you all so much. I am beyond thrilled to be here with all of you today as we celebrate the second anniversary of "Let's Move." It's a birthday. (Applause.)

And I want to start by thanking Pastor Hunter and Becky for, oh, that very kind introduction. We love those two people very dearly. They are tremendous role models to our family, to their community, to this nation. And I am grateful that they're hosting us here today. So let's give them a wonderful round of applause. (Applause.) Thank you so much.

I also want to thank Nemours for their support for today's events and for their partnership in so many of our "Let's Move" initiatives.

And finally, I want to thank all of you. We have got folks here from more than 120 congregations and organizations representing at least 15 different faiths and denominations. But we are all (applause)—that's wonderful. That is wonderful. And you're here on a Saturday morning, which is another wonderful thing. (Laughter.) Now, that's some commitment. Like that. (Laughter.)

But we are all here today for one very simple reason—because we love our children, and we are determined to build a future that is worthy of their promise.

That's what so many of you are doing every day in your congregations and in

Delivered February 11, 2012, at Let's Move! Faith and Communities Event, Longwood, Florida, by Michelle Obama.

your communities. Whether you volunteer with a homeless ministry of a food bank, whether you're fighting for better health care or a cleaner environment, every day, so many of you are taking on the most urgent challenges of our time.

Every day, you're serving God by serving others. Every day, you're proving that when we come together to do good works, no challenge is too big, no problem too hard, and there is no such thing as a hopeless cause. No such thing. And that, more than anything else, is the story of "Let's Move."

It's the story of a very serious challenge—a challenge that many of us believed was too big, too complicated, too entrenched for us to solve. And that problem is our epidemic of childhood obesity—the fact that right now, one-third of our children are overweight or obese. And they're at risk for serious conditions like diabetes, cancer, heart disease that undermine their health, that diminish their prospects, and they cost our economy billions of dollars each year.

But the story of "Let's Move" is also the story of individuals and organizations from every sector of our society who have stepped forward to meet this challenge. It's the story of food manufacturers who've pledged to cut 1.5 trillion calories from their products. Companies like Goya Foods that are giving our family the information they need to make healthy choices about what they eat. Local grocers and national chains like Walgreens, SuperValu—they're building new supermarkets and selling fresh food in 1,500 underserved communities in this country. (Applause.)

Our restaurants are stepping up, transforming their kids' menus, loading them with healthier options. Our mayors out there across the country, they're planting gardens, they're refurbishing parks. Congress passed historic legislation to provide healthier school meals for millions of our children. (Applause.) More than 3,400 professional chefs have signed up to help local schools improve their menus.

And then there are our celebrities—everyone from Beyonce to LeBron to Drew Brees are serving as role models, inspiring our kids to dance, dribble and pass their way to a healthier life.

And it's important to know that all these folks are doing these things not just as business leaders who are concerned about their bottom lines—not just as elected officials serving their constituents, or as celebrities promoting a cause. They're doing this as parents and grandparents who care about our nation's children. They're doing it as citizens who know that we as a country cannot fulfill our promise unless our children can fulfill their promise. (Applause.)

And they're doing it because they know that when children here in one of the nations—richest nations on Earth aren't getting the nutrition they need, when one in three of our children is on track to develop diabetes in their lifetimes, that means it's time for us to act. Because this isn't who we are, and it certainly isn't who we want to be.

We know that something better is possible for our children. And we are determined to solve this problem once and for all. But we know that if we truly want to end our obesity epidemic so that our kids can have a healthier future, then we have to understand, how did we get here in the first place, how did we wind up here?

So I want you all to think back, think way back—especially the grown folks like me—think back to when many of us were kids, all those years ago. Now, the children, you might not even understand how life was back then. (Laughter.) Most of us led reasonably healthy lives. We walked to and from school every day—rain or shine. (Applause.) Amen. And in Chicago, where I was raised, we did it in the hail, sleet, snow, gale-force winds. (Applause.) Yes, I sound just like my grandfather. Never thought I would. (Laughter.)

Back then, our TVs only had a few channels—you remember that? (Laughter.) Just a handful of channels. And when those Saturday morning cartoons were finished, we were done with TV. That was it. It was over. (Laughter.) Once American Bandstand and Soul Train were over—(applause)—you had to go outside and play—right? And back then, playing did not involve a screen or a remote control. (Laughter.) It meant actually moving your bodies. (Laughter.) It meant riding bikes, jumping double-dutch, playing tag until our mothers called us in for dinner.

And then when we ate that dinner, we all sat around the table as a family. (Applause.) Yes. And our food wasn't fancy. Because we didn't have a lot of money, the portion sizes had to be reasonable—right? (Laughter.) There was always a vegetable on the plate. (Applause.) And we ate whatever we were served. (Applause.) My mother never cared whether my brother or I liked what was on our plate. (Laughter.) We either ate what was there, or we went to bed hungry. That was the bottom line.

And in those days, we hardly ever ate out. Fast food was considered a rare treat. In fact, I tell this story often, but I can still remember the time that my brother and I convinced our grandmother to let us have takeout burgers and fries for lunch. Now, we were shocked when she finally agreed. We could barely contain our excitement. So when the food arrived, Grandma unwrapped the burger, put it on a plate—because you had to eat on a plate no matter what you were eating—(laughter)—put the fries on a plate. We were sitting there all excited, and then what does she do? She opened up a can of peas. (Laughter.) She opened up a can of peas. And to our horror, she served us two scoops each. My brother and I, we were like, "Grandma, no!" (Laughter.) Because fast food or not, my grandma, she believed in feeding her family a balanced meal at every single meal. Every single meal. (Applause.)

See, back then, our society was structured so that healthy eating and exercise were just natural parts of kids' lives—all our lives. We didn't have to think about it; that was just the way it was.

But today, unfortunately, it's the exact opposite. It's the exact opposite. Many kids no longer attend neighborhood schools, so instead of walking or riding their bikes to school, they're taking a bus or car. Instead of just a few hours of cartoons on weekends, there are entire networks devoted to children's programming and the Internet is available 24/7. That was just never an option for us. So today, when our kids go and "play," that often means they're sitting in one place for hours, clicking, typing, texting away—not moving a lick.

And for many folks, those wholesome family meals are, unfortunately, a thing of the past. See, a lot of our families today are living in communities without a single grocery store, so they have to buy their food at places like gas stations or corner stores, places with few, if any, healthy options.

And frankly, a lot of parents today are just plain tired. Folks are working longer hours to make ends meet and everyone is under more stress. And as much as we all hate to admit it, sometimes it's just easier to park the kids in front of the TV, so that we can get a little time to pay the bills, do the laundry, just get a few hours of peace right? Just a little peace, that's all we want. (Laughter.)

Sometimes it's just easier to pick up something from the drive-through, pop something in the microwave. And if we're being honest with ourselves, we have to admit that even when we do cook, we don't always make the healthiest choices.

And that's really where this gets personal and emotional—probably why some people think this is a very complicated issue. You see, for so many of us, food is more than just nourishment for our bodies. It's how we knit our families and our communities together. It's how we pass down traditions from generation to generation.

How many of us find ourselves looking forward to that fried chicken and mac and cheese, pound cake, after church on Sunday? (Laughter.) Some people come to church just for the fried chicken. (Laughter.) How many of us have those warm, wonderful memories of family and friends gathering in the kitchen? We still do that at the White House. It's a little, bitty kitchen—big, old house, everybody sitting in the kitchen. No matter where—you're sitting in the kitchen. I'm not cooking, but— (laughter and applause)—but we still like the kitchen. (Laughter.) Dirtying every pot, cooking everyone's favorite dishes, talking, laughing, sharing stories late into the night. That's family.

Whether it's Christmas supper, Passover Seder, Iftar dinner, so many of our most sacred holidays revolve around food. All those familiar smells and tastes, and the memories that go along with them—all of that brings us joy and comfort. Times may be tough and money may be tight, but at least we can still serve up Uncle Joe's ribs or Abuela's arroz con pollo—huh? (Applause.) That's how we show our families that we care about them. Right?

No matter what culture we come from, no matter what faith we believe in, for so many of us, food is love. Food is sometimes all we have. And that is a beautiful thing and we don't ever want to give that up—right? And fortunately, we don't have to. Fortunately, we don't have to. We can still show that love, we can still honor those traditions, and we can do it in a way that's healthy for everyone, especially our kids. But we're going to have to make some changes, some modifications to adapt these traditions to our way of life today.

And ultimately, that's what "Let's Move" is really trying to do. We know that government doesn't have all the answers; know that there's no one-size-fits-all program or policy that will solve this problem. Every family and every community is different. Each of us needs to make the changes that fit with our budgets, our beliefs, and our tastes.

And that's really where all of you come in. That's why today was such an important part of our celebration. Because that is what our faith communities do best—you inspire and empower people to make meaningful changes in their lives. Sometimes folks won't do it if it wasn't said right here—right? You serve as a beacon for those who are lost, a refuge for those who've been forgotten. You're there for people during some of the most important moments of their lives, offering counsel on family matters, providing comfort in times of crisis, guiding folks on every mile of their journeys. That's why people come.

And our faith communities don't tend only to folks' spiritual health but to their emotional and their physical health as well. Think for a moment about the scripture that tells us that your bodies are temples given to you by God. That is a core teaching of so many of our faiths— a teaching that calls us to honor and nourish the bodies we've been blessed with, and to help others do the same.

> *And for many folks, those wholesome family meals are, unfortunately, a thing of the past. See, a lot of our families today are living in communities without a single grocery store, so they have to buy their food at places like gas stations or corner stores, places with few, if any, healthy options.*

So it's no accident that this church hosts classes to help folks lead healthier lives. It's no accident that, long before we ever started "Let's Move," so many congregations were already sponsoring health ministries and fitness classes, hosting food pantries and summer nutrition programs for our kids.

So as part of "Let's Move," we wanted to work with you from the very beginning. We wanted to learn from our faith communities. And we wanted to do everything we could to support and highlight your magnificent efforts. And that's why we started a special program called Let's Move Faith and Communities to challenge more of our organizations and congregations to take up this cause.

And just like everywhere else, the response to this initiative has been overwhelming. All kinds of faith communities have been stepping up. Muslim community leaders are hosting sports tournaments to encourage young people to get active. The Jewish Community Centers Association is working with JCCs around the country to grow gardens, and to get fresh food into underserved areas, and they're creating early child wellness programs.

Groups like the National Council of Churches have joined with an organization called Ample Harvest to help gardeners donate fresh produce to 4,700 of their local food pantries. (Applause.) The National Baptist Convention is aiming to have health ambassadors at all of their nearly 10,000 churches by September. (Applause.) And some of their churches have already created "no fry" zones in their congregations. (Applause.) Now, it's been a little tough. (Laughter.) But with just a little effort, the congregations have accepted this. They're also hosting "Taste Test Sundays" where people can sample healthy food.

Altogether, the members of Let's Move Faith and Communities have sponsored more than 1,000 summer nutrition sites providing millions of healthy meals for children in need. And these congregations and communities have walked more than 2.8 million miles. That's very impressive. (Applause.) Very impressive.

And let's not forget that all of this represents the efforts of just a tiny fraction of our faith and community organizations. Just a tiny fraction. That's what they've done in just a short period of time.

So just imagine what we could achieve if every single organization and every single congregation in America got involved in this way. Just imagine. Imagine how many children we could feed. Imagine how many miles we'd walk. Imagine how many lives would be transformed.

So today, I have just one simple request for congregations and organizations across America, and that is: Join us. Join us. Be a part of this effort. Join us. If you're in a leadership role, make wellness a priority both with words and with deeds. Talk about the importance of healthy eating and physical activity with your members. Get organized. Get organized by creating a wellness council or a ministry, appointing a health ambassador to lead the charge.

There are so many natural leaders in our congregations who are just waiting to be tapped. Maybe there's a gardener who's been growing food in her backyard who wants to help the church out. Or maybe there's a nurse or a dietitian, a community health worker, who's eager to share their expertise. Maybe there's somebody who's just a great cook—right—and knows how to make some good, healthy snacks that taste good, too, right?

And once you've gotten organized, I want you to take action. Don't hold back. On this one, the sky should be the limit. You can host cooking classes or a farmers market. I just tried Zumba, which is like—that was pretty good. (Applause.) See! We've got a lot of Zumbas. We're Zumbaing after church—man, look out. (Laughter.)

You can take your youth group on a weekend hike, or better yet, a weekly jog. They will love the time spent with an adult. You can try substituting fresh fruit and vegetables for those donuts and coffee cake after service—right?

And anyone who is interested for additional ideas, tools, resources, you can go directly to the website at Letsmove.gov. There are so many fun things, ways people are doing—there are so many creative activities happening in congregations and in communities across the country. And I hope you all will be inspired to do even more.

And whatever you do, I want to know about it. Tell me about it. Whatever you're doing out in your congregations, I want you to email me, I want you to write me. Even better, I want you to send me a video of what you're doing. Because today, I'm announcing—listen up—that "Let's Move" is starting a video contest—and we're asking faith and community organizations to show us the best examples of the healthy changes that you're making. And you know what, the winners—you know what we're going to do? We're going to invite them to the White House this summer. (Applause.) Come on to the White House! Our top entrees. Because I want to meet you all in person; I want to hear about all that you're doing. So, hopefully that's a little incentive. Maybe a little fun—the funnier, the better. You've seen me—I love fun. (Laughter.)

So I really do hope that all of you, here and congregations and organizations across this country, will embrace these efforts on behalf of our children. Because we all know that we are our children's first and best role models. No matter what they see or hear, we're it. And if we embrace this work, our kids will embrace it. If we're excited about it, then they will be excited about it, too.

It won't be easy. But our faith communities have never shrunk from a challenge right? From slavery to civil rights, from poverty to human rights, so many of our congregations have been a force for justice and equality. (Applause.) Right? So many have been the righteous voice for the least among us, working every day, in ways large and small, to repair our world. And today, once again, we need all of you to help lead the way on this important issue. We need your vision. We need your moral passion. As it says in this church's vision statement, it says, "A vision is a clear mental picture of a preferable future. It sees the future through the eyes of faith."

We all know the future we want for our kids. We all know that, right? No matter who those kids are, we know what we want for our kids. We want them, every single one of them—every single one of them—to be healthy and whole. We want them to have opportunities that we never dreamed of. We want them to have families of their own that love them. We want them to have communities that support and sustain them. And we want them to have the strength and the energy and the stamina to live their lives to the fullest—and to raise their own children to do the same. That's how we build community. That's how we do it.

Again, while it won't be easy to make that vision a reality, I have faith that together, we will get where we need to go. I mean, it's the same faith that so many of you share—"the substance of things hoped for, and the evidence of things not seen." (Applause.) And with that faith, and with that hope, let us join together—every single one of us—and work together in this campaign for our children's lives.

Let's finish what we started—this wonderful journey—and give our kids everything they need for the bright, healthy futures they all deserve.

I look forward to working with you all in the months and years to come. Thank you all and God bless. (Applause.)

About Michelle Obama

Michelle Obama is the current First Lady of the United States of America. She is the wife of President Barack Obama, and has been First Lady since his inauguration as president in January 2009. Obama was born Michelle LaVaughn Robinson on January 17, 1964, in Chicago, Illinois. She attended Princeton University and graduated in 1985 with a bachelor's degree in sociology. Obama earned her law degree from Harvard Law School in 1988. After graduating from Harvard Law, Obama joined Sidley and Austin, the Chicago law firm where she would meet her future husband, Barack Obama. She left Sidley and Austin in the early 1990s and worked as an assistant to Chicago mayor Richard Daley. In 1996, Obama joined the University of Chicago as associate dean of student services. She also worked as vice president of community and external affairs for the university's medical center. Her primary initiatives as First Lady include fighting childhood obesity and supporting the families of military veterans.

The Rising Importance of Family Medicine

By Margaret Chan

Margaret Chan, the director-general of the World Health Organization, addresses an audience of physicians at the 2013 World Congress of the World Organization of Family Doctors. Chan outlines the primary challenges facing modern medicine in the twenty-first century, including an aging population of unprecedented size, rising obesity rates, and drug-resistant bacterial diseases. She warns of the possibility of a "post-antibiotic era," in which common infections no longer respond to existing medications and therefore become fatal. Due to the rising rates of chronic disease, she emphasizes the importance of family medicine in providing long-term and comprehensive care to manage and prevent these diseases. Likewise, Chan asserts that, while hospitals and specialists are essential, primary care is vital for providing the best possible care at the lowest cost.

Excellencies, honorable ministers, family doctors, ladies and gentlemen, I thank WONCA [World Organization of Family Doctors] for organizing this world congress. The work of WHO and WONCA shares much common ground, especially in the priority we give to primary care and prevention.

Given the unique health challenges of the twenty-first century, this common ground has risen in importance. It is good to see our joint work receiving well-deserved attention.

I thank the Czech Republic for hosting this event in the beautiful city of Prague. We can all enjoy its monuments, its showcase modern architecture, and the many visible signs of its rich history as a center of trade, culture, and architecture.

I welcome this opportunity to address an audience of family doctors. Your profession also has a rich history, with many achievements to showcase.

Your work continues a long and noble tradition. The first physicians were generalists. Family doctors have always been the backbone of health care. Family doctors have always been the bedrock of comprehensive, compassionate, and people-centered care.

Today, you are the rising stars who offer our best hope of coping with a number of complex and ominous trends. Your talents and skills are needed, and wanted, now more than ever before.

My passion for family medicine is personal as well as professional.

My first career choice was to be a teacher of young children. Then I followed my

Delivered June 26, 2013, at the World Congress of the World Organization of Family Doctors, Prague, Czech Republic, by Margaret Chan.

heart in the most literal sense possible. My future husband had chosen medicine as a career. I adapted my plans accordingly. I followed him to Canada where we undertook our medical studies together.

I have never regretted either of those two decisions. Not the career or the husband.

I have now worked in public health for 35 years. Much has changed, of course. But the rate and complexity of these changes has accelerated most dramatically since the start of this century. These changes have fundamentally altered the landscape of medical care, the nature of threats to health, and the strategies for their prevention.

Ladies and gentlemen,

In our world of radically increased interdependence, health everywhere is being shaped by the same powerful forces, like demographic aging, rapid urbanization, and the globalization of unhealthy lifestyles.

Under pressure from these forces, the disease burden has shifted in a fundamental way. Chronic noncommunicable diseases have overtaken infectious diseases as the leading cause of morbidity, disability, and mortality.

This shift has major implications for the organization, financing, and delivery of health care.

Prevention has become problematic. The root causes of chronic diseases reside in non-health sectors. They are profoundly shaped by the products and marketing practices of the tobacco, food, beverage, and alcohol industries.

Obesity is also profoundly shaped by some of these industries, and it is likewise on the rise. WHO data show that rates of obesity have nearly doubled since 1980 in every region of the world.

There are many reasons why not one single country has managed to turn its obesity epidemic around in all age groups. Here is just one. Health budgets are ridiculously tiny when compared with the marketing and advertising budgets of these industries.

Populations are aging at an unprecedented rate. WHO estimates that, within the next five years, the population of people aged 65 and older will outnumber children under the age of five for the first time in history.

The therapeutic arsenal for clinical care has changed, in ominous ways. As drug resistance continues to increase, medicine is losing its front-line antimicrobials at an alarming rate. For some forms of drug-resistant tuberculosis, second-line medicines are failing as well. For some diseases, like gonorrhea, the cupboard is nearly bare.

Some experts say that medicine is moving back to the pre-antibiotic era. No. With so few replacement drugs in the pipeline, we are moving to a post-antibiotic era where many common infections will once again kill.

This will be the end of modern medicine as we know it. In a post-antibiotic era, sophisticated interventions, like hip replacements, organ transplants, cancer chemotherapy, and care of preterm infants, will become far more difficult or even too dangerous to undertake.

At the same time, new medical technologies, interventions, devices, and drugs for chronic diseases are being developed and introduced with unprecedented speed. They come at a heavy cost.

Medicine is one of the few areas of technical innovation where new products are nearly always much more costly, more sophisticated, more difficult to use, and more likely to malfunction.

This is certainly not the case with other areas of technology, like flat-screen TVs or computers and hand-held devices, where products keep getting easier to use and cheaper to buy.

In terms of actually being able to afford the latest technical innovations, health care in many countries is approaching the limit, the tipping point where constantly rising costs become unsustainable.

As the Lancet Oncology Commission observed, cancer care in wealthy countries operates in a culture of excess: excessive diagnostic tests, excessive interventions, and excessive promises that create unrealistic expectations for patients and their families.

These expectations, in turn, lead patients to undergo end-of-life interventions that are toxic, painful, disconcerting, and extremely expensive, yet of no proven benefit to patients. As doctors, this was not the kind of service meant when we took the Hippocratic oath.

These trends are universal, and they bring universal challenges to service delivery everywhere. Everywhere, costs are soaring, budgets are shrinking, and public expectations for health care are rising.

And there are other problems. We live in an era of inequalities that are getting worse instead of better. Our world is dangerously out of balance, also in matters of health.

A world that is greatly out of balance is neither stable nor secure. This point was vividly demonstrated in 2011, when protests and demonstrations against social inequalities made the headlines and toppled governments.

Gaps, between and within countries, in income levels, opportunities, health outcomes, and access to care, are greater today than at any time in recent decades.

According to a major study from the Organization for Economic Cooperation and Development, income inequalities have reached their highest level in half a century.

The difference in life expectancy between the richest and poorest countries now exceeds 40 years. Total annual government expenditure on health ranges from as little as US $1 per person to more than US $7,000.

The rise of costly and demanding chronic diseases is certain to increase these gaps and inequalities even further. In 2010, the USA alone spent US $124 billion on cancer care. Worldwide, some 30 countries, including 15 in sub-Saharan Africa, do not possess a single radiation therapy machine.

Against this backdrop, prevention and primary care come to the fore as never before. The ground for this shift has been well-prepared. International public health has learned some major lessons since the late 1970s.

Ladies and gentlemen,

At the international level, approaches to the organization of health services and the provision of care have undergone some recent pendulum swings. The swings have been dramatic, highly visible, hotly debated, and played out on the global stage.

In 1978, the Declaration of Alma launched the health for all movement based on primary health care. It articulated a set of guiding principles and ethical values, including equity, solidarity, and the need for fairness in access to health care. It positioned primary care as the springboard for a larger social and political movement towards more equitable care.

These noble ambitions were followed almost immediately by an oil crisis and a global recession. As resources for health declined, selective approaches using packages of interventions gained favor over the intended aim of fundamentally reshaping health care.

AIDS emerged and exploded. Fueled by the AIDS epidemic, tuberculosis returned with a vengeance. The malaria situation deteriorated to the point that it was said to be "stable," since it could hardly get any worse.

The 1980s became known as the "lost decade for development." The pendulum swung away from broad-based programs of equitable care towards the urgent management of high-mortality diseases.

At the turn of the century, the Millennium Declaration, with its eight development goals, marked the start of the most ambitious attack on human misery in history, including the misery caused by disease.

Commitment to the health-related goals brought out the best in human creativity and generosity. Innovative ways were found to scale up the delivery of life-saving interventions. Funding increased nearly three-fold.

But commitment to the goals also stimulated the creation of numerous global health initiatives focused on a single disease or set of interventions, such as childhood vaccines. When confronted with weak capacities in recipient countries, many of these initiatives built their own parallel systems for procurement, delivery, financial management, monitoring, and reporting.

The delivery of care became fragmented. Some eye-catching and mind-boggling statistics began to emerge. In a single year, Viet Nam dealt with more than 400 donor missions to review health projects or the health sector. In a single year, Rwanda has to report to various donors on 890 health indicators, with nearly 600 relating to HIV and malaria alone.

With the rise of chronic diseases, the swing is now firmly in the direction of integrated, comprehensive, people-centered primary care. As health professionals now recognize, these diseases cannot be prevented or managed in the absence of a strong primary care infrastructure.

A health system where primary care is the backbone and family doctors are the bedrock delivers the best health outcomes, at the lowest cost, and with the greatest user satisfaction.

One statistic makes the point. In some countries where chronic diseases are the principal health burden, family doctors manage 95 percent of the health problems while absorbing only 5 percent of the health budget.

Some would argue that this satisfaction on the part of users extends to healt care providers as well. Some would say that family doctors enjoy the most satisfying and rewarding careers in medicine.

The work of a family doctor is hard and demanding. You don't earn the highest pay. Your waiting rooms may have patients in every age group, with every imaginable symptom and complaint, with the full spectrum of challenges modern medicine is expected to address.

But you also have the satisfaction of getting to know your patients over time, and watching their lives and health evolve. Family doctors do the detective work that deepens the diagnosis to include the social and environmental causes of ill health.

Studies show that patients want care that is accessible and affordable. Above all, they want care that responds to them as people, in their unique family and social situations. People do not want to be treated like a collection of specialized body parts. They don't want to have bits and pieces fixed. They want to be treated as people with social and spiritual lives.

In a trend that started in the early years of the AIDS epidemic, many people now seek out their own medical information. They teach themselves how to read and understand research reports.

They search the many web sites that offer medical information. They come for consultations well-informed and ready to question, challenge, and make their own decisions. This can enrich the doctor-patient dialogue, but it also increases demands.

The use of social media can have a dark side, as we know very well from resistance to childhood immunization, out of unfounded fears of an increased risk for autism. This, too, makes the job of preventive care even harder.

Family doctors are the linchpin in the continuum of care. Some of your patients will need specialist treatment in hospitals. You coordinate this part of their care.

Your patients age. They develop multiple co-morbidities that may need treatment by multiple specialists. You remain the guardian of the whole person, making sure that treatments ordered by different doctors do not result in dangerous drug interactions and that contraindications are respected.

In 1978, the Declaration of Alma launched the health for all movement based on primary health care. It articulated a set of guiding principles and ethical values, including equity, solidarity, and the need for fairness in access to health care.

Specialized models of medical care are not an ideal approach to the management of aging populations. Family doctors, who are in the best position to cultivate long-term relationships with patients, are uniquely well-placed to help people age in good health, stay in their homes as long as possible, remain socially engaged, and find the right mix of specialized care when needed.

This integrated approach extends to multidisciplinary teamwork that includes nurses. In fact, one of the reasons why the

WHO Surgical Safety Checklist has been so successful is the fact that it engages the whole team, including nurses. All are given shared responsibility and equally important roles in protecting patients from dangerous or deadly errors.

In 2011, the United Nations General Assembly convened a special session on the prevention and control of noncommunicable diseases. This was only the second time in history that a health issue commanded such a high level of political attention.

As the Political Declaration issued by this event clearly stated, prevention must be the cornerstone of the global response to these deadly, demanding, and costly diseases.

Since the start of this century, WHO has made some significant contributions to population-wide prevention through adoption of a number of international instruments. The WHO Framework Convention on Tobacco Control is one especially strong example, as its provisions are legally binding.

Other instruments provide global strategies and policy options for reducing the harmful use of alcohol, and improving diets, nutrition, and physical activity. WHO Member States have also adopted recommendations for reducing the marketing of unhealthy foods and beverages to children.

Yet even if all these strategies were implemented to perfection, we would still have clinical cases of heart disease, cancer, diabetes, and chronic respiratory diseases, and these patients must be managed in growing numbers.

Prevention is rightly the cornerstone for the global response. But at the individual level, the personal level, family doctors are the cornerstone for both prevention and care.

Ladies and gentlemen,

Sometimes in technical meetings, when data and statistics are being discussed in the abstract, I have to remind participants to stop for a moment. Go back to the basics. Remember the people.

This is what makes our work matter, whether as family doctors or public health officials.

Health systems are social institutions. They do much more than deliver babies and pills, the way a post office delivers letters. Properly managed and financed, a well-functioning health system contributes to social cohesion and stability. At a time when so many world events give cause for international outrage, social cohesion and stability are prized assets everywhere.

Health systems must have specialists and hospitals, of course. But they must also have primary care doctors who care about prevention. They must have doctors who know their patients long enough and well enough to truly manage the totality of health in all its multiple dimensions, including mental and spiritual needs.

The dignity which every human being has at birth vanishes so easily in the labyrinth of high-tech, specialized, and depersonalized medical care. For patients, being able to talk to a doctor and undergo a professional examination has therapeutic value but also social value as a ritual.

Technology and computers can never substitute for the human side of the doctor-patient relationship. A long-term relationship that instills trust builds motivation.

Motivated people are the ones most likely to accept personal responsibility for maintaining good health.

Primary care is our best hope for the future. Family doctors are our rising stars for the future.

Out of the ashes built up by highly specialized, dehumanized, and commercialized medical care, family medicine rises like a phoenix, and takes flight, spreading its comprehensive spectrum of light, with the promise of a rainbow.

This is the ancient historical covenant between doctors and patients, and this is where the health and medical professions need to return. I encourage all of you to continue to cultivate the human side of medicine.

Thank you.

About Dr. Margaret Chan

Margaret Chan is the director-general of the World Health Organization (WHO). She has served in the position since November 2006, having previously worked as the WHO's director of the Department for Protection of the Human Environment, director of communicable diseases surveillance and response, and the representative of the director-general for pandemic influenza. She was born in 1947 in Hong Kong. Chan earned her medical degree from the University of Western Ontario and joined the Hong Kong Department of Health in 1978. She was appointed director of health in Hong Kong in 1994, and held this position during the first human outbreak of avian flu in 1997 and the SARS scare in the early 2000s. Chan joined the WHO in 2003, and after two years was named assistant director-general for communicable diseases. She was elected to her second five-year term as the director-general of the WHO in July 2012.

The Growing Movement for Universal Health Coverage

By Jim Yong Kim

In this speech delivered to the World Health Assembly in Geneva, Switzerland, World Bank Group president Jim Yong Kim calls upon world leaders to pursue universal health coverage as a means of eradicating absolute poverty. Kim draws a correlation between health care costs and poverty, citing statistics showing that health expenses force one hundred million people into poverty every year. He asserts a strong parallel between inequalities in health care availability and broader economic inequality. Mexico, Thailand, and Turkey are some of the countries Kim names as examples of the economic good that reformed health care systems focused on providing service to impoverished communities can do. Kim discusses five ways the World Bank Group plans to support member countries in their efforts to move toward a universal coverage system. The organization's goal, he says, is to end extreme poverty by 2030, and the only way to do so is through affordable health services for all people worldwide. Health care delivery, Kim repeatedly asserts, is one of the primary obstacles to providing universal health care. Traditional models must be reconsidered, he says. Point-of-service fees, for example, can be eliminated through a variety of sustainable financing options. Kim calls universal coverage a "systems challenge" and assures health ministers that the World Bank Group will provide valuable connections and support networks to help countries overcome any obstacles they might meet.

Mr. President, Director-General Dr. Margaret Chan, Excellencies, colleagues and friends:

We stand at a moment of exceptional possibility. A moment when global health and development goals that long seemed unattainable has moved within our reach. A moment, also, when dangers of unprecedented magnitude threaten the future of humankind. A moment that calls us to shed resignation and routine, to rekindle the ambition that has marked the defining chapters of global public health.

A generation must rise that will drive poverty from the earth. We can be that generation.

A generation must rise that will end the scourge of inequality that divides and destabilizes societies. We can be that generation.

A generation must rise that will bring effective health services to every person in every community in every country in the world. We will be that generation, and you—members of this Assembly—will lead the way.

Delivered May 21, 2013, at the World Health Assembly, Geneva, Switzerland, by Jim Yong Kim.

Yes, I'm optimistic. I'm optimistic because I know what global health has already achieved—what you have achieved.

In 2011, global average life expectancy reached 70 years, a gain of six years since 1990. The global child mortality rate has fallen 40 percent in the same period. In the ten years since Dr. Lee Jong-wook announced WHO's commitment to support countries in scaling up antiretroviral treatment for AIDS, 9 million people in developing nations have gained access to this life-saving therapy. These are just a few of the milestones of recent progress.

I have another reason to be optimistic. I know global health is guided by the right values.

Thirty-five years ago, the Alma-Ata Conference on Primary Health Care set powerful moral and philosophical foundations for our work. The Declaration of Alma-Ata confirmed the inseparable connection between health and the effort to build prosperity with equity, what the Declaration's authors called "development in the spirit of social justice."

Alma-Ata showed the importance of primary health care as a model of health action rooted in the community; responsive to the community's needs; and attuned to its economic, social and cultural aspirations. Alma-Ata set the bar high. But we continue to struggle to provide effective, high-value primary health care to all our citizens. Unfortunately, none of WHO's 194 Member States has yet built the perfect health care system. We can all get better and we know it.

But in the grand spirit of Alma-Ata, we must focus again on the link between health and shared prosperity. And, this time, we must turn our loftiest aspirations into systems that build healthier, more productive, more equitable societies.

For what Alma-Ata did not do was provide concrete plans or effective metrics for delivering on its admirable goals. In many cases, frontline efforts inspired by Alma-Ata lacked strategy; evidence-based delivery; and adequate data collection. This shouldn't have been surprising, and I'm certainly not criticizing global health leaders of that time. Indeed, many of the architects of Health For All are my heroes to this day.

Today, we have resources, tools and data that our predecessors could only dream of. This heightens our responsibility and strips us of excuses. Today we can and must connect the values expressed at Alma-Ata to strategy and systems analysis; to what I have been calling a "science of delivery"; and to rigorous measurement. And we must actually build healthier societies.

The setting for this work is the growing movement for universal health coverage.

The aims of universal coverage are to ensure that all people can access quality health services, to safeguard all people from public health risks, and to protect all people from impoverishment due to illness: whether from out-of-pocket payments for health care or loss of income when a household member falls sick.

Every country in the world can improve the performance of its health system in the three dimensions of universal coverage: access, quality, and affordability. Priorities, strategies and implementation plans will differ greatly from one country to another. In all cases, countries need to tie their plans to tough, relevant metrics. And international partners must be ready to support you. All of us together must prevent "universal coverage" from ending up as a toothless slogan that doesn't challenge us, force us to change, force us to get better every day.

The good news is that many countries are challenging themselves, measuring outcomes and achieving remarkable progress. Turkey launched its "Health Transformation Program" in 2003 to provide access to affordable, quality health services for all. Formal health insurance now covers more than 95 percent of the population. The health reform is one of a bundle of factors that have contributed to Turkey's health gains. Between 2003 and 2010, Turkey cut its infant mortality rate by more than 40 percent.

Whether a country's immediate priority is diabetes; malaria control; maternal health and child survival; or driving the "endgame" on HIV/AIDS, a universal coverage framework can harness disease-specific programs diagonally to strengthen the system.

Thailand's universal coverage reform dates from 2001. The program has substantially increased health care utilization, especially among the previously uninsured. And, as of 2009, the program had already reduced by more than 300,000 the number of Thai people suffering catastrophic health care costs.

And let me acknowledge that Thailand launched its universal coverage program against concerns over fiscal sustainability initially raised by my own institution, the World Bank Group. Thailand's health leaders were determined to act boldly to provide access for their whole population. Today the world learns from Thailand's example.

Many other countries are also advancing. And the growing momentum for universal health coverage coincides with a new chapter in the global fight against poverty.

Last month, the organization I lead, the World Bank Group, committed to work with countries to end absolute poverty worldwide by 2030. For the first time, we've set an expiration date for extreme poverty.

And we know that fighting absolute poverty alone is not enough. That's why we've set a second goal. We'll work with countries to build prosperity that is equitably shared, by nurturing economic growth that favors the relatively disadvantaged in every society. We'll track income growth among the poorest 40 percent of the population in every country and work with country leaders to continuously improve policy and delivery, so countries can achieve economic progress that is both inclusive and sustainable—socially, fiscally, and environmentally.

To end poverty and boost shared prosperity, countries need robust, inclusive economic growth. And to drive growth, they need to build human capital through investments in health, education and social protection for all their citizens.

To free the world from absolute poverty by 2030, countries must ensure that all of their citizens have access to quality, affordable health services.

This means that, today as never before, we have the opportunity to unite global health and the fight against poverty through action that is focused on clear goals.

Countries will take different paths towards universal health coverage. There is no single formula. However, today, an emerging field of global health delivery science is generating evidence and tools that offer promising options for countries.

Let me give just one example. For decades, energy has been spent in disputes opposing disease-specific "vertical" service delivery models to integrated "horizontal" models. Delivery science is consolidating evidence on how some countries have solved this dilemma by creating a "diagonal" approach: deliberately crafting priority disease-specific programs to drive improvement in the wider health system. We've seen diagonal models succeed in countries as different as Mexico and Rwanda.

Whether a country's immediate priority is diabetes; malaria control; maternal health and child survival; or driving the "endgame" on HIV/AIDS, a universal coverage framework can harness disease-specific programs diagonally to strengthen the system.

As countries advance towards universal health coverage, there are two challenges we at the World Bank Group especially want to tackle with you. These two areas are deeply connected to the goals on poverty and shared prosperity I described a moment ago.

First, let's make sure that no family, anywhere in the world, is forced into poverty because of health care expenses. By current best estimates, worldwide, out-of-pocket health spending forces 100 million people into extreme poverty every year, and inflicts severe financial hardship on another 150 million. This is an overwhelming form of affliction for people, as the anguish of impoverishment compounds the suffering of illness. Countries can end this injustice by introducing equitable models of health financing along with social protection measures such as cash transfers for vulnerable households.

Second, let's close the gap in access to health services and public health protection for the poorest 40 percent of the population in every country. Improving health coverage and outcomes among the poorer people of any country is critical to building their capabilities and enabling them to compete for the good jobs that will change their lives. We have to close health gaps, if we're serious about reducing economic inequality, energizing countries' economies and building societies in which everyone has a fair chance.

The issue of point-of-service fees is critical. Anyone who has provided health care to poor people knows that even tiny out-of-pocket charges can drastically reduce their use of needed services. This is both unjust and unnecessary. Countries can replace point-of-service fees with a variety of forms of sustainable financing that don't risk putting poor people in this potentially fatal bind. Elimination or sharp reduction of point-of-service payments is a common feature of all systems that have successfully achieved universal health coverage.

Now let me tell you five specific ways the World Bank Group will support countries in their drive towards universal health coverage.

First, we'll continue to ramp up our analytic work and support for health systems.

Universal coverage is a systems challenge, and support for systems is where the World Bank Group can do the most to help countries improve the health of your people.

I was recently in Afghanistan, where the Bank Group has been working with the government and other partners to rebuild the country's health system. In Afghanistan, this abstract term "health system" quickly becomes personal. Let me tell one story. Several years ago, Shakeba, a young woman from Parwan province, gave birth at home, because there was no health center she could go to. She developed complications and lost her baby. Earlier this year, Shakeba gave birth to another child—in the delivery room of a recently-opened health center, with modern equipment and skilled personnel. Shakeba and her new baby are thriving. Improving health systems literally means life or death for many mothers and children.

The number of functioning health facilities in Afghanistan grew more than four-fold from 2002 to 2011. During this time, the country reduced under-five mortality by more than 60 percent.

Middle-income countries may face very different challenges. Many middle-income countries I visit are suffering from an epidemic of hospital-building. In some countries, I've seen brand-new, ultra-sophisticated emergency facilities where specialists are preparing to treat, for example, complicated emergencies like diabetic ketoacidosis. But when patients are released from these facilities, they can't get adequate support in the routine, daily management of illnesses like diabetes, because the primary care system has been starved of financing. It makes no sense to pour resources into responding to downstream complications, without investing in upstream prevention and disease management that could often keep those complications from happening in the first place.

When countries anchor their health systems in robust primary care and public health protection, health care costs can be controlled. We will work with all countries to do just that.

Our second commitment is that we will support countries in an all-out effort to reach Millennium Development Goals 4 and 5, on maternal mortality and child mortality.

Reaching these two MDGs is a critical test of our commitment to health equity.

We must continue to focus on the MDGs, even as we prepare for the post-2015 development agenda. The MDGs have given energy and focus to everyone in the global development community. We have not finished the job. Now is the time to do it.

Last September at the United Nations General Assembly, I announced that the World Bank Group would work with donors to create a funding mechanism to scale up support for MDGs 4 and 5. Since then, we have been expanding our results-based financing for health, focusing on the maternal and child health goals. Our results-based financing fund has leveraged substantial additional resources from the International Development Association, IDA, the World Bank Group's fund for the poorest countries. This has been an unquestioned success: the trust fund has multiplied resources for maternal and child health. Over the past five years, we have leveraged $1.2 billion of IDA in 28 countries, including $558 million for 17 countries since last September alone. Now we are working with Norway, the United Kingdom and other partners to expand this effort.

Results-based financing is a smart way to do business. It involves an up-front agreement between funders and service-providers about the expected health results. Payment depends on the delivery of outcomes, with independent verification. Results-based financing also allows citizens to hold providers accountable. It puts knowledge and power in ordinary people's hands.

These programs all have rigorous impact evaluations. In Rwanda, the impact evaluation showed officials that performance incentives not only increased the coverage and quality of services, but also improved health outcomes. The study found that babies were putting on more weight, and that children were growing faster.

Our third commitment is that with WHO and other partners, the World Bank Group will strengthen our measurement work in areas relevant to universal health coverage. In February, the Bank and WHO agreed to collaborate on a monitoring framework for universal coverage. We'll deliver that framework for consultation with countries by the time of the United Nations General Assembly in September.

We don't have enough data. For example, we don't yet measure the number of people forced into poverty by health expenditures in every country each year. We will work with countries and partners to make sure we get better data so countries can achieve better outcomes.

Fourth, we will deepen our work on what we call the science of delivery. This is a new field that the World Bank Group is helping to shape, in response to country demand. It builds on our decades of experience working with countries to improve services for poor people. As this field matures, it will mean that your frontline workers—the doctors and nurses, the managers and technicians—will have better tools and faster access to knowledge to provide better care for people.

Distinguished ministers, as you move towards universal coverage, tell us where you're hitting barriers in delivery. We'll connect you and your teams to global networks of policymakers and implementers who have faced similar problems. We'll mobilize experienced experts from inside and outside the World Bank Group, including from the private sector, where much of the best delivery work happens.

Fifth and finally, the World Bank Group will continue to step up our work on improving health through action in other sectors, because we know that policies in areas such as agriculture, clean energy, education, sanitation, and women's empowerment all greatly affect whether people lead healthy lives.

Mexico has done an impressive job in this respect. Mexico's Seguro Popular, for instance, works in concert with the Oportunidades cash transfer program. Oportunidades has increased poor people's spending capacity and reduced the depth of poverty. It has also raised school enrollment and access to health services among the poor. Meanwhile, Seguro Popular has reduced out-of-pocket health care payments and catastrophic health expenditures, especially for the poorest groups. All countries can't match Mexico's resources. But promising options for similar types of action exist for all countries.

When ministers of health seek to integrate expanded health coverage with efforts to reduce poverty, the World Bank Group's policy advice, knowledge resources and convening power are at your disposal. For instance, we can help facilitate discussions with ministries of finance. We saw promising steps in this direction at the meeting of African health and finance ministers in Washington last month.

But specific actions from the World Bank Group must be part of a wider change in how we work together as a global health community.

The fragmentation of global health action has led to inefficiencies that many ministers here know all too well: parallel delivery structures; multiplication of monitoring systems and reporting demands; ministry officials who spend a quarter of their time managing requests from a parade of well-meaning international partners.

This fragmentation is literally killing people. Together we must take action to fix it, now.

Aligning for better results is the approach of the International Health Partnership, or IHP+. And it's gaining momentum. Earlier today, Director-General Margaret Chan and I took part in an IHP+ meeting. It's inspiring to see more and more countries taking charge, setting the agenda based on strong national plans, and making development partners follow the lead of governments.

We are reconfirming our shared commitment to IHP+ as the best vehicle to implement development effectiveness principles and support countries driving for results. But, honorable ministers, we must hold each other accountable. We all have to be ready to pound the table and demand that we stop the deadly fragmentation that has hindered the development of your health systems for far too long. The stakes are high and the path will be difficult, but I know we can do it.

My friends,

Together, we face a moment of decision. The question is not whether the coming decades will bring sweeping change in global health, development and the fundamental conditions of our life on this planet. The only question is what direction that change will take:

Toward climate disaster or environmental sanity;

Toward economic polarization or shared prosperity;

Toward fatal exclusion or health equity.

Change will come—it's happening now. The issue is whether we will take charge of change: become its architects, rather than its victims. The gravest danger is that we might make decisions by default, through inaction. Instead, we must make bold commitments.

Since the turn of the millennium, we have experienced a golden age in global health, shaped by the achievements of the leaders in this hall. But will history write that the golden age expired with its hopes unfulfilled, its greatest work barely begun? That it sank under the weight of economic uncertainty and leaders' inability to change, to push ourselves beyond our old limits?

We know what the answer must be. The answer that the peoples of all our nations are waiting for—those living today and those yet to be born.

We can do so much more. We can bend the arc of history to ensure that everyone in the world has access to affordable, quality health services in a generation.

Together, let's build health equity and economic transformation as one single structure, a citadel to shelter the human future.

Now is the time to act.

We must be the generation that delivers universal health coverage.

We must be the generation that achieves development in the spirit of social and environmental justice.

We must be the generation that breaks down the walls of poverty's prison, and in their place builds health, dignity and prosperity for all people.

Thank you.

About Jim Yong Kim

Jim Yong Kim is the current president of the World Bank Group, having replaced Robert B. Zoellick in July 2012. Born in South Korea in 1959, Kim moved to Muscatine, Iowa, at the age of five. He graduated magna cum laude from Brown University with a bachelor's degree in human biology in 1982, received his MD from Harvard Medical School in 1991, and earned a PhD in anthropology from Harvard in 1993. Kim cofounded Partners in Health—a Boston-based health care organization that provides services to some of the world's poorest communities—in 1987. Kim was instrumental in the 2003 launch of the World Health Organization's (WHO) 3 by 5 Initiative—a global effort to treat three million new HIV patients by 2005—and was the director of the WHO's Department of HIV/AIDS from 2004 to 2006. In 2006, Time magazine placed Kim on its 100 Most Influential People list in recognition of his work with 3 by 5, and for his efforts battling drug-resistant tuberculosis in Peru. He was named president of Dartmouth College in 2009, becoming the first Asian American president of an Ivy League institution. President Barack Obama nominated Kim to head the World Bank in March 2012.

3

The Debate on Gun Control

Residents of Sandy Hook, Connecticut, in the United States, listen to speakers during a rally on the National Mall in Washington, DC, January 26, 2013. Spurred by the Newtown, Connecticut elementary school massacre, gun control activists participate in the One Million Moms for Gun Control.

Pro-Gun Ownership and Anti-Gun Violence

By Mark E. Kelly

In testimony before the United States Senate Committee on the Judiciary, retired astro-naut and Navy captain Mark E. Kelly presents the position that he and his wife—for-mer Congresswoman Gabby Giffords, who was the victim of an assassination attempt in 2011—take on gun violence. Both Giffords and Kelly own firearms, he says, and both feel the right to do so must be preserved. Steps need to be taken, however, to re-duce the level of gun violence in America, Kelly says. He tells the story of the attempt on Giffords's life, and outlines the ways in which it might have been prevented. Kelly then presents a plan for addressing what he and Giffords feel are the underlying issues behind gun violence. These proposed measures include closing a private sales loophole in background check requirements, removing limitations on funding for gun violence research at the Centers for Disease Control and Prevention (CDC), enacting federal gun trafficking legislation, and setting boundaries on the lethality of legally available firearms. Kelly urges partisan civility and cooperation on the matter, and expresses his belief that a consensus can be reached that both preserves Second Amendment rights and protects the public from gun violence.

Thank you, Chairman Leahy and Ranking Member Grassley, for inviting me here today. I look forward to a constructive dialogue with your committee. I also want to take the opportunity to congratulate Gabby's friend and much respected former col-league, Jeff Flake, on his new role as Arizona's junior Senator.

As you know, our family has been immeasurably affected by gun violence. Gab-by's gift for speech is a distant memory. She struggles to walk, and she is partially blind. Her right arm is completely paralyzed. And a year ago she left a job she loved serving the people of Arizona.

But in the past two years, we have watched Gabby's determination, spirit, and intellect conquer her disabilities.

We aren't here as victims. We're speaking to you today as Americans.

We're a lot like many of our fellow citizens following this debate about gun vio-lence:

- We're moderates. Gabby was a Republican long before she was a Democrat.

- We're both gun owners, and we take that right and the responsibilities that come with it very seriously.

Delivered January 30, 2013, at the Hart Senate Office Building, Washington, DC, by Mark E. Kelly.

- And we watch with horror when the news breaks to yet another tragic shooting. After 20 kids and six of their teachers were gunned down in their classrooms at Sandy Hook, we said, this time must be different. Something needs to be done.

We are simply two reasonable Americans who realize we have a problem with gun violence, and we need Congress to act.

At 10:10 am on January 8, 2011, a young man walked up to Gabby at her constituent event at a Safeway in Tucson, leveled his gun, and shot her through the head. He then turned down the line and continued firing. In 15 seconds, he emptied his magazine. It contained 33 bullets; there were 33 wounds.

As the shooter attempted to reload, he fumbled. A woman grabbed the next magazine, and others tackled and restrained him.

Gabby was the first victim. Christina-Taylor Green, nine years old, born on 9/11 2001, was shot with the thirteenth bullet or after. And others followed.

The killer in the Tucson shooting suffered from severe mental illness. He is a paranoid schizophrenic who had been deemed unqualified for service in the United States Army and exhibited increasingly bizarre behavior as he spiraled toward murder. At Pima Community College, his disruptions led to run-ins with the campus police and his expulsion, but was never reported to mental health authorities.

On November 30, 2010, he walked into a sporting goods store, passed a federal NICS [National Instant Criminal Background Check System] background check, and walked out with a Glock 19 semiautomatic handgun. He had never been legally adjudicated as mentally ill, and, even if he had, Arizona at the time had over 121,000 records of disqualifying mental illness it had not submitted to the background check system.

Looking back, we can't say with certainty, "Only if we had done this, it wouldn't have happened." There isn't a single action or law that could have elegantly prevented the Tucson shooting from being written into the history books.

Gabby is one of roughly 100,000 victims of gun violence in America every year. Behind every victim lays a matrix of failure and inadequacy—in our families, communities, and values; in our society's approach to poverty, violence, and mental illness; and, yes, in our politics and in our gun laws.

One of our messages is simple: The breadth and complexity of the problem of gun violence is great, but it is not an excuse for inaction.

As you know, there's another side to our story.

Gabby is a gun owner. I am a gun owner.

We have our firearms for the same reasons millions of Americans just like us have guns—to defend ourselves, our family, and our property, and to go hunting or target shooting.

We believe wholly and completely in the Second Amendment of our Constitution—and that it confers upon all Americans the right to own a firearm for protection, collection, and recreation.

We take that right very seriously, and we would never, ever give it up—just like Gabby would never relinquish her gun, and I would never relinquish mine.

But rights demand responsibility. And this right does not extend to terrorists. It does not extend to criminals. It does not extend to the mentally ill.

When dangerous people get guns, we are all vulnerable—at the local movie theater, worshipping at church, conducting our everyday business, exercising our civic responsibilities as Americans, and—time after time after time—at school, on our campuses, in our children's classrooms.

When dangerous people get dangerous guns, we are all the more vulnerable. Dangerous people with weapons specifically designed to inflict maximum lethality upon others have turned every corner of our society into places of carnage and gross human loss.

Our rights are paramount. But our responsibilities are serious. And as a nation we are not taking responsibility for the gun rights our founders conferred upon us.

Gabby and I are pro-gun ownership. We are anti-gun violence.

And we believe that in this debate Congress should look not toward special interests and ideology, which push us apart, but toward compromise, which brings us together. We believe whether you call yourself pro-gun or anti-gun violence, or both—that you can work together to pass laws that save lives.

We have some ideas for you.

Fix background checks. Currently up to 40 percent of all gun transfers are made through private sales and without background checks. Not surprisingly, 80 percent of criminals reported obtaining their weapons through private sales with no background check. This makes a mockery of our background check system. Congress should close the private sales loophole and strengthen the background check system by requiring states and the federal government to supply the necessary records.

Remove the limitations on the CDC and other public health organizations on collecting data and conducting scientific research on gun violence. As a fighter pilot and astronaut, I saw the value of using data to achieve our military and scientific objectives. We wouldn't have gotten to the Moon or built the International Space Station without robust use of data to make informed decisions. It is simply crazy that we limit gun violence data collection and analysis when we could use that knowledge to save lives.

Enact a federal gun trafficking statute with real penalties for people in the business of helping criminals get guns. Let's get law enforcement the tools they need to stop violent criminals from killing people with illegal guns.

And, finally, let's have a careful and civil conversation about the lethality of the firearms we permit to be legally bought and sold. You can't just walk into a store and buy a machine gun, but you can easily buy a semi-automatic high-velocity assault rifle and/or high-capacity

Behind every victim lays a matrix of failure and inadequacy—in our families, communities, and values; in our society's approach to poverty, violence, and mental illness; and, yes, in our politics and in our gun laws.

ammunition magazines. We should come together and decide where to draw that line in such a way that it protects our rights and communities alike.

This country and this Congress can find a commonsense consensus on preventing gun violence and protecting our inviolable Second Amendment rights. We went to the Moon and back within a decade of deciding we were going to do it. We have prevailed over adversaries big and small. Surely when the safety of our communities, our schools, and our children is at stake, our politics can provide a path toward compromise, and not an obstacle that can't be overcome.

Thank you.

About Mark E. Kelly

Mark Kelly is a retired American astronaut and the husband of former United States congresswoman Gabrielle Giffords. Kelly was born on February 21, 1964, in Orange, New Jersey. His identical twin brother, Scott, is also an astronaut; they are the only siblings to have both been to outer space. Kelly graduated from the US Merchant Marine Academy in 1986 with a bachelor's degree in marine engineering and nautical science. He earned a master's degree in aeronautical engineering from the US Naval Postgraduate School in 1994. In 1987, Kelly became a naval aviator. From 1993 to 1994, Kelly trained at the US Naval Test Pilot School. His first space shuttle mission was in 2001, as pilot of the Endeavour *on a trip to the* International Space Station. *Kelly became a prominent gun-control advocate following an assassination attempt on his wife in January 2011. In 2013, he and Giffords founded a political action committee called* Americans for Responsible Solutions.

The Human and Economic Cost of Gun Violence

By James Johnson

In a speech presented before the US Senate Judiciary Committee, Baltimore County police chief James Johnson urges Congress to implement stricter gun control measures, including background checks for firearm purchasers, bans on assault weapons, and limiting high-capacity ammunition-feeding devices (magazines) to ten rounds. Speaking on behalf of the National Law Enforcement Partnership to Prevent Gun Violence, Johnson backs up his argument by presenting statistics on the number of firearm-related deaths in the United States and the financial burden associated with gun violence. He asserts that the current background check system is not viable and that more thorough screenings can help prevent guns from falling into the hands of criminals and the mentally ill. Johnson also explains why, in his view, these commonsense measures will save lives without violating Second Amendment rights.

Mr. Chairman, Ranking Member, and Members of the Committee, I want to thank you for the opportunity to testify today. I am here on behalf of the National Law Enforcement Partnership to Prevent Gun Violence, an alliance of the nation's law enforcement leadership organizations concerned about the unacceptable level of gun violence in the United States.

The Partnership, founded in 2010, includes: the Commission on Accreditation of Law Enforcement Agencies; Hispanic American Police Command Officers Association; International Association of Campus Law Enforcement Administrators; International Association of Chiefs of Police; Major Cities Chiefs Association; National Association of Women Law Enforcement Executives; National Organization of Black Law Enforcement Executives; Police Executive Research Forum; and the Police Foundation.

We mourn those lost to gun violence, including the twenty children in Newtown, along with the six brave adults whose lives were cut short by a deranged individual armed with firepower originally designed for combat, not for gunning down innocent members of our communities.

More than thirty homicides occur in America each day. Two thousand children, ages eighteen and under, die of firearm-related deaths in the US every year. In 2011, for the first time in fourteen years, firearms were the leading cause of death for police officers killed in the line of duty. In just the two-week period after the Newtown massacre, six police officers were killed and 10 injured in 12 separate shootings.

Delivered January 30, 2013, at the Hart Senate Office Building, Washington, DC, by James Johnson.

In a one-week period in 2011, the Police Executive Research Forum (PERF) found that gun crime in six cities cost more than $38 million, and in the year 2010 cost the entire country more than $57 billion.

We urgently need Congress to address the rising epidemic of gun violence. Law enforcement leaders support the President's comprehensive approach, which includes enhancing safety at educational institutions and addressing mental health issues. But on behalf of my colleagues across the nation, I am here today to tell you that we are long overdue in strengthening our nation's gun laws. Doing so must be a priority for Congress.

The organizations in the National Law Enforcement Partnership to Prevent Gun Violence are united in urgently calling on Congress to:

- Require background checks for *all* firearm purchasers;

- Ensure that prohibited purchaser records in the National Instant Criminal Background Check System (NICS), are up-to-date and accurate; and

- Limit high-capacity ammunition-feeding devices to ten rounds.

Seven of our nine groups, including the largest organizations among us, also support a ban on two assault weapons and Senator Feinstein's legislation.

Federal law prohibits dangerous individuals, such as convicted felons and those with mental health disqualifiers, from possessing firearms. While background checks are required for purchases through federally licensed gun dealers, no check is required for private sales, such as those through Internet postings, print ads or gun shows.

From November 2011 to November 2012, an estimated 6.6 million firearm transactions occurred without a background check. Up to 40 percent of firearm transactions occur through private individuals rather than licensed gun dealers. Allowing 40 percent of those acquiring guns to bypass background checks is like allowing 40 percent of airline passengers to board a plane without going through airport security.

Last October, in Brookfield, Wisconsin, seven women were shot by a prohibited purchaser who was under a domestic violence restraining order. The shooter answered an online ad and was able to buy a gun without a background check. Had the sale required a check, this tragedy could have been prevented.

Background checks work. They stopped nearly 2 million prohibited purchases between 1994 and 2009. We already have a national background check system in place. Therefore, extending background checks to *all* firearm purchasers can easily be implemented—and should be, without delay.

> **The common-sense measures we are calling for will not infringe on Second Amendment rights, but will ensure that we keep guns out of dangerous hands and excessive firepower out of our communities.**

States can't do it alone. Interstate firearms trafficking is a serious problem that must be addressed federally. The problem is rampant: According to the ATF, [Bureau of Alcohol, Tobacco and Firearms] in 2009, 30 percent of guns recovered at crime scenes had crossed state lines.

Submissions to NICS must be improved, especially mental health and drug abuse records. The 2007 massacre at Virginia Tech is a tragic example of a prohibited purchaser slipping between the cracks due to incomplete NICS records.

The ban on assault weapons and high-capacity ammunition magazines must be reinstated. Like assault weapons, high-capacity magazines are not used for hunting, do not belong in our homes and wreak havoc in our communities. Banning these magazines will reduce the number of bullets a shooter can use before having to reload. Reloading can provide a window of time in which to take down a shooter, as we saw in Tucson.

In 1998, four years after the assault weapons and high-capacity ammunition magazine ban was enacted, the percentage of firearms with large-capacity magazines recovered by Virginia police decreased and continued to drop until it hit a low of 9 percent in 2004, the year the ban expired. It hit a high of 20 percent in 2010, according to a *Washington Post* analysis.

After the 1994 law expired, 37 percent of police agencies saw increases in criminals' use of assault weapons, according to a 2010 PERF [Police Executive Research] survey.

I have been in law enforcement for nearly thirty-five years, and have seen an explosion in firepower since the assault weapons ban expired. It is common to find many shell casings at crime scenes these days, as victims are being riddled with multiple gunshots.

The common-sense measures we are calling for will not infringe on Second Amendment rights, but will ensure that we keep guns out of dangerous hands and excessive firepower out of our communities.

Generations of Americans, including our youngest ones, are depending on you to ensure they will grow up and fulfill their roles in the great human experience. None of us can fail them. I urge you to follow the will of the American public and stand with law enforcement to enact these common-sense public safety measures.

Thank you.

About James Johnson

James Johnson is the chief of police for the Baltimore County Police Department and chair of the National Law Enforcement Partnership to Prevent Gun Violence. He began his career in law enforcement as a Baltimore County cadet in 1979, working in the 911 center. Johnson has a master's degree in applied behavioral science from Johns Hopkins University and a bachelor's degree in criminal justice from the University of Baltimore. He has served at every rank in the city's police department, including patrolman, corporal, sergeant, lieutenant, captain, and commander. Johnson was promoted to major in 2000 and tasked with commanding the western patrol division. From 2003 to 2006, he held the rank of colonel, and served as head of the human resources bureau. After a brief stint commanding the operations bureau, Johnson was appointed chief of police by County Executive Jim Smith in 2007. In 2010, County Executive Kevin Kamenetz reappointed Johnson to the post.

Stricter Gun Control Legislation: A Waste of Time

By Orrin Hatch

In an address to the US Senate Judiciary Committee, Senator Orrin Hatch, Republican of Utah, discusses essential criteria for effective gun control legislation. He contends that Congress must look back to past legislative experience, including a ten-year ban on federal assault weapons that he says had no impact on reducing gun violence, in order to assess the impact of future laws on curbing gun violence. Past legislative experience, in other words, reveals that most efforts for stricter gun control are futile because they have no effect on gun violence. He highlights underlying factors that do contribute to gun violence, including issues with mental health treatment and screenings, excessive violence in the media, ineffective background checks, and breakdown of the family unit. He asserts that none of these contributing factors have been included in current proposals and that they must be addressed in order to achieve an effective response to gun violence. Hatch emphasizes that whatever new legislation concerning gun violence entails, it must never infringe upon Second Amendment rights.

The recent mass shootings in this country have left us heartbroken and searching for answers. There has been a call to act by the Obama Administration, Members of Congress and the American public to find legislative solutions to curb gun violence. If we are to deal with this very complex problem via legislative solution, any legislation must meet three criteria. First and foremost, the legislation must be consistent with honoring the Second Amendment. Secondly, we must provide policy that draws from past legislative experience. Thirdly, we must consider and address all possible contributing factors to identify the root causes of this problem. Any legislation that fails to meet all three criteria is destined to be ineffective and a disservice to victims and their family members.

To date, legislative efforts have been a single-minded approach to the problem, additional gun control measures to include banning so-called assault weapons, banning so-called high-capacity magazines and heavier penalties for straw-purchasers.

Going forward, each of these legislative efforts will be individually analyzed to determine whether they are consistent with the principles of the Second Amendment. Any review of this legislation will include applying the principles discussed in recent decisions of the US Supreme Court and debated by Members of Congress. Whether they comport with the Second Amendment remains to be seen. However,

Delivered January 30, 2013, at the Hart Senate Office Building, Washington, DC, by Orrin Hatch.

what is certain is that all of the current proposals fail to satisfy the second and third criteria.

All of these legislative efforts fail to recognize the lessons learned from past legislative experience in this area, the second necessary criteria for a successful solution. History has shown that gun control legislation has had little to no effect on stemming these types of incidents. A ten year federal ban on assault weapons resulted in no discernible decrease in gun violence. Each and every one of the current proposals ignores the evidence and data that stricter gun control does not lead to a decrease in gun violence. The renewed efforts for stricter gun control are a waste of time, effort and resources as they have been proven ineffective.

In addition, these legislative actions fail to satisfy the third criteria, which is to consider and address all of the possible contributing factors to identify the root causes of this problem. Experts in the area of these types of shootings have identified common contributing causes, some of which include various issues with mental illness and treatment, violence in our culture through media, breakdown of the family unit, breakdowns in background checks for weapons purchases, response times of law enforcement, and the emergency action plans for schools. None of the identified contributing factors have been considered by the current proposals.

As we move forward, we must focus on a carefully considered, comprehensive approach that includes all of the factors discussed above. Anything less is a disservice to victims and their families.

About Orrin Hatch

Orrin Hatch is the senior United States senator from Utah. Having first been elected in 1976, Hatch is now in his seventh term, making him the most senior Republican in the Senate. Hatch was born on March 22, 1934, in the town of Homestead, in Pennsylvania's Allegheny County, where he spent his early school years in the Pittsburgh public school system. Hatch graduated with a bachelor's degree from Brigham Young University in 1959, and went on to get his law degree from the University of Pittsburgh Law School in 1962. He practiced law in Pennsylvania before moving to Utah in 1969, where he continued to practice until his election to the Senate. He was chairman of the Committee on Labor and Human Resources from 1981 to 1987, and chairman of the Committee on the Judiciary from 1995 to 2001, and then again from 2003 to 2005. He is currently a ranking member of the Senate Committee on Finance, and serves on the board of directors for the Holocaust Memorial Museum in Washington, DC.

A Father's Appeal to Ban Assault Weapons

By Neil Heslin

In this speech, Neil Heslin, the father of Jesse Lewis, a six-year-old boy who was killed during the Sandy Hook Elementary School shooting in Newtown, Connecticut, urges members of Connecticut's state legislature to implement a ban on assault weapons. During his emotional testimony, he recalls dropping off his son at Sandy Hook Elementary on the morning of December 14, 2012, the day when Adam Lanza shot and killed twenty children and six adults. He tells of the events after the shooting and the heartbreak he experienced from losing his son. Heslin asserts that high-capacity weapons belong on the battlefield, not American streets. He points out that the majority of mass shootings, including those in Aurora and Columbine, Colorado, were the result of assault weapons purchased illegally. Heslin concludes that, while work needs to be done in other areas such as mental health, banning assault weapons is the first step in preventing another massacre like Sandy Hook.

Good morning. My name is Neil Neslin. Jesse Lewis was my son. He was six years old. He was a victim at Sandy Hook. I'm here today to just hopefully get the word out that changes have to be made.

I will tell you a little about Jesse. He was a boy that loved life, lived it to the fullest. His mother and I are both separated. He spent equal amount of time with both of us. And, he was my son, he was my buddy, he was my best friend.

I never thought I would be here speaking because, asking for changes on my son's behalf. And I never thought I would [inaudible] the happiest day in my life was the day he was born. He's my only son, my only family. And the worst day of my life was the day when this happened. I was raised in a household with guns and weapons. In fact, I started skeet shooting when I was eight years old. I was educated on the safety of guns. My father was an avid hunter. I was hunting ever since I was eight or ten or twelve years old with him. I am not a gun owner now.

I think a lot of changes need to be made, as for the safety of handling the guns, regulations of the guns, handguns, long-arms, whatever you want to classify as an assault weapon. [Interruption in speech.] Heading back to where I left off. I was raised with firearms and hunting and skeet shooting. I am not in favor of banning guns or weapons. I'm in favor of, would like to see a lot stricter regulations, being on a federal regulation and on a state level. There's a lot of things that should be

Delivered January 28, 2013, at the hearing before the Gun Violence Prevention Working Group at the Legislative Office Building, Hartford, Connecticut, by Neil Heslin.

changed to prevent what happened, mental health being a big part, going back to the basics, better parenting. When I was raised, I was raised to respect my parents and my elders, not to kill my mother when she was sleeping. It just shocked me what happened in Newtown. I looked at these weapons that were presented by the state police here—the so-called assault weapons, meaning military-style or military-look, you can categorize and classify it however you want—I still can't see why any civilian, or anyone in this room in fact, needs weapons of that sort. They're not going to use them for hunting, or even for home protection. The semi-automatic weapon is the most inaccurate weapon out

> *We do not need these weapons on the streets or in our homes. And I ask everybody to think about it, and everybody in this room, whether you're in favor of guns or in favor of banning them, to try to work together, to come up with reasonable changes that work.*

there. The sole purpose of the semi-automatic, those AR-15s, or AK-47s, is to put a lot of lead out in the battlefield quickly. And that's what they do. And that's what they did at Sandy Hook Elementary, the school on the 14th. That was not just a killing—that was a massacre. Those children and those victims were shot apart, and my son was one of them.

This picture I brought with me today was taken six years ago; it was my son when he was six months old and myself. That was my mother's Christmas gift that year. My mother passed away five years ago. Ironically on the same day Jesse perished.

I just hope some good can come out of this, changes for mental health, ban on assault weapons. I just can't fathom why any of us need that, in our society or in our home. Why do we need thirty-round magazines or cartridges? There's no one in this room here that has the capability, mentally or physically, to take on twenty people or fifteen people where you would need thirty rounds of ammunition. There's no reason for it. I hope everybody in this room can realize that and see that.

There's a lot of people here that are in favor of guns and not changes. If they open their eyes and their minds, and supported changes, it would give them more rights if it were on a federally regulated program. It would give them more rights to take hunting weapons in and out of different states. I think both sides really need to work together to pass regulations that work for everybody.

I am never going to have my son back. I accepted what happened that day when it happened. I didn't like it. I couldn't change it. He wouldn't want me to sit around crying or feeling bad. I'm not trying to do something to help him or help the other victims. That school was a beautiful place. It was like Mayberry, going to that school in the morning. I never saw anybody that wasn't happy there. We dropped him off that morning at 9:04, I saw the clock, I walked him into that class, into the school. He gave me a hug and a kiss, and I gave him a kiss back, and he said goodbye. He said I love ya, and he said I loved mom too. We were supposed to go back and make gingerbread houses that day. We never made it. Twenty minutes after that, my son was dead.

There's no reason why Adam Lanza's mother should have had those weapons in that home, locked up or not locked up, with a child that apparently had mental issues. I think a lot of it goes back to mental issues. Years ago when we had Bellville, Fairfield Hills, and people were committed. You never heard of crimes like this. And I think that's a big thing they have to focus on, along with gun control.

The place to start is banning these weapons. There's no reason for these; there's no place on the street for them. Another argument that people have is, well, that criminals will have these weapons. You are never going to take the weapons away from criminals, or drug dealers, or people on the streets that have them. You have to make very strict penalties for that. Not a slap on the wrist. Not probation. You've got to make mandatory, harsh jail terms for those people. If they're convicted of committing a crime with a weapon, whether it's a robbery, a holdup, an assault, there's got to be strict penalties. You're not going to take, banning the firearms, you're not going to get them away from the criminals.

We do not need these weapons on the streets or in our homes. And I ask everybody to think about it, and everybody in this room, whether you're in favor of guns or in favor of banning them, to try to work together, to come up with reasonable changes that work. And I think one place to start is with the regulations on background checks, through background checks, for everyone who purchases a weapon. Resales have to have a thorough background check. I think a ban on high-capacity magazines in assault-type weapons needs to be in place. More strict guidelines for people that own them, such as the state has, the federal government has with machine guns.

I just can't believe what happened in Newtown. We dropped Jesse off at 9:04, and an hour-and-half later I was back at that school, and it was like a military installation. Swat team members, families hysterical, state police from all over the state, FBI—it was unbelievable. Students were there looking to be reunited with their parents, parents looking for their children. I was looking for my son; I was looking for his classroom. They were never to be found. What some of the surviving students' parents told me, my son Jesse yelled—run, run now! He was in Mrs. Soto's class, ten of the students survived. My son wasn't one of them. I hope those words helped some of the students survive. I just hope that some change can come out of it that's positive and good.

Newtown is a broken community. I see the people up there, they're heartbroken with heavy hearts. I had the opportunity to go into Chalk Hill School where these children are, and it wasn't a good feeling, it was a very sad feeling. And it's something that should have never happened.

Getting back to these high-capacity weapons. We are not living in the Wild West; we're not a Third World nation. We have the strongest military in the world. We do not need to defend our home with weapons like that. I just hope that everybody in this room, as I said before, can support change. Ban assault weapons and high-capacity clips in magazines, and that's a step in the right direction. And support federal changes in regulations. I don't know how many people have young children or children, but just try putting yourself in the place that I'm in or these other parents that are here, and having a child that you lost. It's not a good feeling. It's not a good feeling to look at your child lying in a casket. Or look at your child with a bullet wound to the forehead. It's a real sad thing.

I ask, is there anybody in this room that can give me a good reason or challenge this question—why anybody in this room needs to have one of these assault-style or military weapons or high-capacity clips? Not one person can answer that question. [From audience members: *Second amendment. Our rights.*] We are all entitled to our own opinion, and I respect their opinions and their thoughts. But I wish they'd respect mine and give it a little thought, and realize that it could have been their child that was in that school that day.

And I don't think any of the massacres or shootings in this country—I believe they all happened with assault weapons or assault-style weapons, high-capacity clips. Aurora, Columbine, Sandy Hook. I believe they were all purchased legally, too. Not to say that assaults like that couldn't happen in another way. But we need to cut down on the guns, those types of guns. There's no reason for it, and they cause destruction; they cause massacre. And that is what they were made to do. I just ask that they can place a ban on them. That is all I have to say at this time.

About Neil Heslin

Neil Heslin is the father of Jesse McCord Lewis, a six-year-old who was one of the twenty-six people killed in the December 2012 Sandy Hook Elementary School shooting. He has since become an advocate for gun-control efforts, appearing before the Senate Judiciary Committee during a hearing on proposed legislation to ban assault weapons and high-capacity magazines, and a Connecticut State Legislature subcommittee reviewing the state's gun laws.

A More Accountable Gun Culture

By Alan Lowenthal

In a speech delivered on the House floor, California Democrat Alan Lowenthal supports a proposed ban on high-capacity magazines and military-style assault weapons. Lowenthal opens with an anecdote about Peggy McCrum, the Long Beach chapter leader of the Brady Campaign to Prevent Gun Violence, whose brother Robert Kelly was fatally shot by a total stranger while walking to his car. On paper, Kelly was just another statistic, Lowenthal says, but, like all victims of gun violence, he was a human being with a future and a life cut short. Invoking the mass shootings in Newtown, Connecticut, and Aurora, Colorado, Lowenthal declares his support for a ban on assault rifles and high-capacity magazines. Americans have the right to feel safe in the streets, schools, and movie theaters of their country, he says. And while Second Amendment rights must be protected, there ought to be recognized, commonsense limits to its reach, according to Lowenthal. But efforts to reduce gun violence must go beyond bans, he says. Improvements to the mental health and criminal background check systems will do much to address the core issues behind America's gun violence problem, according to Lowenthal. He closes with a call to action for a more accountable gun culture that strikes a balance between the constitutional right to firearms ownership and the general public's right to feel safe.

Madame Speaker, I want to thank the gentlelady from California for calling us together to discuss this important issue.

I stand here today to join my colleagues as we put forth responsible solutions to reduce gun violence in our communities and throughout our country.

It was my honor to introduce from my district Peggy McCrum, the Chapter Leader of the Long Beach Area Brady Campaign to Prevent Gun Violence at yesterday's press conference hosted by the Brady Campaign and Mayors Against Illegal Guns. Three decades ago, her brother Robert Kelly was shot and killed by a complete stranger as he was walking to his parked car—unaware of the perils that awaited him.

It can be all too easy to see Robert as a statistic on a crime map, but he—like all victims of senseless violence—was much, much more. He was a son, a brother, and a loved one. He was 28 years old; a graduate of Cal State Long Beach who was excited about starting his career at an accounting software firm. That future . . . his future . . . ended all too soon at the hands of a criminal with a gun. To date, the killer has not been found.

Delivered February 2, 2013, at the US House of Representatives, Washington, DC, by Alan Lowenthal.

None of us are statistics. We are all living, breathing, caring people with real lives and hopes and dreams, and we all deserve the freedom to feel safe from gun violence, be it in our schools, our movie theaters, or our streets.

Peggy's brother Robert, the victims of tragedies like the Newtown and Aurora mass shootings, and the thousands of Americans whose lives are ended each year by gun violence, will never be forgotten; they should serve as a reminder to us of the fragility of human life and our ability as members of Congress to enact commonsense legislation necessary to prevent such horrific tragedies from continuing to devastate innocent Americans.

These children, their parents, and all of the families who have been affected by the senseless acts of violence that left our country shocked and in disbelief are counting on us to do something—anything to ensure that they have the freedom to feel safe in their schools and communities.

I stand here today in open support of a ban on military-style assault weapons and high-capacity magazines, similar to the gun laws we have in California. These instruments of mass destruction have no place in our society outside of the military, and I thank all of my colleagues on the Gun Violence Prevention Task Force, especially Congressman Thompson and Congresswoman Pelosi, for leading the charge on this effort.

The tragedy of gun violence will not be solved by banning assault weapons and ammunitions alone. We must strengthen our current background check system, as well as the National Instant Criminal Background Check System (NICS); we must increase access to mental health services; we must increase the student-to-counselor ratio in our children's schools; and we must lift the research ban on the Centers for Disease Control (CDC) and the National Institute of Health (NIH). All of these commonsense proposals are crucial to achieving meaningful reforms that will save countless lives.

As a community psychologist, I understand that the early identification and treatment of mental illnesses is the key to preventing potentially harmful acts. That being said, I am proud to cosponsor Congresswoman Barbara Lee's Student Support Act and Congresswoman Grace Napolitano's Mental Health in Schools Act. Both of these bills will address the growing mental health needs in our nation's 95,000 public schools.

The American people want action, and they are demanding a plan. My colleagues, I stand here wanting and demanding a plan. As the President said in his State of the Union address, these victims deserve a vote.

However, I do not, I repeat, I do not believe in taking away any American's Second Amendment right. Just as you cannot yell "fire" in a movie theater, I believe you cannot own weapons capable of killing 20 school children in a matter of seconds. The United States Supreme Court ruling on *Heller v. DC* clearly stated that there are, indeed, limitations to the Second Amendment, and I stand with that ruling. *Heller v. DC* was not meant to strip gun owners of their rights; it was meant to instill a greater sense of responsibility that comes with owning a gun.

I am in favor of protecting an individual's right to own a gun; I also want to help

> *Just as you cannot yell "fire" in a movie theater, I believe you cannot own weapons capable of killing 20 school children in a matter of seconds.*

create a more accountable gun culture—one that upholds Americans' constitutional right to bear arms, and keeps us safe from harm. The constitutional right to own a gun and the God-given human right to feel safe from gun violence is not mutually exclusive.

To conclude, we must all continue to listen to the victims, the survivors, and even those who speak out against gun law reforms; we will not be able to reach common ground on this issue unless we keep an open mind to all of the voices of the American people.

Thank you. I now yield back the balance of my time to the gentlelady from California.

About Alan Lowenthal

Alan Lowenthal is a United States Congressman representing California's Forty-Seventh District. A Democrat, Lowenthal was elected to the House in November 2012. He was born on March 8, 1941, and grew up in the New York City borough of Queens. In 1962, he earned a bachelor's degree in psychology from Hobart College. Lowenthal received a PhD from Ohio State University in 1967. He moved to Long Beach, California, in 1969, and accepted a teaching position at California State University, Long Beach, where he taught courses on community psychology until 1998. Lowenthal was elected to the Long Beach City Council in 1992, and served for six years before running for the California State Assembly. He won a seat representing the Fifty-Fourth District, and was reelected to a second term in 2000, and a third in 2002. In 2004, he was elected to the California Senate, where he served two terms.

The Right to Bear Arms Is an Individual Right

By Chris Stewart

In a speech delivered on the House floor, Congressman Chris Stewart, Republican of Utah, defends the right to private firearms ownership. He addresses recent acts of gun violence, cautioning that they should not be used as justification for stricter gun-control legislation. In 2008, the Supreme Court struck down a District of Columbia handgun ban in District of Columbia v. Heller, *ruling that the Second Amendment to the United States Constitution protects the individual right to possess firearms in the home and within federal enclaves for lawful purposes like self-defense. Stewart invokes this ruling to support the claim that gun ownership is an individual right, and argues that, while firearm violence is a social problem that needs addressing, sufficient laws to prevent gun violence are already in place but are not being adequately enforced. He cites survey data on private firearm use as a means of self-defense, and makes reference to statistics on the proportion of violent crimes that involve guns. Stewart's remarks, which came amid the 2013 budget sequestration, call for spending cuts and reforms to balance the budget. It is irresponsible of the Obama administration, says Stewart, to push gun-control legislation at a time when the country's fiscal stability is in danger. He says proposed legislation doesn't address the real issues behind America's culture of violence, and asserts that violence in the media and an inadequate mental health system are the core problems.*

I had the great blessing of growing up on a family farm. I know what it's like as a kid to be so excited to go hunting with my brothers and my father that you can't sleep the night before. I also had the great privilege of serving for fourteen years as a pilot and an officer in the United States Air Force. There I learned a little bit about defending the nation through an adequate show of force. I also, by the way, qualified as an expert marksman in small arms.

Recent and saddening acts of violence have brought conversations about guns to the national stage. These acts of violence, as terrible as they are, should not be used by the White House as justification to revoke the rights outlined in the Constitution. The Second Amendment clearly states that "the right of the people to keep and bear arms, shall not be infringed." Our Founding Fathers created this amendment to protect citizens from government tyranny. In 2008, the Supreme Court stated emphatically that the right to bear arms is an individual right. Today, it continues to assure Americans' rights to defend themselves against the evil people in the world.

Based on survey data from a study in the year 2000, US civilians do use guns to

Delivered March 6, 2013, at the US House of Representatives, Washington, DC, by Chris Stewart.

> *We already have laws in place to prevent unlawful citizens from purchasing firearms, and instead of creating new harsher laws, we need to do a better job of enforcing the ones we already have in place.*

defend themselves and others from crime at least 990,000 times per year. It's critical that we continue to protect this personal and absolute right.

While gun-related violence is indeed tragic, it's important to note that it only accounts for a small portion of the violent crimes committed in the US. Specifically, the US Department of Justice has said that of the roughly 5 million violent crimes committed in the United States during 2008, only about 8 percent were committed by offenders visibly armed with a gun.

Most of those crimes committed with guns were committed with guns that have already been illegal. The US Justice Department conducted a survey in the 1990s that found that about 79 percent of State Prison inmates that carried a firearm during the offense that sent them to jail received their gun either through an illegal source or through family and friends. This shows that creating stricter laws to ban guns will not solve any problems. We already have laws in place to prevent unlawful citizens from purchasing firearms, and instead of creating new harsher laws, we need to do a better job of enforcing the ones we already have in place.

At a time when sequestration just went into effect, and our country is on a path to bankruptcy, it's unacceptable that the White House continues to push its gun control agenda. We already have gun laws in place, and we need to be focusing on getting our country back onto a path towards fiscal sanity. We need President Obama and his administration to show leadership. We need to ensure that America maintains its leading role in the world. To do that, we need to budget and spend responsibly. We need to replace President Obama's sequester with commonsense spending cuts and reforms. Most importantly, we need the President to demonstrate an understanding of the nation's need to balance our budget and get us on a path to fiscal sanity.

That is the great fight of our day. That is the great challenge that we are facing. My heart bleeds for the victims of gun violence whether they're in Newtown, or in New York, or in my home district. But the President's proposals will not help. They aren't designed to address the core problems of mental health or a culture that is steeped in violence—violence that is thrust upon our children through a media that is bent upon making more money through the violence they propagate. Mr. Speaker, let's concentrate our attention on the greatest challenge of our day, not on a bandaid of additional laws that are designed to do nothing but to make some liberals feel better.

About Chris Stewart

Chris Stewart, a Republican, represents Utah's Second Congressional District in the United States House of Representatives, having assumed office in January 2013. He was born on July 16, 1960, in Logan, Utah. He graduated from Utah State University in 1984, with a bachelor's degree in economics. After college, Stewart served in the Air Force for fourteen years as a pilot, flying the B-1B bomber and rescue helicopters. In June 1995, Stewart and a crew of fellow pilots set the world record for fastest flight around the world. He is the former president and CEO of the Shipley Group, a firm that provides consulting services with a focus on environment and energy concerns, interpersonal communication, and project management. Stewart has published sixteen books, both fiction and nonfiction. In 2011, The Miracle of Freedom: 7 Tipping Points That Saved the World—*coauthored by Stewart and his brother Ted—appeared on national best-seller lists, and was endorsed by conservative radio and talk show host Glenn Beck.*

One Man with Courage Makes a Majority

By Joe Manchin

In this speech delivered on the Senate floor, Senator Joe Manchin of West Virginia debunks what he says are several myths propagated by the National Rifle Association (NRA) regarding a background checks bill he proposed in collaboration with Pennsylvania's Pat Toomey, a Republican. Manchin—a Democrat and lifelong NRA member who was endorsed by the organization throughout much of his political career—accuses the powerful lobbying group of spreading false information about the legislation he and Senator Toomey hope to pass through the Senate. He quotes the claims made in NRA literature, and goes on to refute criticisms of the bill point by point. Manchin also cites inconsistencies in the NRA's stance on background checks, pointing to 1999 congressional testimony from the organization's executive vice president, Wayne LaPierre, in which LaPierre endorsed background checks as a reasonable precaution in gun sales. He accuses the organization of criticizing the bill on false pretexts in an effort to drum up political opposition and bolster their membership ranks. To illustrate the necessity for a more thorough background checks system, Manchin presents evidence that al-Qaeda encourages members to take advantage of lax laws and buy guns online in the United States. He mentions a New York Times *article that calls Internet firearms markets a "gun show that never ends." Manchin closes his remarks by outlining the ways the proposed legislation would benefit gun owners while keeping firearms out of dangerous hands before once again denouncing the NRA's campaign of misinformation.*

Mr. President, as most of my colleagues here in the Senate know, I am a proud gun owner and an A-rated lifetime card-carrying member of the National Rifle Association.

I agree wholeheartedly with the mission of the NRA—which is to defend the Second Amendment rights of all law-abiding Americans, to promote firearms and hunting safety and marksmanship and to educate the general public about firearms.

I carry my NRA membership card with me everywhere I go. I've got it with me now.

And ever since I became a member, I have read all the magazines and all the bulletins they have sent me—and I never had any reason to question their credibility.

So I was surprised when the latest alerts from the NRA was filled with misinformation about the firearms background check legislation that Senator Toomey and I are trying to get the Senate to pass.

Delivered April 17, 2013, at the US Senate, Washington, DC, by Joe Manchin.

The NRA is telling its members that our legislation would—and I quote—"criminalize the private transfer of firearms by honest citizens, requiring lifelong friends, neighbors and some family members to get federal government permission to exercise a fundamental right or face prosecution."

Not a word of that is true, Mr. President.

When Background Checks Were Reasonable

Now, I remember when the NRA used to feel a lot different about background checks—and it wasn't that long ago.

Back in 1999, their executive vice president, Wayne LaPierre, testified before Congress that background checks were reasonable.

In fact, he said it over and over and over again—and I quote:

> We think it's reasonable to provide for instant checks at gun shows just like at gun stores and pawn shops.

> We think it's reasonable to provide mandatory instant criminal background checks for every sale at every gun show. No loopholes anywhere for anyone. That means closing the Hinckley loophole so the records of those adjudicated mental ill are in the system.

> We think it's reasonable to make gun show instant checks just like gun store instant checks.

How is it "criminalizing" now to do criminal and mental health checks on gun buyers and it wasn't back then in 1999? What has changed? Absolutely nothing.

Look, I would be okay with the NRA making the case that, well, we thought background checks were reasonable, but the government didn't do them right and didn't enforce them. Because the government didn't—and that's one of the things our legislation is going to fix.

But I'm not okay with the NRA—or any organization, for that matter—deliberately putting out false information about our legislation just to pump up political opposition to it or just to pump up their membership rolls and dues accounts.

So I would hope that whoever at the NRA put out the untrue information about our legislation would correct it as quickly as possible.

The Internet is a vast marketplace for guns. In 2000, the Department of Justice estimated that 80 online firearm auction sites and approximately 4,000 other sites offered guns for sale.

Losing Credibility

I don't want my friends to lose their credibility, because in this town, once you lose your credibility, you've got nothing.

Mr. President, it is simply not true that our legislation criminalizes private transfers of guns among family, friends and neighbors, as Senator Toomey and I explained in detail here on the Senate floor yesterday.

But I don't have to explain it to the NRA. They've read the bill. They know the facts. So maybe this was just a mistake.

Why We Are Here

Mr. President, I understand that some of our colleagues believe that supporting our legislation is risky politics. But I think they're dead wrong because about 90 percent of Americans support the idea of criminal and mental illness background checks for gun sales. And it isn't often that we get to vote on any issue with that level of support from Americans.

But even if the politics are risky, remember the words of Andrew Jackson: "The brave man inattentive to his duty is worth little more to his country than the coward who deserts in the hour of danger."

Old Hickory also said: "One man with courage makes a majority."

I didn't get into public service as a career—I did it to fix things. And right now few things need fixing more than our gun laws as they relate to background checks for gun show and Internet sales.

Al Qaeda and Gun Shows

Our gun laws are so outdated and so out of whack that even Al Qaeda has figured out how to exploit them to arm themselves against us.

I'm sure all of you have seen the video of this guy—Al Qaeda terrorist Adam Gadahn—telling sympathizers how to get their hands on guns in America, with almost no questions asked.

He says—and I quote—"America is absolutely awash with easily obtainable firearms. You can go down to a gun show at the local convention center and come away with a fully automatic assault rifle, without a background check and, most likely, without having to show an identification card. So what are you waiting for?"

Mr. President, our legislation will shut this guy up.

A Gun Show That Never Ends

If Al Qaeda's enthusiasm for gun show sales isn't chilling enough, you should read today's *New York Times* article about how easy it is for criminals to buy and sell guns on the Internet.

Not only is it quick and easy, it's anonymous—you don't have any idea who you are dealing with. One of the people in the article describes these Internet sales as a "gun show that never ends." And I would add—never closes.

The Internet is a vast marketplace for guns. In 2000, the Department of Justice estimated that 80 online firearm auction sites and approximately 4,000 other sites offered guns for sale.

That was more than a dozen years ago, and we all know how the Internet has expanded since then.

The online market may now exceed gun shows in terms of sales volume. For example, the National Shooting Sports Foundation surveyed owners of modern sporting rifles in 2010 and found that 10 percent of them had purchased their firearms at gun shows whereas 25 percent had purchased them online.

Common Sense—Myth and Fact

Believe me, I understand the political stakes for my colleagues who come from states with strong gun cultures. I come from West Virginia, and no state has a higher regard for the Second Amendment rights to bear arms than my state.

But West Virginians also are guided by common sense. And they are persuaded by the unvarnished facts. And when they read our legislation, they understand that all we are doing is using common sense to protect the safety of the public, especially our kids, and, at the same time, protect the Second Amendment rights to bear arms.

John Adams once said that "facts are stubborn things." And I'm pretty stubborn myself. So I'm going to go through our legislation again and tell you what is the myth out there and what is fact about our legislation.

Let's start with the myth that the NRA is repeating to their members.

Myth: This legislation will require background checks when a gun owner sells, loans or gives a firearm to a relative, neighbor or friend.

Fact: Current law exempts such transfers from background checks, and our bill does nothing to change that.

You can loan your hunting rifle to your buddy without any new restrictions or requirements. Or you can give or sell a gun to your brother, your neighbor, your co-worker without a background check.

You can post a gun for sale on the cork bulletin board at your church or your job without a background check. We are not going to do anything to turn law-abiding gun owners into criminals.

Myth: Nothing in this legislation would have prevented or will prevent any tragic mass shootings in the future.

Fact: We have no way of knowing what future tragedies will be prevented by our bill, and that is the point. But it's just common sense that keeping guns out of the hands of criminals and the dangerously mentally ill will save lives.

As one of the Newtown parents, Francine Wheeler, said, "Please help us do something before our tragedy becomes your tragedy."

Our bill will ensure that States get records into the NICS database.

We know that if all the proper records were in NICS, as our amendment provides, it would have prevented the Virginia Tech shooting, where the shooter should have been a prohibited purchaser but was not because the records were not in the system.

Our bill will prevent felons from buying guns at gun shows and online. It would also prohibit the types of transactions that al Qaeda suggested in a promotional video. It would require background checks on all transactions online and at gun shows.

Myth: Our amendment creates or will lead to a national registry.

Fact: Current law prohibits the creation of a national registry. Our bill reiterates the prohibition in three separate places. Let me read them:

Section 122(c) prohibits the establishment of a national gun registry.

(c) PROHIBITION OF NATIONAL GUN REGISTRY.—

Section 923 of title 18, United States Code, is amended by adding at the end the following:

(m) The Attorney General may not consolidate or centralize the records of the— (1) acquisition or disposition of firearms, or any portion thereof, maintained by—

(A) a person with a valid, current license under this chapter;

(B) an unlicensed transferor under section 922(t); or

(2) possession or ownership of a firearm, maintained by any medical or health insurance entity.'

Section 102. Findings. Congress reaffirms prohibition of a national firearms registry.

(2) Congress supports and reaffirms the existing prohibition on a national firearms registry.

Section 103. Rule of Construction. This section clearly states that the bill does not allow for the creation or establishment of a national registry. "Nothing in this title, or any amendment made by this title, shall be construed to expand in any way the enforcement authority or jurisdiction of the Bureau of Alcohol, Tobacco, Firearms, and Explosives; or allow the establishment, directly or indirectly, of a Federal firearms registry." Our bill also creates a serious penalty for any government employee seeking to misuse records to create a registry: a felony with up to 15 years in prison.

Myth: Our amendment imposes a universal background check.

Fact: This is not a universal background check. Our bill simply extends existing law to apply to all commercial sales, including gun shows and online. Private sales will not require background checks.

Again, all family transfers would not require background checks. Friends, family and neighbor sales would all be allowed without a background check. Also, loaning your gun to your buddy for the weekend hunting trip would still be allowed.

Myth: A doctor can put me into the National Instant Criminal Background Check System (NICS) because I am being treated for PTSD or some other mental condition.

Fact: A doctor cannot put someone into NICS under current law or under our bill. A person has to be adjudicated as mentally ill by a court before being placed into NICS. Our bill does not change current federal medical privacy law; it simply clarifies that States are not prohibited from entering mental health records into NICS.

Myth: This amendment would unfairly burden veterans.

Fact: Our amendment provides additional protections for our veterans.

This amendment fixes an outdated law and allows active duty service members and their spouses to purchase guns in their home state, as well as their duty station. Current law unfairly restricts them to only buying guns in the state where they are stationed.

This amendment requires notification of veterans who have already been placed in the NICS by the Department of Veterans Affairs; some veterans may not even know they are in NICS. Once they are notified, the amendment allows every veteran in NICS to appeal for removal. There are currently over 150,000 veterans in NICS because they have had a fiduciary—someone to manage their finances—designated for them.

This amendment creates a fair appeals process for veterans who may have been wrongly or automatically categorized as unfit to own or purchase firearms.

This amendment establishes an appeals process for veterans by allowing them to appeal to an independent board or a court before being placed in the NICS system.

This amendment protects a veteran's right to bear arms until he or she has exhausted the appeals process, which is different from the current system in which veterans are "guilty until proven innocent."

Myth: There is no need for a Commission on Mass Violence. Every bill currently before the Senate establishes studies of some sort.

Fact: Our bipartisan commission does not focus solely on guns. Instead, it will examine our culture of mass violence by bringing together acknowledged experts in the fields of firearms, school safety, media, and mental health to look at all the possible root causes of the problem.

As a nation, we must look at all aspects of our culture of violence. We must rethink our treatment of the mentally ill. We must redesign our schools to keep our kids safe. And we must challenge a popular culture that accepts stomach-churning violence in our movies and video games.

Myth: Why create new background check requirements when current ones aren't even being enforced?

Response: We agree that more background check violations need to be prosecuted, and our amendment contains the following language supporting increased prosecutions:

SEC. 102. FINDINGS.

Congress finds the following:

Congress believes the Department of Justice should prosecute violations of background check requirements to the maximum extent of the law.

SEC. 143. DUTIES OF THE COMMISSION.

Study.—

(2) MATTERS TO BE STUDIED.—In determining the root causes of these recurring and tragic acts of mass violence, the Commission shall study any matter that the Commission determines relevant to meeting the requirements of paragraph (1), including at a minimum—

(J) the role of current prosecution rates in contributing to the availability of weapons that are used in mass violence; we must also acknowledge that background checks do work in keeping guns out of the hands of people who should not have them.

Last year, 88,000 people were denied firearms when they failed a background check. Our amendment will ensure even more people who should not have guns do not get guns.

Myth: Criminals will never get a background check.

Fact: We don't expect criminals to submit to background checks—that is why they are criminals, and frankly, this argument is just silly.

Our amendment reduces the number of places where a criminal can buy a gun. Right now, a criminal can buy a firearm at a table or out of someone's trunk at a gun show, through an online sale from the same state, or through a newspaper ad because no background check is required for these kinds of sales.

Our bill closes those avenues to criminals, making it harder for criminals to get guns. Period.

Benefits for Gun Owners

I have told my friends at the NRA that they should like this legislation not only because it will keep guns out of the dangerous hands, but it also benefits gun owners in a number of ways.

It prohibits the Attorney General from consolidating or centralizing records into a National Gun Registry. Any person who knowingly does so would be imprisoned for 15 years.

It clarifies and fixes interstate travel laws for sportsmen traveling long distances across states to hunt or shoot.

It allow dealers to complete transactions at gun shows that take place in a state for which they are not a resident.

It includes a requirement that if a background check at a gun show does not result in a definitive response from NICS within 48 hours, the sale may proceed. Current law is three business days.

It requires the FBI to give priority to finalizing background checks at gun shows over checks at store front dealerships.

It authorizes use of a state concealed carry permit in lieu of a background check for all transfers with permits that expire every five years.

It would permit interstate handgun sales from dealers.

And it would allow active military to buy firearms in their home states.

Facts and Evidence

Mr. President, those are the facts, and no amount of spin will change them. And in a debate this important to the course of our country, we need to begin with the facts.

Facts are indeed stubborn things. And as John Adams also said of them: ". . . whatever may be our wishes, our inclinations, or the dictates of our passion, they cannot alter the state of facts and evidence."

About Joe Manchin

Joe Manchin is the junior United States senator from West Virginia. A Democrat, Manchin won the special election to fill the vacant seat of the late Robert Byrd in November 2010 and was reelected to a full term in 2012. Prior to joining the Senate, Manchin served as West Virginia's secretary of state from 2000 to 2004, and as West Virginia's thirty-fourth governor from 2005 to 2010. He was chairman of the National Governors Association during the last year of his term. Manchin was born on August 24, 1947, in Farmington, West Virginia. He earned a bachelor's degree from West Virginia University in 1970. Manchin was a member of the West Virginia House of Delegates from 1982 to 1986, and a member of the state Senate from 1986 to 1996. He unsuccessfully ran for governor of West Virginia in 1996. Manchin has three children with his wife, Gail, and currently lives in Fairmont, West Virginia.

Families Are Saying Enough Is Enough

By Kristen Gillibrand

In a speech delivered on the Senate floor, Senator Kristen Gillibrand of New York speaks in support of the Stop Illegal Trafficking in Firearms Act—a piece of legislation that would give law enforcement greater ability to investigate and prosecute those involved in illegal gun trafficking networks. Gillibrand urges her fellow senators to stand up for victims of gun violence, using the authority of the legislature to protect Americans from mass shootings and daily gun crimes alike. Public opinion is behind stricter gun laws, Gillibrand says, citing a 90-percent rate of support among Americans for expanded background checks. She gives statistics on black market trafficking in firearms and describes the ways current laws fall short in their ability to fight the illegal market. Gillibrand touts the bipartisan nature of the Stop Illegal Trafficking in Firearms Act, and calls for compromise and commonsense reform.

I rise to urge my colleagues on both sides of the aisle to join a strong bipartisan coalition which is taking real action to end senseless, deadly gun violence. This includes truly commonsense reforms which have nothing to do with infringing on our Second Amendment rights and the Second Amendment rights of our law-abiding citizens.

We have seen the Newtown parents here in Washington bravely telling their stories. They deserve better than this body turning their backs on them. The families of Aurora deserve better than this body turning their backs on them. The families of the more than 30 people who die every single day at the hands of gun violence deserve more from this body.

My friends, it is simply time to act. Today is the day for this body to show the American people their voices matter. When 90 percent of Americans demand us to expand background checks, we can deliver.

We should be able to agree we no longer need military-style weapons and ammunition clips on our streets. We should be able to agree it is time to crack down on the illegal handguns being trafficked on our streets into the hands of criminals.

Four years ago I met the parents of Nyasia Pryear-Yard. Nyasia was a beautiful 17-year-old honor student killed in the prime of her life by an illegal handgun when she was just spending time with her friends.

I vowed to Nyasia's parents and classmates I would stop the flow of illegal guns which make their way onto our streets and into the hands of criminals by finally making gun trafficking a federal crime and holding offenders accountable with stiff

Delivered April 17, 2013, at the US Senate, Washington, DC, by Kristen Gillibrand.

penalties. We have the opportunity today to give law enforcement the tools and resources they need and have long asked for. This is not a Republican or a Democratic idea. It is a smart idea and the action Nyasia's parents deserve from us.

According to the New York City mayor's office, 85 percent of the guns used in crimes come from out of state. At least 90 percent of those guns are illegal. They are illegally trafficked into our cities and State. Of all the laws we have on the books today, effectively none are directly focused on preventing someone from driving from one state to another with stricter gun laws, parking their car in a parking lot, and selling hundreds of firearms directly into the hands of criminals. It is shocking to me as a mother and as a lawmaker.

Instead, prosecutors primarily rely on laws which prohibit making false statements in connection with the purchase of a firearm. These are paperwork violations with penalties too low to be effective law enforcement tools.

Over the past 3 fiscal years, more than 330,000 guns used in violent crimes show telltale signs of black market trafficking, 420,000 firearms were stolen, and thousands of guns with obliterated serial numbers were recovered by law enforcement. While law enforcement is working overtime to track down illegal guns and apprehend those who traffic these weapons, current law restricts their ability to investigate and prosecute these crimes.

We can all agree this simply makes no sense and leaves all our communities vulnerable. All across this country in small towns and big cities, families are saying enough is enough. It is time to get serious and do something to prevent the next tragedy.

Now we are able to do so. Our bipartisan Stop Illegal Trafficking in Firearms Act would empower law enforcement to investigate and prosecute illegal gun traffickers, straw purchasers, and their entire criminal networks. This bill is not everything I wanted when I set out on this mission in 2009, but it is a good bipartisan compromise. It is a compromise I urge my colleagues on both sides of the aisle to support. If you do, we can stop the illegal flow of guns which are coming into our city neighborhoods, reduce gun violence, and reduce senseless gun death.

Law enforcement officials across the country need this legislation to protect our communities from illegal weapons. If you are a responsible, law-abiding gun owner watching this, you should support this legislation too. My friends who are Second Amendment supporters, gun owners, and hunters support this commonsense legislation.

I am urging all my colleagues on both sides of the aisle to join us. Stand with families in our communities all across the country who are looking to

> *Over the past 3 fiscal years, more than 330,000 guns used in violent crimes show telltale signs of black market trafficking, 420,000 firearms were stolen, and thousands of guns with obliterated serial numbers were recovered by law enforcement.*

us to take action. It is time to prevent the next senseless tragedy, prevent the next death, and the next Nyasia Pryear-Yard.

I urge you to stand with the brave men and women of our law enforcement at every level who are asking us to take these critical commonsense measures needed so they can do a better job for us and keep our families safer.

About Kirsten Gillibrand

Kirsten Gillibrand is the junior United States Senator from New York. A Democrat, Gillibrand was appointed to fill the New York US Senate seat left vacant by Hillary Clinton when she became secretary of state in 2009. Gillibrand was elected to her first six-year Senate term in 2012, winning sixty of the state's sixty-two counties. Prior to becoming a member of the Senate, Gillibrand served in the House as representative for New York's Twentieth Congressional District from 2007 to 2009. Though considered a part of the conservative-leaning Blue Dog coalition in the House, Gillibrand has since defined herself as a progressive Democrat, aggressively supporting causes like the repeal of the military's Don't Ask, Don't Tell policy on homosexuals, and greater transparency in government. Born on December 9, 1966, in Albany, Gillibrand earned her law degree from UCLA in 1991. She served as special counsel to Andrew Cuomo when he was secretary of Housing and Urban Development under the Clinton administration, and went on to join Hillary Clinton's US Senate campaign in 1999.

4

Immigration Reform

Immigration and workers rights supporters march in support of immigration reform in Los Angeles, May 1, 2013. May Day is the day workers around the globe rally for support of their issues of wages, job security, health care, and, in the United States, immigration reform.

"How Do You Define 'American'?"

By Jose Antonio Vargas

In testimony before the Senate Judiciary Committee, Jose Antonio Vargas—a Pulitzer Prize–winning journalist and immigration activist—discusses his status as an undocumented immigrant, and challenges lawmakers to define "American." His remarks come amid national debate on immigration reform measures and the government's approach to America's approximately eleven million undocumented immigrants. Vargas was brought to America from the Philippines by his grandfather, who paid for Vargas's passport and green card. Vargas tells of how, upon applying for a driver's permit at the age of sixteen, he discovered that the green card his grandfather had given him was a fake. As a student at Mountain View High School in Mountain View, California, Vargas says, he decided to become a journalist in an effort to "write my way into America." Vargas is part of a growing movement of immigrants going public with their undocumented status. He describes the America he and others like him know, and talks of the teachers and benefactors who protected and helped him overcome the obstacles associated with being an undocumented immigrant. Vargas urges lawmakers to consider the humanity of the populations that immigration reform will most heavily impact and bemoans the connotations of calling undocumented immigrants "illegals." He invokes the late Senator Ted Kennedy, who once wrote, "Immigration is in our blood . . . part of our founding story," and closes his remarks by asking the committee, "How do you define 'American'?"

Thank you, Chairman Leahy, Ranking Member Grassley, and distinguished members of this Committee.

I come to you as one of our country's 11 million undocumented immigrants, many of us Americans at heart, but without the right papers to show for it. Too often, we're treated as abstractions, faceless and nameless, subjects of debate rather than individuals with families, hopes, fears, and dreams.

I am in America because of the sacrifices of my family. My grandparents legally emigrated from the Philippines to Silicon Valley in the mid-1980s. A few years later, Grandpa Teofilo became a US citizen and legally changed his name to Ted—after Ted Danson in "Cheers." Because grandparents cannot petition for their grandkids—and because my mother could not come to the United States—grandpa saved up money to get his only grandson, me, a passport and green card to come to America. My mother gave me up to give me a better life.

I arrived in Mountain View, California, on August 3, 1993. One of my earliest memories was singing the National Anthem as a 6th grader at Crittenden Middle

February 13, 2013, at the US Senate Judiciary Committee Testimony, Washington, DC, by Jose Antonio Vargas.

School, believing the song had somehow something to do with me. I thought the first lines were, "Jose, can you see?"

Four years later, I applied for a driver's permit like any sixteen-year-old. That was when I discovered that the green card that my grandpa gave me was fake.

But I wanted to work. I wanted to contribute to a country that is now my home. At age seventeen, I decided to be a journalist for a seemingly naive reason: if I am not supposed to be in America because I don't have the right kind of papers, what if my name—my byline—was on the paper? How can they say I don't exist if my name is in newspapers and magazines? I thought I could write my way into America.

As I built a successful career as a journalist—paying Social Security and state and federal taxes along the way—as fear and shame, as denial and pain, enveloped me—words became my salvation. I found solace in the words of the Rev. Martin Luther King, quoting St. Augustine: "An unjust law is no law at all."

Ultimately, it took me twelve years to come out as an undocumented American—because that is what I am, an American. But I am grateful to have been able to tell the truth. And in the past few years, more undocumented people, particularly young DREAMers, are coming out, telling the truth about the America we experience.

We dream of a path to citizenship so we can actively participate in our American democracy. We dream of not being separated from our families and our loved ones, regardless of sexual orientation, no matter our skill set. This government has deported more than 1.6 million people—fathers and mothers, sons and daughters—in the past four years.

We dream of contributing to the country we call our home.

In 21st century America, diversity is destiny. That I happen to be gay, that I speak Tagalog, my first language, and want to learn Spanish—that does not threaten my love for this country. How interconnected and integrated we are as Americans makes us stronger.

Sitting behind me today is my Filipino American family—my grandma Leonila, whom I love very much; my Aunt Aida Rivera, who helped raised me; and my Uncle Conrad Salinas, who served, proudly, in the US Navy for twenty years. They're all naturalized American citizens.

I belong in what is called a mixed-status family. I am the only one in my extended family of twenty-five Americans who is undocumented. When you inaccurately call me "illegal," you're not only dehumanizing me, you're offending them. No human being is illegal.

Also here is my Mountain View High School family—my support network of allies who encouraged and protected me since I was a teenager. After I told my high school principal and school superintendent that I was not planning to go to college because I could not apply for financial aid, Pat Hyland and Rich Fischer secured a private scholarship for me. The scholarship was funded by a man named Jim Strand. I am honored that Pat, Rich and Jim are all here today. Across the country, there are countless other Jim Strands, Pat Hylands, and Rich Fischers of all backgrounds who stand alongside their undocumented neighbors. They don't need to see pieces of paper—a passport or a green card—to treat us as human beings.

This is the truth about immigration in our America.

As this Congress decides on fair, humane reform, let us remember that immigration is not merely about borders. "Immigration is in our blood . . . part of our founding story," writes Senator Ted Kennedy, former chairman of this very Committee, in the introduction to President Kennedy's book, *A Nation of Immigrants*. Immigration is about our future. Immigration is about all of us.

> *We dream of not being separated from our families and our loved ones, regardless of sexual orientation, no matter our skill set. This government has deported more than 1.6 million people—fathers and mothers, sons and daughters—in the past four years.*

And before I take your questions, I have a few of my own:

What do you want to do with me?

What do you want to do with us?

How do you define "American"?

Thank you.

About Jose Antonio Vargas

Jose Antonio Vargas is an American journalist who has written for the New Yorker, *the* Huffington Post—*where he launched the Technology and College pages*—Rolling Stone, *and the* Washington Post. *While with the* Post, *he was part of the reporting team that won a Pulitzer Prize in 2008 for coverage of the Virginia Tech shooting massacre. Vargas—who was born in the Philippines and raised in the United States from the age of twelve—made headlines when he publicly revealed his status as an undocumented immigrant in an essay for the* New York Times Magazine *in June 2011. In the years following, he was featured on the cover of* Time *along with other undocumented immigrants, founded Define American—an advocacy group aimed at raising awareness of immigration issues—and wrote and directed a documentary film about his life called* Documented. *Vargas graduated from Mountain View High School in California in 2000, and San Francisco State University in 2004.*

Living Under the Threat of Deportation

By Benita Veliz

When political activist Benita Veliz introduced Cuban American journalist Cristina Saralegui at the 2012 Democratic National Convention (DNC), she made history as the first illegal immigrant to address a national political party convention in the United States. She is best known for her work in support of the proposed DREAM (Development, Relief, and Education for Alien Minors) Act. First introduced in 2001, the DREAM Act offers pathways to permanent residency for individuals who arrived in the United States as minors and have lived in the country for at least five years. Although it has undergone various incarnations, the basic provision of the bill includes temporary legal residency for aliens who work toward a college degree or enlist for military service. Permanent legal residency becomes open to them upon completion of their education or military enlistment. The DREAM Act has been introduced in the United States Congress a number of times but has never been approved by legislators. Critics of the bill believe that it rewards the practice of illegal immigration and will encourage others to enter the United States illegally. US President Barack Obama voiced his strong support of the DREAM Act in 2010, when it was approved in the House before being voted down in the Senate. In her remarks to the DNC, Veliz reviews her personal history and educational achievements, while noting that she has lived her life in fear of deportation. She also speaks in praise of Obama's support of the DREAM Act and highlights Saralegui's support of Obama's 2012 reelection campaign. The following is a copy of a speech, as prepared for delivery, by Benita Veliz, DREAM Act Activist at the Democratic National Convention on Wednesday, September 5, 2012.

My name is Benita Veliz, and I'm from San Antonio, Texas. Like so many Americans of all races and backgrounds, I was brought here as a child. I've been here ever since.

I graduated as valedictorian of my class at the age of 16 and earned a double major at the age of 20. I know I have something to contribute to my economy and my country. I feel just as American as any of my friends or neighbors.

But I've had to live almost my entire life knowing I could be deported just because of the way I came here.

President Obama fought for the DREAM Act to help people like me. And when Congress refused to pass it, he didn't give up. Instead, he took action so that people like me can apply to stay in our country and contribute. We will keep fighting for reform, but while we do, we are able to work, study and pursue the American dream.

Delivered September 5, 2012, at the Democratic National Convention, Charlotte, North Carolina, by Benita Veliz.

President Obama has fought for my community. Now it's my honor to introduce one of the leaders in my community who is fighting for him. From her television show to her magazines to her radio network, she is truly an icon: ladies and gentlemen, Cristina Saralegui.

About Benita Veliz

Benita Veliz was eight years old when her parents brought her to Texas from Mexico in 1993. When she was sixteen, Veliz graduated from San Antonio's Thomas Jefferson High School as the valedictorian of her class. She subsequently received a full scholarship to attend St. Mary's University in San Antonio, Texas, where she double majored in biology and sociology. While attending college she volunteered at a children's hospital and supported herself by waiting tables at a Mexican restaurant. The DREAM Act, a congressional bill that would allow children of undocumented immigrants to earn citizenship after graduating from high school and attending college or serving in the military, was the focus of her honor's thesis. Veliz continues to be an advocate for immigration reform.

The Opportunity of Immigration Reform

By Thomas J. Donohue

In this speech delivered to the US Chamber of Commerce Immigration Summit, chamber president and CEO Thomas J. Donohue addresses immigration reform from a business standpoint. Donohue calls the current immigration system broken, and says that it is working against America's economic, business, security, and labor interests, leaving the country at a competitive disadvantage. Where many people see a problem, Donohue says, he sees an opportunity. Calling immigration reform a complex issue with far-reaching impacts, and deriding those who inject fear and misinformation into the debate, Donohue says that it is a top priority for the chamber and of great personal importance. He claims that immigration reform has the potential not only to secure the country's borders, but to open up economic avenues for immigrant populations and to allow the United States to retain US-educated foreign talent that, under current laws, might not be able to remain in the country. Donohue specifically endorses a proposed bill drafted by a bipartisan group of eight Senators, and praises its temporary worker program, its visa provisions, and its national employee verification system. Strong leadership that brings about effective and decisive reform of America's immigration system, Donohue says, will show the world that America still holds true to the principles upon which it was built.

Good morning everyone, and thank you for coming.

We are here today to address one of the compelling challenges of our time—ensuring that our great country can compete and win in the global race for talent . . . that we can secure the lives and livelihoods of all Americans . . . and that we can reaffirm our proud and honorable legacy as an open and welcoming society.

Immigration reform has been a top priority of the Chamber's for years—and it is a deeply personal priority of mine.

We can take great encouragement in the fact that this time, so many groups and individuals from across society and across the political spectrum have joined forces to build support for reform.

But we must take nothing for granted. Immigration is a difficult issue. It encompasses a complex bundle of impacts, interests, and emotions. We must respect all points of view in this important debate—even those that differ from our own. At the same time, we should have little patience for those who decide to prey on fear and misunderstanding—or those who put their own short-term political interests above the national interest.

Delivered April 26, 2013, at the US Chamber of Commerce Immigration Summit, Washington, DC, by Thomas J. Donohue.

The fact is that our current immigration system is broken. Everybody knows it. It's not serving the interests of our economy, our businesses, our workers, or our collective security.

America cannot compete and win in a global economy without the world's best talent, hardest workers, or biggest dreamers. We cannot sustain vital programs for the elderly and needy without more workers—both low skilled and high skilled—to grow our economy and tax base.

Our current system, quite frankly, isn't cutting it. It has failed to fully secure our border. It has failed to keep us informed about just who is coming to our country and whether they leave when they are supposed to leave. It has failed to provide us with the workers we need and the skill levels we need to ensure a strong and growing economy. Gaps and shortages in our workforce put American jobs at risk— because if companies can't find all the workers they need here, then they will be forced to move all the work where the workers are.

We can do better and we must do better. Immigration reform isn't just a problem to be solved, it's an opportunity to be seized.

Few understand this reality better than the bipartisan group of eight Senators—and we are honored to have two of them here today. Their bill has tough, practical measures to secure our borders while allowing people and commerce to flow efficiently and lawfully in and out of our country. It proposes a thoughtfully designed, temporary worker program that would allow employers to use immigrant labor when US workers are not readily available. It better ties visas to market demands. It helps ensure we don't educate the best foreign talent in the world and then send it away.

It makes E-Verify a national employee verification system. It's a system we can support as long as there is strong preemption language for state and local laws . . . no obligation to re-verify the entire current workforce for private employers, which would cost a fortune and take forever . . . and a safe harbor for good faith efforts by employers.

And the bill provides a path out of the shadows for the 11 million undocumented immigrants who live in the United States today—with the understanding that they will meet strict conditions, such as paying civil penalties and back taxes and learning English.

There is no doubt that there will be additional input and analysis through Senate hearings and amendments. That's how it should be. We support a transparent and open process and debate. Given the broad support this bill has garnered from business and labor . . . from conservatives and liberals . . . and from faith-based and civil groups, I'm optimistic that this time we have an excellent chance at getting immigration reform done.

As a vigorous national debate continues, let's not forget who we are, or what this nation was built on—the dreams and hard work of those who came here seeking a better life.

This is a moment that cries out for principled, courageous leadership, leadership that puts it all on the line to build a brighter and more hopeful future for our children and grandchildren.

We need this leadership on many serious issues—deficits, debt, entitlement reform, education, and national security, just to name a few. Let's start with immigration reform. Let's show the world that America still has the capacity to do great things.

> *As a vigorous national debate continues, let's not forget who we are, or what this nation was built on—the dreams and hard work of those who came here seeking a better life.*

I just returned from Europe where we were busy promoting a new jobs and a growth trade pact between the United States and the European Union. We found and generated a lot of enthusiasm for that, but everywhere we went, Europeans also wanted to talk about immigration. There was a sense that if our country could get this done, it would cement our global leadership for years to come. America would be acting like America once again.

Thank you very much.

About Thomas J. Donohue

Thomas J. Donohue is the president and chief executive officer of the United Sates Chamber of Commerce, having assumed that post in 1997. For thirteen years prior to joining the chamber, Donohue was president and CEO of the American Trucking Associations. Before that, he worked as US deputy assistant postmaster general, as well as vice president of development at Connecticut's Fairfield University. He was born in New York City in 1938, graduated from St. John's University with a bachelor's degree, and earned his master's in business administration from Adelphi University in 1965. Throughout his career, Donohue has served on the board of directors for a number of different entities, including the Union Pacific Corporation and Marymount University. From 1999 to 2008, he was director of XM Satellite Radio Holdings, and from 1996 to 2013, he was director of Sunrise Senior Living. Under Donohue's leadership, the Chamber of Commerce has become one of the most powerful lobbying forces in Washington, DC.

Life in the Shadows

By Eric Holder

In an address to the Mexican American Legal Defense and Educational Fund (MALDEF) at the organization's 2013 Awards Gala in April 2013, Attorney General Eric Holder addresses the issue of civil rights in the United States. Specifically, Holder addresses a recent legal challenge to the Voting Rights Act of 1965 before the United States Supreme Court. At issue in the case, Shelby County v. Holder, *is a provision in the law (section 5) stipulating that certain states and local governments obtain federal permission before making alterations to their voting laws and practices. Holder speaks in support of the Voting Rights Act, which he believes succeeds in preventing discriminatory changes in voting procedures in states with a history of government-sanctioned prejudice against racial minorities. These procedures include changes in early voting regulations, redistricting, and photo identification requirements. Critics of section 5 argue that it is a relic of a bygone era and no longer necessary. Holder states his belief that while racial equality has improved in America, the nation is not yet ready to abandon this provision of electoral law. Holder also recounts the history of the American civil rights movement more broadly and MALDEF's role in improving voting rights. He also addresses MALDEF's work in support of the Violence Against Women Act. Other issues discussed include labor rights, human trafficking, and immigration reform. MALDEF's 2013 Award Gala honored the career achievements of Ken Salazar, secretary of the US Department of the Interior; Alejandro Mayorkas, director of US Citizenship and Immigration Services; and Anna Maria Chávez, CEO of Girl Scouts of the USA.*

Thank you, John, for those kind words—and thank you all for such a warm welcome. It's a pleasure to be in such great company this evening. And it's a privilege to join so many friends, colleagues, committed partners, and distinguished award recipients for tonight's important celebration.

I'd like to thank Tom Saenz for his strong leadership since becoming President and General Counsel of the Mexican American Legal Defense and Educational Fund in 2009. I'd like to acknowledge the hard work of MALDEF's national Board of Directors, regional office leaders, professional staff, supporters, and sponsors—not only in ensuring that this organization remains America's leading "law firm of the Latino community," but in advancing equality , opportunity , and justice. And I'd like to thank tonight's honorees—Anna Maria Chávez, Director Mayorkas, and

---

Delivered April 24, 2013, at the Mexican American Legal Defense and Educational Fund Awards Gala, Washington, DC, by Eric Holder.

my good friend Secretary Salazar—for their leadership of these essential efforts; for the remarkable achievements we've gathered to celebrate; and for the service that each of them has rendered—to their communities and their country—by helping to build engagement, address disparities, and overcome injustice wherever it is found.

Tonight's Awards Gala presents an important opportunity for everyone here to renew our shared commitment to this work—and to the cause of equality that we've come together to advance. This cause has served as a unifying vision, and a rallying cry, since the day MALDEF was founded—four and a half decades ago—when a group of concerned citizens gathered in San Antonio, Texas, to put forward a vision of hope in a time of difficulty, and a year defined by national tragedy.

During the spring and summer of 1968—with the shocking murders of Dr. Martin Luther King, Jr. and Senator Robert F. Kennedy—the country, and the Civil Rights Movement, were badly shaken. In cities and towns across America, peaceful activists faced misguided legal actions, abusive words, and threats of violence. In East Los Angeles, California, thousands of Latino high school students walked out of their classrooms to protest discrimination in the public school system. And, although our nation had made significant strides since the days of Bull Connor, the Freedom Rides, and the bombing of the 16th Street Baptist Church—in 1968, the future of the progress to which Dr. King, Senator Kennedy, and so many others had dedicated their lives was anything but certain.

Yet MALDEF's founders were not only undaunted—they were defiantly optimistic. With assistance from the Ford Foundation, and help from other civil rights groups—such as LULAC and the NAACP—MALDEF built a strong base of support and began to intervene in civil legal aid cases. Over the next 45 years—as this organization grew, and its work broadened—your dedication to the values of equity and inclusion has remained steadfast. Through educational outreach, legislative advocacy, community engagement, and principled litigation, you've consistently fought to secure the rights of immigrants and underserved populations. You've played a key role in high-profile policy debates and Supreme Court cases. And you've taken difficult stands—often against long odds and steep opposition— to expand education and employment, to bridge longstanding divisions, and to see that justice is done.

In a variety of ways, MALDEF has helped to bring about meaningful changes—from America's schools and workplaces, to our housing and lending markets, border areas, and immigrant communities. Time and again, you've stood up—and spoken out—for equal opportunity and equal rights. And as we assemble tonight, here in our nation's capital, your efforts are continuing to make a powerful difference—particularly, when it comes to our ongoing struggle to safeguard the single most fundamental, and most powerful, right of American citizenship: the right to vote.

As you know, in recent years, we've seen an unprecedented number of lawsuits challenging the constitutionality of one of our most effective tools for preventing discrimination in our elections systems: Section 5 of the Voting Rights Act of 1965. This landmark provision was a signature achievement of the Civil Rights Movement. It requires all or parts of fifteen states with histories of discrimination to obtain approval, from either the Justice Department or a panel of federal judges, for any proposed changes in voting procedures or practices—including redistricting plans, early voting procedures, and photo identification requirements—some of which may disproportionately impact young, poor, elderly, and minority voters.

> *As it stands, too many employers game this system by hiring and exploiting undocumented workers. Far too many people are relegated to living in the shadows—without the rights, dignity, and legal protections they deserve.*

There has long been a national, bipartisan consensus that this important law is not only necessary—but good—for our democracy. Unfortunately, despite this consensus, and the overwhelming Congressional majority that voted to reauthorize the Voting Rights Act in 2006, the Supreme Court recently heard a case challenging Section 5—contending that it is no longer constitutional, and arguing that our nation has moved beyond the realities that prompted its passage and its recent renewal.

Let me be clear: while this country has indeed changed, and real progress has been made—thanks to groups like MALDEF and many others—we are not yet at a point where the most vital part of the Voting Rights Act can be described as unnecessary or a product of a flawed political process. That's why today's Justice Department has vigorously defended Section 5 as an indispensable tool for eradicating discriminatory election practices. It's why MALDEF has stood shoulder-to-shoulder with us in this effort—filing an amicus brief arguing that Section 5 must be upheld, and working hard to safeguard the rights of language minorities.

And it's why—no matter the outcome of this important case—my colleagues and I will remain committed to the aggressive and appropriate enforcement of every federal voting and civil rights protection that's on the books. What we cannot—and will not—do is stand by and allow the slow unraveling of an electoral system that so many have sacrificed so much to construct. We must not countenance procedural abuses or consider unwise proposed changes—such as shortened voting periods— that are inconsistent with the historic ideal of expanded participation in the process. We must take action, together, to address long lines—which are unnecessary and may depress turnout among certain voting populations. And we must speak out against recent proposed changes in how electoral votes are apportioned in specific states—and call such proposals what they are: blatantly partisan, unfair, divisive, and not worthy of our nation.

Above all, we must stand together to honor the basic principles of equal treatment and fair representation that have always been at the center of our identity as a nation; that have driven MALDEF to fight for expanded access and social change in the public arena; and that have stood at the core of the Justice Department's recent efforts to enforce voting laws and a range of other essential civil rights protections. Especially over the past four years—under the leadership of Assistant Attorney General and Secretary of Labor-designate Tom Perez—the Department's Civil Rights Division has taken this work to new heights—striving to reduce violence, eliminate bias, and combat intimidation. We've significantly increased hate crime prosecutions. And we have opened a record number of inquiries into local police departments and other agencies to ensure constitutional policing practices.

In addition, we have taken steps to address discrimination in schools—and to protect the right of all children to enroll, regardless of immigration status. Through our Office on Violence Against Women, we're implementing legislative improvements like the reauthorized Violence Against Women Act—which MALDEF helped to secure, and which includes increased protections for immigrants, LGBT men and women, and women in tribal communities. And we're building reinvigorated partnerships with key international authorities—particularly Mexican leaders—to combat the repugnant practice of human trafficking.

Over the past four years, these efforts have enabled the Department to charge a record number of human trafficking cases. Just yesterday, I traveled to Mexico City—and met with my Mexican counterparts—to discuss the Administration's plans to build on this work, and to address other shared law enforcement and criminal justice challenges. I was proud to help strengthen the bonds of friendship that the United States has forged with Mexico and other allies throughout Latin America—and to reaffirm my personal and professional commitment to the values that our people have always shared.

Yet I recognize that—although we can be encouraged by these recent steps forward, and by the remarkable progress we've seen in the years since MALDEF was founded—there's also no denying that significant obstacles remain before us. Among these challenges, none is more important—or more urgent—than the need to enact commonsense, comprehensive legislation that reforms, improves, and makes more fair our nation's broken immigration system.

As it stands, too many employers game this system by hiring and exploiting undocumented workers. Far too many people are relegated to living in the shadows—without the rights, dignity, and legal protections they deserve. And the escalating costs of this broken system—in terms both economic and moral—are simply too much to bear.

As President Obama has made clear, it is long past time to reform our immigration system in a way that is fair; that guarantees that all are playing by the same rules; and that requires responsibility from everyone—both the people who are here in an undocumented status and those who hire them. Creating a pathway to earned citizenship for the 11 million unauthorized immigrants in this country is essential. The way we treat our friends and neighbors who are undocumented—by creating a mechanism for them to earn citizenship and move out of the shadows—transcends the issue of immigration status. This is a matter of civil and human rights. It is about who we are as a nation. And it goes to the core of our treasured American principle of equal opportunity.

Like many of you, I have been encouraged to see that the bipartisan reforms currently under discussion in the US Senate are consistent with these basic principles. I look forward to working with Members of Congress and groups like MALDEF to help refine and improve these proposals. The Senate Judiciary Committee's markup of legislation next month will provide us all with an opportunity to do this. And, as this debate unfolds, I am optimistic that—if we continue to work together—we can move forward to make our nation stronger, more secure, and more prosperous by building a fair and effective system that lives up to our heritage as a nation of laws—and, never let us forget, a nation built by immigrants. After so many years of work by MALDEF and many others, today, our shared goal of meaningful reform is a real possibility. Just as in the past you have opened the doors of educational opportunity and protected the rights of Latinos at the ballot box—so, today, can we stand together in achieving commonsense, comprehensive immigration reform, and honoring the American story in its most basic form.

For centuries, courageous women and men from every corner of the globe have set their sights on our shores, driven by little more than their hope for a better life and their dream for a brighter future for their children. Many have crossed vast oceans, harsh deserts, and great cultural divides to make that dream a reality.

This is the dream that, many years ago, inspired my own family to come to this country—just as it has inspired so many of yours. Although I am a native New Yorker—by birth as well as upbringing—I'm proud to say I was raised in a home infused with traditions and values that my father and all my grandparents brought with them from the great island of Barbados. I was fortunate to spend many of my formative years in a neighborhood that was populated largely by immigrants—among wonderful, hardworking people who championed education, understood the importance of family, and constantly reinforced the value of tolerance and respect.

These principles are reflected in this Justice Department's efforts to enforce protections against racial and ethnic discrimination—as well as existing immigration laws. They will continue to guide our work to fairly adjudicate immigration cases, and to hold accountable employers who knowingly hire undocumented workers or engage in illegal or discriminatory practices. And they drove the Administration, just last summer, to announce that certain young people—brought to this country illegally by their parents through no fault of their own, but who pose no risk to public safety or national security and who enrich our nation—may now receive relief from removal and apply for work authorization through the Deferred Action for Childhood Arrivals process. Thanks to MALDEF and many others in the legal community, many young people were given the basic information and the legal assistance they needed to come forward and request relief under this process. Their dream must be ours as well.

This common-sense approach to focusing our enforcement resources will help to make our immigration policy not only more efficient and cost-effective—but more just. It represents a step in the right direction—but it's far from a permanent solution. And, by itself, it will never be enough. The time for comprehensive immigration reform is now.

So, as we gather this evening—to celebrate the positive steps we've taken, and to discuss the challenges ahead—we must also seize this chance to reaffirm our collective resolve to build on the record of achievement we've established. Although we come together, as your founders did, in an hour of need—it's also a time of significant opportunity, and limitless promise.

Thanks to the work of committed leaders and passionate advocates in this room—and our partners throughout the Obama Administration and across the country, and patriots and friends like Ken Salazar—I am confident that the months ahead will be marked by deeper engagement between government leaders, policy makers, and advocates from across the political spectrum. I am eager to see where each of you will help to lead us from here. And I am optimistic about the dialogue we will build—and the country and future we will create—together.

Thank you.

About Eric Holder

Eric Holder is the current Attorney General of the United States. He was sworn in on February 3, 2009. Holder was born in the Bronx borough of New York City, on January 21, 1951. He attended Stuyvesant High School, and earned his bachelor's degree in American history from New York's Columbia University in 1973. He earned his law degree from Columbia in 1976. From 1976 to 1988, he was a member of the Public Integrity Section with the US attorney general's office. In 1988, President Ronald Reagan nominated Holder as an associate judge on the Superior Court of the District of Columbia. He served in that capacity until 1993, when he became the US attorney for Washington, DC. In 1997, President Bill Clinton appointed Holder deputy to Attorney General Janet Reno. Prior to the confirmation of John Ashcroft, Holder served as acting attorney general from January 20, 2001, to February 2, 2001. He subsequently returned to private practice, working as a litigation partner at the law firm Covington & Burling LLP. In 2007, he became senior legal advisor to the presidential campaign of then senator Barack Obama. Obama nominated Holder to the post of US Attorney General on December 1, 2008.

Puerto Ricans Are US Citizens, but Our Citizenship Is Second Class

By Pedro R. Pierluisi

In an address to the League of United Latin American Citizens (LULAC), Congressman Pedro Pierluisi, Resident Commissioner of Puerto Rico, discusses the issues of comprehensive immigration reform and citizenship for residents of Puerto Rico. The speech took place at the 84th Annual LULAC National Convention and Exposition in Las Vegas, Nevada. Pierluisi states his belief that individuals born outside the United States have made lasting and significant contributions to the country's development and growth. He compares the status of illegal immigrants in the United States to residents of Puerto Rico, stating that both are treated differently because of their place of birth. Although Puerto Rico remains an unincorporated territory of the United States, numerous policies enacted by the United States Congress have an impact on the lives of the people who live there. These include decisions on economic policy and immigration. Pierluisi discusses the results of a November 2012 referendum on Puerto Rico's political status. The majority of Puerto Ricans voted against maintaining the island's current political status and expressed their preference for a move toward statehood. Pierluisi describes the Puerto Rico Status Resolution Act, legislation he introduced to initiate the process of making Puerto Rico a state. He commends LULAC for their support of this initiative, which he introduced to Congress in 2013.

Thank you for the warm introduction, Tony.

Buenas noches a todos. I want to begin by thanking LULAC, which strives every day to seek justice for Latinos in the United States. I particularly want to thank Margaret, Brent, Ivonne Quiñones, and my friend Elsie Valdés. LULAC is a national treasure, and I am honored to be with you tonight.

My remarks will be very brief, because I know you are anxious to continue enjoying the good food and the good company. I just want to touch upon two public policy issues that are distinct—and ought to be treated as such by policymakers—but that share an important principle in common, namely, the principle of equality.

The issues are, on the one hand, the need to create a reasonable path to US citizenship for millions of undocumented immigrants in the United States by enacting comprehensive immigration reform and, on the other hand, the imperative to create a path to full and equal US citizenship for millions of American citizens residing in Puerto Rico by enacting federal legislation to facilitate the territory's transition to a democratic and dignified political status.

Delivered June 21, 2013, at the LULAC National Convention, Las Vegas, Nevada, by Pedro R. Pierluisi.

LULAC is to be commended for its moral clarity on immigration and Puerto Rico's status. This organization understands that each subject—while different in key respects—raises fundamental questions about the nature of our democracy and the meaning of American citizenship. How we answer these questions will demonstrate what we stand for, and who we aspire to become, as a nation.

As a member of the House Judiciary Committee's Subcommittee on Immigration and Border Security, I strongly support comprehensive immigration reform that includes a path to citizenship. I also support enhanced border security, but I oppose the cynical efforts being made by some politicians to require a level of border security that is unattainable in a free and open society before undocumented immigrants can take the first steps on the journey to citizenship.

America has always been—and remains today—a work in progress. And since the country's founding, the hard work of perfecting our Union has often been carried out by intrepid men and women born outside of America, immigrants from other shores who chose to leave behind everything and everyone they know, who came here in search of economic opportunity or to escape poverty or persecution, and whose character, passion and talent have enriched the life of this nation and replenished its spirit.

These men and women are the engine of our economy. Without them, this country could not function. They get up early and go to bed late. They toil day and night, for low wages and little recognition. They may lack the proper documents, but they have tremendous dignity. They deserve a chance to become citizens of the nation that their labor has helped build and sustain. And so it is vital for political leaders to give them that chance by enacting sensible legislation.

I am a Puerto Rican and, as such, a natural-born American citizen. But, I must tell you, I can relate to the experience of the undocumented immigrant in this country. Those of us who are from Puerto Rico know how it feels to be excluded or treated differently because of our place of birth. Puerto Ricans are US citizens, but our citizenship is second class.

Like our immigrant brothers and sisters, we, too, aspire to be treated equally by the country to which we have given so much. And we are making our aspirations heard loud and clear.

Last November, Puerto Rico exercised its right to self-determination by holding a free and fair vote on the question of our political status. The results demonstrate that a clear majority of my constituents do not wish to maintain the current status, which deprives us of the most fundamental democratic rights. To the extent that the people of Puerto Rico ever gave their consent to the current status, that consent has now been withdrawn. The results further demonstrate that, for the first time in Puerto Rico's history, there are more people who want Puerto Rico to become a state than who want to continue the status quo.

It is now essential for the US government to respond by enacting legislation to offer Puerto Rico one or more of the status options that would provide its people with a full measure of self-government.

In April, President Obama sought an appropriation from Congress to conduct the first federally sponsored vote in Puerto Rico's history to "resolve" the territory's status.

And, last month, I introduced the Puerto Rico Status Resolution Act, which outlines the rights and responsibilities of statehood, and then asks the people of Puerto Rico if they accept those terms. If a majority of voters say yes, the bill provides for the President to submit legislation to admit Puerto Rico as a State after a transition period.

> *Those of us who are from Puerto Rico know how it feels to be excluded or treated differently because of our place of birth. Puerto Ricans are US citizens, but our citizenship is second class.*

My bill has already been cosponsored by over 80 Members of Congress from both political parties, representing districts all over this great land.

Just as I have faith that the US government will act to reform our unprincipled immigration laws, I have faith that it will fulfill its legal and moral obligation to facilitate Puerto Rico's transition to a democratic and dignified status. And I know that LULAC, because of its ironclad commitment to equality, will continue to remain at the forefront of both of these fights.

About Pedro Pierluisi

Congressman Pedro Pierluisi—a Democrat from Puerto Rico—is the island's current resident commissioner in Washington, DC, and its only representative in Congress. Pierluisi was born in San Juan on April 26, 1959. He graduated from Tulane University in New Orleans with a bachelor's degree in American history in 1981, and received a JD from the George Washington University Law School in 1984. Pierluisi was attorney general of Puerto Rico from 1993 to 1996. During this time, he was a member of the National Association of Attorneys General and served as the group's eastern region chairman in the last year of his term. He returned to private law practice before deciding to run for the post of resident commissioner of Puerto Rico in 2008. He was elected and went on to win a second term in Congress in the November 2012 general election. Pierluisi currently serves on the Committee on the Judiciary, the Committee on Natural Resources, and the Committee on Ethics.

Success on Immigration Reform Runs Through the Border

By Mitch McConnell

Speaking on the floor of the United States Senate on June 27, 2013, US Senate Minority Leader Mitch McConnell, Republican from Kentucky, discusses the issue of comprehensive immigration reform. Specifically, McConnell addresses why he has chosen not to vote in favor of an immigration reform bill before the Senate. According to McConnell, the legislation fails to adequately address the issue of border security. He states his belief that changes to existing immigration law should secure the United States border and prevent illegal immigrants from entering the country. Recounting his wife's experience as an immigrant from Taiwan, McConnell articulates his belief in the importance of legal immigration. McConnell states that millions of undocumented aliens currently reside in the United States and that millions more will enter the country unless new immigration legislation addresses border security. Certain features of the legislation are praised by McConnell, including its focus on skills-based immigration and reformed visa programs— both of which he implies will result in benefits to the American economy. He criticizes his Democratic colleagues in the Senate for what he sees as their failure to properly consider the issues of border security. Although the Senate approved the legislation discussed by McConnell in this address in June 2013, the legislation failed to gain approval in the House of Representatives.

At the outset of this debate I expressed my hope that we could do something about our nation's broken immigration system.

Millions of men and women are living among us without any documentation or certainty about what the future will bring for themselves or their families. Many of those who come here legally end up staying here illegally. We have no way of knowing who or where they are. And current law simply doesn't take into account the urgent needs of a modern, rapidly changing economy.

Beyond all this, it's long been a deep conviction of mine that from our earliest days as a people immigration has been a powerful force of renewal and national strength. Most of the people who've come here over the centuries have come as dreamers and risk-takers, looking for a chance at a better life for themselves and their children.

I can think of no better example of this than my wife, who came here at the age of eight in the cargo hull of a ship, because her parents didn't have the money for a plane ticket. When she entered the third grade at a public high school in New York, she

Delivered June 27, 2013, at the US Senate, Washington, DC, by Mitch McConnell.

didn't speak a word of English. And yet, in just a few short decades she'd be sworn in as a member of the President's cabinet, an honor and an opportunity she could have hardly guessed at when she first arrived here as a girl.

> *One thing I'm fairly certain about is that we'll never resolve the immigraiton problem on a bipartisan basis either now or in the future until we can prove that the border is secure as a condition of legalization.*

This is the kind of story that has made this nation what it is. Legal immigration made it possible. So yes, I had wanted very much to be able to support a reform to our nation's immigration laws. I knew it would be tough, and the politics aren't particularly easy either. But the fact is, our constituents didn't just send us here to name post offices and pass Mother's Day resolutions. They sent us here to tackle the hard stuff too.

Broad bipartisan majorities agree that our immigration system needs updating. In my view, we had an obligation to our constituents to at least try to do it, together, and, in the process, show the world that we can still solve big national problems around here. And reaffirm the vital role that legal immigration has played in our history.

So it's with a great deal of regret, for me at least, that the final bill didn't turn out to be something I can support.

The reason is fairly simple. As I see it, this bill just doesn't meet the threshold test for success that I outlined at the start of this debate. It just doesn't say to me, at least, that we've learned the lessons of 1986, and that we won't find ourselves right back in the same situation we found ourselves in after that reform.

If you can't be reasonably certain that the border is secure as a condition of legalization, there's just no way to be sure that millions more won't follow the illegal immigrants who are already here. As others have rightly pointed out, you also can't be sure that future congresses won't just reverse whatever assurances we make today about border security in the future.

In other words, in the absence of a firm, results-based border security trigger, there's just no way I can look my constituents in the eye and tell them that today's assurances won't become tomorrow's disappointments; and since the bill before us doesn't include such a trigger, I can't support it.

It doesn't give me any pleasure to say this, or to vote against this bill. These are big problems that need solving. And I'm deeply grateful to all the members of my caucus and their staffs who devoted so much of their time and worked so hard over a period of many months to solve them. I'm grateful to all of them.

And while I won't be voting for this bill, I think it has to be said that there are real improvements here.

Current immigration policy, which prioritizes family-based immigration, hasn't changed in decades. This bill would take an important step toward the kind of skills-based immigration a growing economy requires. Through new and reformed visa programs, for instance, this bill would provide many of our most dynamic businesses with the opportunity to legally hire the workers they need to remain competitive and expand.

Some industries, like construction, could and should have fared better. But on balance, I think the improvements to legal immigration contained in this bill are a step in the right direction.

We've learned an important lesson in this debate. One thing I'm fairly certain about is that we'll never resolve the immigration problem on a bipartisan basis either now or in the future until we can prove that the border is secure as a condition of legalization. This, to me, continues to be the biggest hurdle to reform.

Frankly, I can't understand why there's so much resistance to it on the other side. It seems pretty obvious to me, and I suspect to most Americans, that the first part of immigration reform should be proof that the border is secure. It's common sense.

Hopefully, Democrats now realize that this is the one necessary ingredient for success and they'll be a little more willing to accept it as a condition for legalization. Because until they do, I for one just can't be confident that we've solved this problem, and I know a lot of others won't be either.

So this bill may pass the Senate today, but not with my vote. And in its current form, it won't become law. But the good news is this: the path to success is fairly clear at this point. Success on immigration reform runs through the border. Looking ahead, I think it's safe to say that's where our focus should lie.

About Mitch McConnell

United States Senate minority leader Mitch McConnell—a Republican—is currently the senior senator from Kentucky. He began his first term in the Senate in 1985. McConnell was born in Louisville, Kentucky, on February 20, 1942. He earned his bachelor's degree from the University of Louisville College of Arts and Sciences in 1964, and subsequently enrolled in the University of Kentucky College of Law, graduating in 1967. After spending a decade working under various elected officials in Washington, DC, McConnell was elected judge-executive for Jefferson County, Kentucky, serving from 1978 to 1985. In 1984, McConnell beat out Democratic incumbent Walter "Dee" Huddleston—who had been in office since 1973—for a seat in the US Senate, becoming the first Republican to win a statewide election in Kentucky since 1968. McConnell has served as Senate Republican leader since 2006, was the majority whip in the 108th and 109th Congresses, and was chairman of the National Republican Senatorial Committee in 1998 and 2000. Now in his fifth term, McConnell serves as a senior member on the Appropriations, Agriculture, and Rules Committees.

Solving Guest Worker Problem Leads to Immigration Reform

By Marco Rubio

Republican Senator Marco Rubio of Florida delivers the keynote address at the 2012 Hispanic Leadership Network (HLN) Conference. The address took place on January 27, 2012, in Miami, Florida. Rubio began his tenure as a US senator in January 2011. The subject of his speech is immigration and the American economy. Rubio begins his remarks by addressing the audience in Spanish. His remarks are momentarily interrupted by political protestors. Although he does not refer to him by name, Rubio is highly critical of President Barack Obama, whom he describes as divisive and interested in political gain. However, he submits that the issue of immigration has been politicized by all politicians. Rubio states his support for a guest worker program and also discusses the Republican Party's approach to the issue of immigration. His speech includes a series of personal anecdotes about his parents and grandfather. Rubio's parents emigrated to the United States from Cuba. He also includes a reading of the poem The Colossus *by Emma Lazarus. Relating the poem to the issue of immigration, Rubio reminds the audience that it is engraved on the Statue of Liberty in New York Harbor. Rubio concludes his speech by discussing his firm belief in the doctrine of American exceptionalism. He asserts that every human being is endowed by God with inalienable rights, regardless of her or his background.*

Thank you, thank you very much. Thank you. That was a very kind introduction, thank you very much. What's this? Rick Sanchez is staring at me, let me just.

(Places magazine with Rick Sanchez cover on the podium)

Makes me nervous. Thank you very much. Is Rick here? No? Thank you.

Unas palabras en español brevemente. Muchísimas gracias por esta oportunidad en este momento tan clave en la historia de este país. Un país que tiene que escoger en este momento una dirección económica que en mi opinión tiene que ser muy distinta a la dirección que esta administración nos lleva.

Lo que ha hecho este país grande es la libre empresa. La habilidad de personas de venir de todas partes del mundo, y de seguir sus sueños económicos y familiares. De poder ir hacia delante y dejar sus hijos en mejor posición de donde empezaron ellos.

Eso nos hace único como país, y tengo el miedo que lo vamos a perder, que la dirección que nos lleva este presidente es una dirección que nos va a robar de algo que nos hace especial y distinto al resto del mundo.

Delivered January 27, 2012, at the Hispanic Leadership Network Conference, Miami, Florida, by Marco Rubio.

Así que estas elecciones van a ser claves y bien importantes, y no hay comunidad en este país que entienda mejor esa realidad económica, que entienda mejor ese sueño americano que la nuestra.

Y es por eso que pienso que la comunidad latina e hispana en este país se debe desempeñar al nivel político de todas maneras posibles. Y les agradezco a todos que han organizado este evento, y que están aquí en el día de hoy, para no solamente escuchar mis palabras, sino las palabras de los candidatos republicanos y de otros invitados y distinguidos que van a estar aquí hoy con nosotros. Muchísimas gracias.

To those that don't speak Spanish, I apologize. I was basically describing how I saved a bunch of money on my car insurance.

So thank you for choosing Miami. It's a great place to do political things. It's a very exciting and vibrant place to do politics.

On my way in today I got a text from a friend who said that someone is flying a plane over the building with a banner that says "Marco, No Somos Rubio," which means "Marco, We're Not Blonde." Which, by coincidence neither am I. So, although if I'm in the Senate for another year I may start being a little bit more grey.

But anyway, thank you for choosing this place and for being a part of this and giving us the opportunity to speak at this key moment in our nation's history.

I want to begin. Obviously, when people talk about Americans of Hispanic descent the first issue that comes to mind is immigration, and rightfully so. Because for people in our community the issue of immigration is not a theoretical one, it's not an issue of statistics, it's not always even an issue of law and order. It's an issue of their lives, and of the people that they love.

Whether you came here from another country yourself, whether your parents did, or whether you've been here generations, there is no one in the community of Hispanic Americans who does not love someone who has found themselves in limbo or in a situation. No one. It's impossible to walk a block in Miami, in Los Angeles, in others, San Antonio, without running into somebody who is being deeply impacted by a broken legal immigration system.

And so when politicians and political figures speak about the issue of migration, they're not just talking about a legal issue. They're speaking about the real lives of real people that so many of us love and care for. And so it is an important issue, not just for our country, but in our community it's a gateway issue.

(Inaudible Protesters in Crowd)

Nope, please. No, no, no, no, no, please. Let me—

(Inaudible Protesters in Crowd)

Yes, let me, may I say something to you? May I say something to you? Will you listen to me for a second? May I say something?

(Inaudible Protesters in Crowd)

No, no, no, listen. These young people, these young people are very brave to be here today. They raise a very legitimate issue. And if you would allow me to, no, no, please, if they would give me the courtesy of finishing my speech where I'm going to speak about this, then I ask that you let them stay because I think they'll be interested in what I'm going to say.

I don't, I don't want them to leave. I want them to stay. These young, let me tell you guys something, these young men and women raise a very legitimate issue. They came here to a crowd that they know may not be friendly to their point of view on some issues, and they had the bravery and the courage to raise their voices. A: I thank God that I'm in a country where they can do that, but B: I want them to hear what I have to say. Because I think number one, I'm not who they think I am, and number two, I don't stand for what they claim I stand for. And so unfortunately, they weren't willing to be a part of that or listen to it, so I'll speak to you. And hopefully those of you with cameras and tape recorders will report it to them and the rest of the world, and the rest of the country.

The immigration issue is critical and it's important because it's a gateway issue to the number one issue on the minds of the people in this community, of all walks of life, and that's economic empowerment.

Let me say that there is no community in America that understands the American dream of economic empowerment better than ours. And the reason is that the number one issue in our community is the desire to accomplish your dreams and hopes and to leave your children and your grandchildren with opportunities that you yourself never had.

Every single day, people lived, obsessed, in this country with that notion. But no community is more obsessed with it than ours. It's the reason why people come here. It's the reason why they work two jobs. It's the reason why your parents gave up their own hopes and their own dreams so that you could do the things they couldn't, so you could be what they could not be, so you could go where they could not go, so the doors that were closed to them were open for you.

Which community in our country understands that better than ours, there is none. It typifies our life. It's who we are, it's why we're here. And it's what's made our country great.

And I would submit to you that there has never been an economic system that provides the opportunity to do that better than the American free enterprise system. No economic system is perfect. But nowhere in the world have more people from all walks of life been able to empower their children and their grandchildren more than they were able to do here in the twentieth century in the American free enterprise system.

And I also submit to you that today it is under assault. That our country today is run by a President that's as divisive as any figure in modern American history, who sadly has chosen the route of dividing Americans against each other for the purpose of gaining votes and political support.

His message is one that basically says to people, the way to protect your job is to raise your boss' taxes. That the way for you to do better off is for someone else to be worse off. That the only way you can climb up the ladder is if we pull some people down.

Now let me tell you, that language is common all over the world. You find it often in the third world. But it's never been who we are.

As I said in a speech at the end of last year, we have never been a nation of haves and have nots. We have always been a nation of haves and soon to haves, a people who have made it and people who believe that given the chance they will make it too. And if we lose that, we lose the essence of what's made us great in terms of economics.

And so, when the choices that are put before us today are dangerous ones, because if we choose this path of pitting people against each other, if we buy into this notion that our economy really can't grow fast enough for all of us to prosper so we're going to have to somehow empower government to distribute the wealth of this country among us, we've chosen to become like everybody else. We've chosen to become like the countries that your parents and grandparents came here to get away from. And that's a powerful message. And that's the message that we need to deliver. And that's the message we need to work on delivering. It's a winning message, but it's a difficult message to get to because the gateway issue of immigration stands in the minds of so many people who we live next to and love.

Our country has a broken legal immigration system. Its status quo is unsustainable.

We don't have a functional guest worker program in a nation that knows that it has, especially in things like agriculture, a need for temporary workers who enter on a temporary basis.

Our nation has a complicated and burdensome visa process, where even if you wanted to enter this country legally, and you wanted to stay here legally, it costs so much money, it's so complicated, so bureaucratic, that it's difficult to comply with.

And by the way, the things I just outlined to you are things of massive, overwhelming support in our country. There is broad bipartisan support across the board for the idea that America needs a legal immigration system that works.

And that's why I have challenged the Republican nominees and all Republicans to not just be the anti-illegal immigration party. That's not who we are, that's not who we should be. We should be the pro-legal immigration party. A party that has a positive platform and agenda on how we can create a legal immigration system that works for America and works for immigrants.

They're all around us. You find them in Home Depot when I drive up in my pickup truck, in the desperate look of faces of men that are looking for work. You find it in homes across this community and this country, where women work hard, long hours— sometimes without documents— to send money back home.

And I think you could find broad bipartisan support today for the idea that our legal immigration system is broken and needs to be modernized. That we need to take into account the needs and realities of the 21st century and tailor a legal immigration system and a visa program that takes care of that.

I think you could find broad bipartisan support for the notion that our immigration laws need to be enforced, that we need some sort of electronic, low-cost, affordable verification system for employers. That we need increased border security and ways to protect our borders. That we need to invest in these technologies and make this possible.

I think you would find broad bipartisan support for the idea that we need a functional guest worker program. Where, from year to year, when there are indeed jobs, for workers from abroad to come into the United States because we need them for our economy to grow and prosper, so that food doesn't rot in the farm fields, so that construction gets finished, or whatever the industry that year may be. A functional guest worker program, where people can apply in their home country, receive a tamper-proof identification card, enter the U.S., we know who you are, we know why you're here, we know where you work, you're here for a defined period of time and then you go home when it's done. And by the way, they want that too.

You know why people overstay visas; you know why people overstay temporary, if they can get the temporary worker visas today? Because they're afraid if they leave they'll never be able to get back in, because it's so complicated and burdensome and broken.

You can find broad bipartisan support for all of these ideas. So why haven't they happened? Well they haven't happened because the issue of immigration is a powerful one politically. And dividing people along the lines of immigration has proven to be rewarding to politicians on the left and on the right.

And so for those of us who come from the conservative movement, we must admit that there are those among us who have used rhetoric that is harsh and intolerable, inexcusable. And we must admit, myself included, that sometimes we've been too slow in condemning that language for what it is.

But, at the same time, on the left, there are those that are using this issue for pure politics. Creating unrealistic and unreasonable expectations among those in the Latino community across this country. Advocating that our country be the only one in the world that has no immigrations laws, and no mechanism for enforcing them. Both sides are guilty of using this issue to divide us. I think that needs to stop.

Now, if you solve the issue of the guest worker program, you solve the issue of the illegal immigration system that you have that needs to be reformed and modernized, you're left with between nine and eleven million people who are in this country undocumented. They came for different reasons. They found themselves in this predicament in different ways, and it's a real challenge for our country.

On the one hand there is not political support for the notion of basically granting eleven million people citizenship or a path thereto in the United States. It's just not there. On the other side, it's not realistic to expect that you're going to deport eleven million people. It doesn't work, we can't do it, and it would offend American sensibilities and rightfully so. What's the solution to it? There is no magic solution to it—that's why it's so complicated. And that's why the politics makes it more complicated.

Now these young people that stood up a moment ago, I think one of the reasons why they're here is because they're concerned about young people. Let me say: I'm confident in what I have said throughout my political career and especially during my campaign for the Senate, that there is broad support in America for the notion that for those children that were brought here at a very young age, by their parents through no fault of their own, who have grown up here their entire lives, and now want to serve in the military or are high academic achievers and want to go to school and contribute to America's future, I think there is broad bipartisan support for the notion that we should somehow figure out a way to accommodate them. Figure out a way to accommodate them in a way that does not encourage illegal immigration in the future.

Unfortunately some of the legislative proposals that are out there today go too far and there's no support for those either. But I think we can solve that problem. And I hope that we, as Republicans and as conservatives, take the lead in solving it. Because it's not just the right thing to do, it speaks to our hopes and dreams as a nation. And it's critical for our economic future.

How about everybody else? I don't have a magic answer for you. This is a difficult issue, and sometimes those of us in public service need to stop pretending like difficult issues have easy answers. They don't. It'll require an open conversation across this country about what we want to do. How can we create and deal with this issue in a way that both honors our legacy as a nation of immigrants but also honors our legacy as a nation of laws? How do we balance those two things? Well that's at the core of this issue. And it must be confronted because the status quo is unsustainable.

This issue is a deeply personal one for so many people in this room. I know it is for me. A few months ago—you may have read about it, maybe you didn't—I got some dates wrong in my parents' immigration history. And it created some difficult, you know, uncomfortable days. It was a blessing in disguise. You know what it made me do? It made me do something that we don't do enough. And that's go back and discover who our parents were when they were our age. What were their hopes and dreams? What did they want out of life? Where did they want to go and what did they want to do with themselves? I had a chance to do that. And from the tattered pages of passports and the yellowed papers of olden documents, from across five decades, I clearly heard the voice of people I never really met.

Of my father who came here as a young man and didn't find instant success. He went to New York—it was too cold. He came to Miami—it was too hard. He went to Los Angeles—it was too California. He went back to Las Vegas the first time. He came back to Miami. He was discouraged. He struggled as a young man who grew up in poverty in Havana after his mom died and then he was struggling here too. He had hopes and dreams for himself. He wanted to own a business and he thought America was the place he could do it and he struggled. And he was discouraged, and he even made plans to go back to Cuba because of that.

I discovered this about my grandfather, who I thought I knew real well, but in fact he grew up in an agriculture family and as a young man he suffered polio. He lost the use of his leg—they sent him to school. He was the only one in his family who knew how to read and write. He got a good job running one of the railroad stations. His family lived comfortably—he had five daughters at the time. It was a heavy undertaking in that climate. And one day, from day to night, he lost his job.

And instantly he was tossed, and his family was, into poverty and struggle. He was a disabled man in early twentieth century Cuba trying to find a way to feed his five—almost six—daughters. Struggling with that. My mother tells the story of how he would spend all day looking for work sometimes having to walk miles and come home at night his knees bleeding because he would trip and fall. Because he didn't have the use of a leg. Tough life.

Why am I different than them? Am I better than them? Why have I had opportunities that they did not have? It was but for the grace of God. That's true of all of us. I've been able to do things they didn't because I'm here, in the single greatest society and the single greatest nation in all of human history. But it reminded me that their stories, although they're gone, are still alive. They're all around us. You find them in Home Depot when I drive up in my pickup truck, in the desperate look of faces of men that are looking for work. You find it in homes across this community and this country, where women work hard, long hours—sometimes without documents—to send money back home.

Of course there are people that abuse the system. But the enormous majority of the people that come here legally and illegally do so because they want a better life for themselves and more importantly for their children. And as we deal with this complicated issue I ask you: What if you were them? What if you lived in a country where your children had no hope and no future? Where your wife stayed up all night crying because she was afraid your son would join a drug gang. Where your children wept each night because you didn't have enough food to feed them. What if you were there? Let me tell you—if I was there, there are very few things I would not do. There is no fence high enough; there is no ocean wide enough that most of us would not cross to provide for them what they do not have.

And that's at the core of this issue and these people that we're dealing with. Yes we have to have laws—they have to be respected. No we cannot legalize eleven million people. But they're people. They're human beings with real lives and real stories. And the complexity of the issue challenges the core and soul of our nation perhaps more than any other issue that we face. Because in the end, without immigration, there would be no America. And we would be just like everybody else. And the challenge of this century on this issue is how can we once again make this issue a source of pride, not a source of conflict. Something that unites us as a people, not divides us. Something that we brag about, not something that we fight over. How can we do that? Well that's what I hope to be a part of. That's what I hope events like this will be a part of. I hope never again that young people will have to stand up in an event like this and hold up a sign—because the issue's been taken care of, in one way or another.

That's what we need to work towards. And it's not easy, and it's difficult, but it must be done. Because you see, throughout ages, even in the world today, most societies teach their people that who you are, is determined by who you come from. Who are your parents? What family were you born into? What neighborhood did you grow up in? What school did you go to, and what social circle do you run in? Because based on that is who you will be.

That's the way it's been for much of human history. That's the way it is today in much of the rest of the world. And then there came America, where we said we didn't care if your parents were poor, if your grandfather was disabled, or your dad was not connected. You can be anything you wanted—in fact we bragged about it, and we welcomed the world to come here and prove that anyone, from anywhere, can accomplish anything.

Today I took the liberty, it's the only thing I wrote for today's speech, well I printed it. I don't have a (inaudible), I apologize. If you go to New York, there is a famous statue there, you may have heard of it, it's called the Statue of Liberty. On it, is engraved the poem from Emma Lazarus, it's called "The Colossus," which speaks to our nation, and who we are. I'm not a big poetry fan, but this one, there's nothing wrong with poetry. Now I'm going to get the poet people upset at me. You got to be careful, every vote counts.

This poem speaks to this battle between those nations who believe that who you are is determined by the circumstances of your birth, and us.

> Not like the brazen giant of Greek fame,
> With conquering limbs astride from land to land;
> Here at our sea-washed, sunset gates shall stand
> A mighty woman with a torch, whose flame
> Is the imprisoned lightning, and her name
> Mother of Exiles. From her beacon-hand
> Glows world-wide welcome; her mild eyes command
> The air-bridged harbor that twin cities frame.
> And she says:
>
> "Keep ancient lands, your storied pomp!" cries she
> With silent lips. "Give me your tired, give me your poor,
> Your huddled masses yearning to breathe free,
> The wretched refuse of your teeming shores.
> Send these, the homeless, the tempest-tost to me,
> I lift my lamp beside the golden door!"

This is who we were. For 225 years, this is who we've been. And the question now is, is this who we will remain? If we lose this, we lose ourselves. If we walk away from this, we walk away from what makes us different, and special, and unique from all the nations on the earth.

This is a great challenge but it's one that must be confronted. For in the end, those of us in the conservative movement draw our strength not only from our laws of man, but from the laws of God. We believe that our nation was not just founded on spiritual principles, but that our adherence to them has caused great blessing upon us. We recognize that the Constitution and our laws are important, but we live our lives with the knowledge that there is a higher law yet, a law that commands us to feed the hungry, and clothe the naked, and be kind to the alien in search of home.

Because America has, I believe, God has blessed her. We are not just great because we're great. We are great because we have been blessed. And with those blessings come responsibilities. Because we're not just blessed so that we can have, we're blessed so we can give.

And what we have given the world, on issue after issue, is a light. A light that shines upon the world, and says that all human beings are endowed by God their creator with rights. That the source of those rights are not your king, your president, your laws or your government, but that you're born with them. And because of that, anything you want to do, you should have a chance to be. Doesn't matter where you were born, or where you came from, or whether your last name ends in a vowel. That's who we have been, and if this century is to be an American Century, we have to figure out a way to make sure that that is who we remain.

So thank you for the opportunity to give you this speech. I appreciate it. Thank you.

About Marco Rubio

Marco Rubio is currently a US senator from Florida. Before joining the Senate on January 3, 2011, he was a member of the Florida House of Representatives from 2000 to 2009. Rubio was born in Miami, Florida, on May 28, 1971. He graduated from South Miami Senior High School in 1989, and earned his bachelor of arts degree from the University of Florida in 1993. Rubio graduated with law degree from the University of Miami School of Law in 1996. His political career began in 1988 when he was elected to the West Miami City Commission. The following year, he was elected to the Florida House of Representatives. He held a number of leadership positions there, including majority leader in 2003 and speaker of the house from 2007 to 2009. In 2009, he entered the race for US Senate and defeated former Florida governor Charlie Crist for the Republican nomination. On November 2, 2010, Rubio defeated his Democratic opponent Kendrick Meek in the general election.

12 Million Undocumented Workers in the Balance

By Rand Paul

Republican Senator Rand Paul of Kentucky delivers the keynote speech at an immigra-tion forum held by the National Hispanic Christian Leadership Conference (NHCLC) and the Latino Partnership for Conservative Principles. The forum was held on June 13, 2013, in Washington, DC. Founded in 1992 by Dr. Jesse Miranda, the NHCLC is an organization representing the Hispanic American evangelical community. The Latino Partnership for Conservative Principles was founded in 2010 and is part of the American Principles Project headed by Princeton law professor Robert George. Paul, who took his seat in the Senate in January 2011, gave remarks concerning the ongoing congressional debate on the issue of immigration in the United States. According to Paul, the human element of the immigration issue is often lost in policy debates. He re-counts the story of his great grandparents emigrating to American from Germany. Paul speaks in support of a modernized visa system and enhanced border security while criti-cizing approaches to immigration policy he believes grant amnesty to those who have entered the United States illegally. Paul's speech includes commentary on his personal religious beliefs. He also discusses the life and work of Jaime Escalante, an East Los Angeles math teacher whose work with immigrant students was celebrated in the 1988 motion picture Stand and Deliver. *Paul believes that more should be done to continue Escalante's legacy of educating Hispanic students and preparing them for high levels of achievement.*

Por favor disculpen mi Espanol. Como creci en Houston-es un poco "espanglish" y un poco Tex Mex.

It's great to be here with you today.

As we continue to debate immigration in Congress this week, I think sometimes the human factor gets lost. When discussing the issue, I think it's important to re-member that we're talking about people, not just policy.

We're not talking about criminals; we're talking about immigrant workers caught up in a failed government visa program.

I think it's always important that we put a human face on immigration and not just talk about numbers and statistics.

I can't think about immigration without thinking about my own family.

My German great-grandparents didn't speak much English when they came to America. They didn't have much, but they also didn't ask for much—all they wanted was an opportunity.

They began in America peddling vegetables. They finally got that opportunity when they started a dairy business in their garage, scraping together a living, raising a family, and constantly working to give their children a better life than they had.

My great-grandfather came to America in the 1880s. His father died after only six months in America. At fourteen, my great-grandfather was alone.

He survived and ultimately thrived in his new country with a new language. In their home and their church they spoke German.

As the son of immigrants, my grandfather, who only had an 8th grade education, would live to see his own children all go to college. They became ministers, professors, doctors and accountants and one of them became a Congressman.

My family's story is like that of millions of others who came to this country. Every generation of immigrants wants these opportunities.

The problem we face today is: How do we now reflect this in our twenty-first century immigration policy?

It is absolutely vital for both the success of our immigration policy and for the purposes of national security that we finally secure our borders.

Not to stop most immigrants from coming—we welcome them and in fact should seek to increase legal immigration.

The Republican Party must embrace more legal immigration.

Unfortunately, like many of the major debates in Washington, immigration has become a stalemate—where both sides are imprisoned by their own rhetoric or attachment to sacred cows that prevent the possibility of a balanced solution.

First, everyone has to acknowledge that we aren't going to deport twelve million illegal immigrants.

If you wish to work, if you wish to live and work in America, then we will find a place for you.

In order to bring conservatives to this cause however, those who work for reform must understand that a real solution must ensure that our borders are secure.

But we also must treat those who are already here with understanding and compassion.

The first part of my plan—border security—must be certified by Border Patrol and an Investigator General and then voted on by Congress to ensure it has been accomplished.

This is what I call, Trust but Verify.

With this in place, I believe conservatives will accept what needs to come next, an issue that must be addressed: what becomes of the twelve million undocumented workers in the United States?

My plan is very simple and will include work visas for those who are here, who are willing to come forward and work.

> *On immigration, common sense and decency have been neglected for far too long. Let's secure our borders, welcome our new neighbors, and practice the values of freedom and family for all to see.*

A bipartisan panel would determine the number of visas per year. High tech visas would also be expanded and have a priority. Special entrepreneurial visas would also be issued.

Fairness is key in any meaningful immigration reform, but this fairness would cut both ways.

The modernization of our visa system and border security would allow us to accurately track immigration.

It would also enable us to let more people in and allow us to admit we are not going to deport the millions of people who are currently here illegally.

This is where prudence, compassion and thrift all point us toward the same goal: bringing these workers out of the shadows and into being taxpaying members of society.

Imagine 12 million people who are already here coming out of the shadows to become new taxpayers,12 million more people assimilating into society. Twelve million more people being productive contributors.

Conservatives are wary of amnesty. My plan will not grant amnesty or move anyone to the front of the line.

But what we have now is de facto amnesty.

The solution doesn't have to be amnesty or deportation—a middle ground might be called probation where those who came illegally become legal through a probationary period.

My plan will not impose a national ID card or mandatory E-Verify, forcing businesses to become policemen.

We should not be unfair to those who came to our country legally. Nor should we force business owners to become immigration inspectors—making them do the job the federal government has failed to do.

After an Inspector General has verified that the border is secure after year one, the report must come back and be approved by Congress.

In year two, we could begin expanding probationary work visas to immigrants who are willing to work. I would have Congress vote each year for five years whether to approve or not approve a report on whether or not we are securing the border.

We should be proud that so many want to come to America, that it is still seen as the land of opportunity.

On immigration, common sense and decency have been neglected for far too long. Let's secure our borders, welcome our new neighbors, and practice the values of freedom and family for all to see.

Embracing immigrants is an American value, but just one of many.

My religion is not something I wear on my sleeve. I try to stay true to my family and my faith. I'm a Christian, a husband and a father. I'm faithful to my wife and my family. I try to be good at all those things, though, of course, we all fall short of perfection in our lives. I try to adhere to the tenets of God's word in the New Testament. I take seriously my oath to defend the Constitution. And I try to fight for truth and my values regardless of the political outcome, regardless of how popular or unpopular they may be.

One thing worth fighting for is life. I don't think a civilization can long endure that does not have respect for all human life, born and not yet born.

We have a great many problems in this country to solve. But I believe there will come a time when we are all judged on whether or not we took a stand in defense of all life from the moment of conception until our last natural breath.

As a teenager, I gave my first public speech in my church. It was an overcoming. My hands shook. My heart pounded. I wondered, can I do this?

But somehow I did. And because I wanted to talk about things that were important, I persisted. I chided my church as a senior in high school for not seeming to care about the not yet born, for looking the other way and for not taking a stand on life.

Though I believe in limited powers for the federal government, I believe, as our founders did, that primary among these powers and duties is the protection of life, that government cannot protect liberty if it does not first protect life.

We must embrace the values of life, liberty and prosperity that will lead this country back to greatness. And we should do so proudly as Christians.

Ultimately, our success in life is measured in man's humanity toward man. This is true of our immigration policies. This is true of our attitude towards our fellow man.

For the American Dream to be achievable for all, we have to have an educational system that believes that all students have the capability to succeed.

Unfortunately, the education establishment seems to casually discard Latinos, blacks, and others into crummy schools with no hope.

I argue that the struggle for a good education is the civil rights issue of our day.

I love the story of Jaime Escalante. They made a movie about him: *Stand and Deliver*.

In the area of East Los Angeles, in 1982, in an environment that values a quick fix over education and learning, Escalante was a new math teacher at Garfield High School determined to change the system and challenge the students to a higher level of achievement.

Escalante was at first not well liked by students, receiving numerous taunts and threats.

As the year progressed, he was able to win over the attention of the students by implementing innovative teaching techniques.

He transformed even the most troublesome teens into dedicated students. While Escalante was teaching basic arithmetic and algebra, he realized that his students have far more potential.

He decided to teach them calculus. To do so, he held a summer course in pre-calculus.

Despite concerns and skepticism of other teachers, who felt that "you can't teach logarithms to illiterates," Escalante nonetheless developed a program in which his students can eventually take AP calculus by their senior year.

Taking the AP calculus exam in the spring of their senior year, his students were relieved and overjoyed to find that they have all passed, a feat done by few in the state.

My dream is that we transform the education monopoly into a thriving, competitive environment where Hispanic students get to choose what school they attend and that no student is forgotten or ignored.

Jaime Escalante will always be remembered for the wonderful things he did for his kids.

Man's humanity towards man is how we will be judged. For the teacher. For the student. For the immigrant. For the unborn. For the next generation.

We, as Christians, should never lose sight of what's important. We, as Americans, should never lose sight of the things we share in common, and do our best to love thy neighbor, every chance we get.

Thank you and God bless.

About Rand Paul

Senator Rand Paul—a Republican—is currently the junior senator from Kentucky, having assumed office in 2011. Paul was born in Pittsburgh, Pennsylvania, on January 7, 1963. He is the son of Ron Paul, a Republican congressman from Texas, and a three-time presidential candidate. Rand Paul did his undergraduate work at Baylor University from 1981 to 1984, but left before earning a bachelor's degree upon his early acceptance to the Duke University School of Medicine, from which he graduated with a medical degree in 1988. Paul completed his residency at Duke in 1993, and went on to practice ophthalmology for seventeen years in Bowling Green, Kentucky, before running for the Senate in 2010. He became a favorite among Tea Party conservatives for his staunchly independent tone and small-government views. Paul currently serves on the following Senate committees: Foreign Relations; Health, Education, Labor and Pensions; Homeland Security and Governmental Affairs; and Small Business and Entrepreneurship.

5

Remaking Business

The board at the New York Stock Exchange shows a new record high before the closing bell on Wall Street in New York City on May 28, 2013. Stocks advanced with the Dow ending at yet another record closing high, closing at 15,409.39 after central banks reassured investors that they will keep policies designed to foster global growth.

A Rose by Any Other Name ...
Would Probably Violate the FTC Act:
Shakespeare, the FTC, and Advertising

By Edith Ramirez

In an address to the American Advertising Federation in April 2013, Federal Trade Commission (FTC) Chairwoman Edith Ramirez addresses the issue of consumer privacy in digital advertising. Ramirez states that honesty and transparency are essential components of a functioning marketplace and a crucial element in the relationship between businesses and consumers. She cites statistics related to the boom in advertising revenue for mobile devices and makes reference to an FTC report on best practices regarding the disclosure of sensitive consumer data. This data includes information on consumer health, location information, mobile device contacts, personal calendars, and photographs. Ramirez also discusses the FTC's work on ensuring that environmental claims made by advertisers are not deceptive. She references the FTC's Green Guides, a set of guidelines for the advertisement of environmentally friendly products, cautioning businesses about using claims of safety and renewability that are too broad. The issue of tracking the online behavior of consumers is also discussed. According to Ramirez, consumers remain uninformed about who is collecting data regarding their behavior on the Internet and how this data is used. She reviews the development and implementation of "do not track" mechanisms on web browsers and other tactics used by web companies to block third-party tracking. Ramirez—whose speech includes topically relevant quotes from Shakespeare—believes it is possible to develop an online environment that meets the needs of both consumers and advertisers.

It is a pleasure to be here today to talk about the FTC's approach to advertising; how we are adapting to our increasingly digital world; green marketing; and the efforts to develop a Do Not Track system. Because these topics are vitally important, I will try to cover them heeding the counsel of Hamlet's mother: "More matter with less art."

I call on Shakespeare this morning because next week is the 449th anniversary of his birth. If any point is worth making, he has made it, and as succinctly and eloquently as it can be made.

As I considered my remarks today, the famous Shakespearean phrase that struck me was "spotless reputation," which comes from *Richard II*. Bolingbrook, the future Henry the Fourth, accuses Mowbray, a fellow duke, of treason (among other crimes) in front of the king, who would very much like the spat to blow over. But

Delivered April 17, 2013, at the American Advertising Federation, Washington, DC, by Edith Ramirez.

Mowbray will have none of it, explaining that he cannot let the attacks on his character stand. He says:

> The purest treasure mortal times afford
> Is spotless reputation—that away,
> Men are but gilded loam, or painted clay.

Of course, you already know this. As advertisers, your reputation—your brand—is everything. And, in fact, you know it better than most, because you pursue a spotless reputation for yourself and for the clients whose reputations you broadcast out into the wide world.

At the FTC, our work to promote truthful advertising and protect consumer privacy dovetails with your mission to promote the spotless reputations of your clients and your own firms. We aim to provide consumers with the information they need to make informed decisions about their purchases and exercise control over their personal data. It is self-evident that this is good for consumers. But it also benefits honest competitors, well-functioning markets, and commercial growth. Honesty and transparency are essential to maintaining a positive brand. Sooner or later, deceptive and opaque practices damage a firm's most important asset—its reputation. And from that, a business may never recover, no matter how clever its ad copy or eye-catching its graphics.

Further, deceptive practices do more than harm the spotless reputation of the offending company. Consumers may lose faith in an entire industry or sales medium if advertising frequently misleads or companies hide information about their products or business practices. By encouraging businesses to be above-board in their advertising and privacy practices, the FTC promotes the consumer trust and confidence that are essential to a thriving, growing marketplace.

We do this proactively and devote substantial resources to educating businesses on how to comply with the law and on best practices that may go beyond what the law requires. This year, the FTC has turned its focus to the mobile environment.

It has been aptly said that "the future of mobile is the future of everything."[1] Today, there are twice as many mobile devices sold as personal computers.[2] Spending on mobile advertising is projected to rise by 77 percent to roughly $7.3 billion this year,[3] and an expected $27.13 billion by 2017, just shy of 45 percent of all digital ad revenue.[4] Finally, there are over one million mobile apps available today, and consumers spend more time on them than they do on the mobile web.[5]

In light of this, the FTC recently issued a report on best practices in the realm of privacy disclosures by mobile operating systems, apps and ad networks, and analytics companies—all of which get access to consumer data through devices that are always with us and always on.[6] We stress the importance of platforms, which are the gatekeepers to the mobile marketplace. For example, we encourage platforms to ensure that apps give just-in-time notice and get express affirmative consent before they access location data, health and financial information, contacts, address books, calendars, photos, and videos.

We hope our report will inform the current efforts of a wide spectrum of stake-holders, led by the Department of Commerce, to develop a self-regulatory code of conduct on mobile transparency. The FTC strongly supports meaningful self-regulation in general and the Department of Commerce process in particular. That undertaking has already made substantial progress in a short period, and we encourage stakeholders to move towards finalizing a code of conduct.

Soon after the FTC issued its report on mobile privacy disclosures, we updated our Dot Com Disclosures, which provide guidance on how to reveal key information in digital advertising.[7] The original Dot Com Disclosures were released in 2000—back when we were just grateful that our phones were cordless and "facebook" referred to the printed guide to your freshman class. It was time for a refresh.

The new guidance makes clear that consumer protection laws apply to ads on a PC, a mobile phone, Twitter, or a social network in the same way those laws apply to ads in print, radio, or TV. As before, our guidance comes down to common sense. If you were a consumer, what would it take for you to notice and understand a disclaimer? Would you click through multiple links just to find information?

If information is needed to prevent an ad from being deceptive, the information must be included, and it must be clear and conspicuous. This applies to the small screen of a mobile device or the 140 characters in a tweet. If a platform does not let you make a clear and conspicuous disclosure when one is required, then the platform should not be used. Period.

When disclosures can be made, they should be "as close as possible" to the claims they qualify—not relegated to the "terms of use" and other contractual agreements. When practical, advertisers should incorporate qualifying information into the underlying claim rather than having a separate disclosure. The screen design should alert consumers that there is more information available, and advertisers should consider how the page will display on different devices. We caution against making consumers scroll down or over to see a disclosure. But if scrolling is necessary, it should, at minimum, be unavoidable, meaning consumers can't go forward with a transaction without viewing the disclosure.

As in the original guidance, we call on advertisers to avoid using hyperlinks for disclosures of product cost or certain health and safety issues. The new guidelines also ask advertisers to label hyperlinks as specifically as possible, and they caution advertisers to consider how their hyperlinks will function on various programs and devices.

"What's in a name?" asks Juliet, in *Romeo and Juliet*'s famous balcony scene, "that which we call a rose by any other name would smell as sweet." At the FTC, we don't mind what you call that rose, as long as you use easy-to-find, easy-to-understand disclosures to document claims and provide essential information about its sweet smell.

Of course, if Juliet were to deliver her soliloquy today, she might amend it to talk about a rose that not only smells sweet but is also grown organically with no petroleum-based inputs, free of pesticides, and with the tiniest of carbon footprints. These days, green roses trump red roses every time. As a native of California—where the

> *We aim to provide consumers with the information they need to make informed decisions about their purchases and exercise control over their personal data. It is self-evident that this is good for consumers. But it also benefits honest competitors, well-functioning markets, and commercial growth.*

environmental movement first took hold—I have been seeing green marketing claims for years. But such advertising is now truly mainstream.

Last fall, in response to this trend, the FTC updated its Green Guides, which help marketers ensure that their environmental claims are not deceptive.[8] In preparation for that, we researched the impact of broad green advertising claims. We found that consumers hear general assertions about a product's eco-friendliness as statements that an item has no negative impact on the environment. Because it's highly unlikely that a marketer can substantiate such an expansive claim, the revised guides caution against painting a product green with a broad brush. Rather, advertisers should use clear and prominent language that limits the claim to a specific benefit or benefits that can be understood and backed up. And they shouldn't imply that any specific benefit is significant if it is, in fact, minor. We also found that, if a certification or seal of approval used in an ad does not convey the basis for the recognition, either through the name or some other means, consumers will believe the product offers a general environmental benefit. Again, our research showed that it is very improbable that marketers can substantiate such broad claims. So advertisers should avoid environmental certifications or seals that are not clear about the basis for the certification.

The updated Green Guides also address the brave new world (another term coined by Shakespeare, by the way—this time in *The Tempest*) of renewable energy claims. Our research showed that advertisers need to be careful in touting that a product or package was "made with renewable energy." Such claims can be misleading unless the main processes used to make the product or package were powered with either renewable energy or non-renewable energy backed by renewable energy certificates. Otherwise, marketers should clearly specify the percentage of renewable energy that powered the manufacture of the product or package.

The FTC recently lodged complaints against Neiman Marcus and two other retailers that demonstrate what a brave new world the realm of green advertising truly is.[9] We charged these companies with violating the Fur Products Labeling Act, legislation passed in 1951, when consumers wanted to make sure that the fur coats they were shelling out for were more mink than mouse. Today, it is just the opposite—high-end shoppers often demand faux over fox. We called out Neiman Marcus for describing several articles of clothing as containing only fake fur when, in actuality, they were made in part of the real thing. Neiman Marcus, as well as the two other retailers, DrJays.com and Revolve Clothing, have agreed to settlements that will, over the next 20 years, punish future violations with fines of up to $16,000 per incident. Quite a "sea change," as Ariel, a character in *The Tempest,* first said.

While the words of Shakespeare are some of the most beautiful and pithy in the English language, he has also stayed so firmly woven into our discourse because of the themes he explored. Of course, one of Shakespeare's favorite themes—one that appears in almost every play—is identity, and most particularly, the consequences of mistaken identity. There isn't a comedy he wrote that doesn't depend on that conceit. But so do many of his tragedies, including *Romeo and Juliet.* Those star-crossed lovers would have never died were it not for a massive miscommunication and misunderstanding about Juliet's health status and intentions. Which makes *Romeo and Juliet* a cautionary tale about the dangers of losing control over how others perceive you.

And that brings me to Do Not Track. Consumer data is the currency of the Web. Targeted advertising helps enable free content and services for consumers. But the amount of behavioral data collected and how it is used are hidden from the very consumers who are tracked and analyzed.

That is not a long-term recipe for success. Consumers regularly report unease with online tracking.[10] And marketers acknowledge that consumer trust is vital to their success.[11] Online publishers complain that they lack knowledge or control over the entities that collect consumer data from their sites and how that data is used downstream.[12] And the profusion of tracking cookies on websites can slow down the loading of web pages, which can cause advertising conversion rates to plummet.[13]

In late 2010, when the FTC first called for Do Not Track, consumers had very few tools for controlling online tracking. There was no effective counterweight to the growing pressure on marketers to collect and analyze more and more consumer data. We therefore advocated the creation of a persistent Do Not Track mechanism that would apply across industry to all types of tracking; be easy to find and use; be effective and enforceable; and allow consumers to stop the collection of nearly all behavioral data gathered across sites and not just the serving of targeted ads.[14]

Our call for Do Not Track set off a burst of activity. All major browsers now permit their users to send out an instruction not to track them across websites, and major online publishers like Twitter and the Associated Press have welcomed this development.[15] The Digital Advertising Alliance has widely deployed an icon-based opt-out system and last year at the White House promised to honor browser-based opt-outs.[16] Microsoft has turned the Do Not Track setting on by default in Internet Explorer 10.[17] Apple has implemented a "Limit Ad Tracking" feature for its mobile devices.[18] And Mozilla has recently begun to test blocking third-party cookies by default.[19]

I am pleased that so many have responded to the FTC's call for greater consumer control over online tracking. But consumers still await an effective and functioning Do Not Track system, which is now long overdue. The Tracking Protection Group of the World Wide Web Consortium (or W3C) has been working for some time to develop a self-regulatory Do Not Track standard. Ad networks, analytics companies, web publishers, browsers, social networks, and privacy groups have been involved in that ongoing effort. The differing viewpoints and interests of this broad range of stakeholders create undeniable challenges, but they also offer the potential of an enduring and broad solution.

I urge all stakeholders to take advantage of this venue to work toward consensus on a Do Not Track tool that gives consumers effective and meaningful privacy protection. This includes both the websites that permit ad networks to track consumers on their sites and the companies who pay for their ads to be targeted with the resulting behavioral data. Web publishers and advertisers are every much a part of the ecosystem as the ad networks and the browsers and they should continue to actively engage on this issue.

These are heady days in the online and mobile world, and the market in personal data collected through tracking is some of the reason for that. One can forgive stakeholders for thinking that it will always be so—for believing that "not all the water in the rough rude sea can wash" the shine off this cyber-economy. But an online advertising system that breeds consumer discomfort is not a foundation for sustained growth. More likely, it is an invitation to Congress and other policymakers in the US and abroad to intervene with legislation or regulation and for technical measures by browsers or others to limit tracking.

I therefore urge all players in the online advertising ecosystem to dive into the W3C process with good faith and a resolution to hammer out their differences to develop a transparent Internet advertising system that meets the needs of consumers and advertisers alike. If that happens, and I believe it can, I hope to join you again next year for Shakespeare's 450th birthday—this time with a speech titled "All's Well That Ends Well."

Thank you.

Notes

1. Dan Frommer, *"The Future of Mobile Is the Future of Everything,"* BUSINESS INSIDER, June 6, 2011, *available at* http://www.businessinsider.com/future-of-mobile-experts-2011-6?op=1.
2. Henry Blodget and Alex Cocotas, *The Future of Mobile,* BUSINESS INSIDER, Mar. 27, 2013, *available at* http://www.businessinsider.com/the-future-of-mobile-slide-deck-2013-3?op=1.3
3. Amy Gesenhues, *EMarketer: Google Still Owns Mobile Ad Market, but Facebook Has Largest Share of Mobile Display Ad Dollars*, MARKETINGLAND, Apr. 4, 2013, *available at* http://marketingland.com/emarketer-google-to-take-more-than-half-of-mobile-advertising-dollars-but-facebook-will-win-majority-of-mobile-display-market-38937.
4. *Ibid.*
5. The Future of Mobile, supra note 2.
6. FTC Staff, *Mobile Privacy Disclosures: Building Trust Through Transparency* (Feb. 1, 2013), *available at* http://www.ftc.gov/os/2013/02/130201mobileprivacy report.pdf.
7. FTC Staff, *.Com Disclosures: How to Make Effective Disclosures in Digital*

Advertising (Mar. 12, 2013), *available at* http://www.ftc.gov/os/2013/03/130
312dotcomdisclosures.pdf.

8. *See* FTC Press Release, *FTC Issues Revised "Green Guides,"* Oct. 1, 2012,
   available at http://www.ftc.gov/opa/2012/10/greenguides.shtm; Guides for the
   Use of Environmental Marketing Claims, 77 Fed. Reg. 62122 (Oct.11, 2012).

9. *See* FTC Press Release, *Retailers Agree to Settle FTC Charges They Marketed
   Real Fur Products as Fake Fur,* Mar. 19, 2013, *available at* http://www.ftc.gov/
   opa/2013/03/neiman.shtm.

10. *See, e.g.*, Meredith Whipple, *CR Survey Finds That Most Consumers Are Still "Very
    Concerned" About Online Privacy*, CONSUMERS UNION BLOG, Apr. 3, 2012,
    http://hearusnow.org/posts/1055-cr-survey-finds-that-most-consumers-are-still-
    very-concerned-about-online-privacy; David Sarno, *Tech Firms' Data Gathering
    Worries Most Californians, Poll Finds*, L.A. TIMES, Mar. 31, 2012, *available
    at* http://www.latimes.com/news/local/la-fi-privacy-poll-20120331,0,2763981.
    story; KRISTEN PURCELL ET AL., PEW INTERNET AND AMERICAN
    LIFE PROJECT, SEARCH ENGINE USE 2012 18-26 (2012), *available at*
    http://pewinternet.org/~/media/Files/Reports/2012/PIP_Search_Engine_
    Use_2012.pdf; Ki Mae Heussner, *Divorcees, Southerners Most Concerned
    About Web Privacy, 90 Percent of Online Adults Worry About Privacy Online,
    Study Shows*, AD WEEK, Feb. 12, 2012, *available at* http://www.adweek.com/
    news/technology/divorcees-southerners-most-concerned-about-web-priva-
    cy-138185; Lymari Morales, *Google and Facebook Users Skew Young, Affluent,
    and Educated*, GALLUP, Feb. 17, 2011, *available at* http://www.gallup.com/
    poll/146159/facebook-google-users-skew-young-affluenteducatedaspx.

11. *See, e.g.*, RESEARCH: *Consumers Feel Better About Brands That Give Them
    Transparency and Control over Ads*, EVIDON BLOG, Nov. 10, 2010, http://blog.
    evidon.com/tag/better-advertising; Interactive Advertising Bureau, Press Re-
    lease, *Major Marketing/Media Trade Groups Launch Program to Give Consumers
    Enhanced Control over Collection and Use of Web Viewing Data for Online Be-
    havioral Advertising*, Oct. 4, 2010, *available at* http://www.iab.net/about_the_iab/
    recent_press_releases/press_release_archive/press_release/pr-1004100; State-
    ment of Pam Horan President, Online Publishers Association, before the House
    Energy and Commerce Subcomm. on Commerce, Manufacturing and Trade,
    Balancing Privacy and Innovation: Does the President's Proposal Tip the Scale?
    (Mar. 29, 2012), *available at* http://energycommerce.house.gov/sites/republi-
    cans.energycommerce.house.gov/files/Hearings/CMT/20120329/HHRG-
    112-IF17-WState-PHoran-20120329.pdf; Statement of John M. Montgomery,
    GroupM Interaction, *The State of Online Consumer Privacy*, Hearing Before the
    S. Comm. on Commerce, Sci., and Transp., 112th Cong. (Mar. 16, 2011),
    available at http://www.iab.net/media/file/DC1DOCS1-432016-v1-John_Mont-
    gomery_-_Written_Testimony.pdf ("We at GroupM strongly believe in pro-
    tecting consumer privacy. It is not only the right thing to do, but it is also good
    for business."); Statement of Alan Davidson, Director of Public Policy, Google
    Inc., *Protecting Mobile Privacy: Your Smartphones, Tablets, Cell Phones and*

Your Privacy, Hearing Before the S. Subcomm. on Privacy, Tech., and the Law, 112th Cong. (May 10, 2011), *available at* http://www.judiciary.senate.gov/pdf/11-5-10%20Davidson%20Testimony.pdf ("Protecting privacy and security is essential for Internet commerce.").

12. John Sternberg, *On Privacy, Publishers Prefer the Sideline*, DIGIDAY, May 12, 2012, *available at* http://www.digiday.com/publishers/on-privacy-publishers-prefer-the-sideline/.

13. Evidon, *The Value of Revealing the Invisible Web*, Sept. 11, 2012, *available at* http://www.slideshare.net/fmsignal/the-value-of-uncovering-the-invisible-web (noting a one second delay in page load time can result in a seven percent decline in conversion, citing data from Wal-Mart).

14. *See, e.g.*, Fed. Trade Comm'n, *Protecting Consumer Privacy in an Era of Rapid Change: Recommendations for Businesses and Policymakers* 52-55 (Mar. 26, 2012), *available at* http://www.ftc.gov/os/2012/03/120326privacyreport.pdf; Prepared Statement of the Federal Trade Commission on Do Not Track (Dec. 2, 2010), *available at* http://ftc.gov/os/testimony/101202donottrack.pdf.

15. Nick Bilton, *Twitter Implements Do Not Track Privacy Option*, N.Y. TIMES, May 17, 2012, *available at* http://bits.blogs.nytimes.com/2012/05/17/twitter-implements-do-not-track-privacy-option/; Hayley Tsukayama, *AP Adopts Mozilla's Do Not Track Header*, WASH. POST, Mar. 31, 2011, *available at* http://www.washingtonpost.com/blogs/faster-forward/post/ap-adopts-mozillas-do-not-track-header/2011/03/31/AF557R9B_blog.html.

16. Press Release, Digital Advertising Alliance, *DAA Position on Browser Based Choice Mechanism*, Feb. 22, 2012, *available at* http://www.aboutads.info/resource/download/DAA.Commitment.pdf.

17. 17 Brendon Lynch, *Advancing Consumer Trust and Privacy: Internet Explorer in Windows 8*, MICROSOFT BLOG, May 31, 2012, http://blogs.technet.com/b/microsoft_on_the_issues/archive/2012/05/31/advancing-consumer-trust-and-privacy-internet-explorer-in-windows-8.aspx.

18. Daniel Eran Dilger, *Apple Adds New "Limit Ad Tracking" Feature to iOS 6*, APPLE INSIDER, Sep. 12, 2013, *available at* http://appleinsider.com/articles/12/09/13/apple_adds_new_limit_ad_tracking_feature_to_ios_6.

19. Alex Fowler, *Firefox to Get Smarter About Third-Party Cookies*, MOZILLA PRIVACY BLOG, Feb. 25, 2013, http://blog.mozilla.org/privacy/2013/02/25/firefox-getting-smarter-about-third-party-cookies/.

About Edith Ramirez

Edith Ramirez is the current chairwoman of the Federal Trade Commission (FTC), having replaced outgoing chairman Jon Leibowitz in March 2013. Ramirez had served as an agency commissioner since April 2010. Prior to joining the FTC, she was a partner at Quinn Emanuel Urquhart & Sullivan LLP. A 1989 Harvard University graduate, she holds a bachelor's degree in history, and she earned her JD from Harvard Law

School in 1992. She served as an editor of the Harvard Law Review *in 1990 and 1991 when Barack Obama was the publication's president. Ramirez began her career in 1992 as a clerk for Judge Alfred T. Goodwin of the United States Court of Appeals for the Ninth Circuit. In 1993, she became an associate at the Los Angeles firm Gibson, Dunn & Crutcher LLP, and worked there until 1996. Ramirez was vice president of the board of commissioners at the Los Angeles Department of Water and Power from 2005 to 2010. In 2008, she served as Latino outreach director in California for then senator Barack Obama's presidential campaign.*

Progress and Opportunity for the Disabled

By Seth D. Harris

In remarks delivered at the Disability Employment Initiative Grantee National Meeting in Washington, DC, then–Acting Secretary of Labor Seth D. Harris discusses the strides made and the challenges yet to be overcome in the effort to achieve an equitable employment environment for people with disabilities. He first describes statistics that show a lack of workforce participation and high unemployment for disabled Americans. Harris says that this is not out of a lack of desire to participate, and he goes on to describe the obstacles that still face disabled Americans looking to enter the workforce today. Discrimination—though significant progress has been made to combat it—is still a major roadblock for people with disabilities, according to Harris, and the Department of Labor is working to combat it through programs that set goals for the employment of people with disabilities by federal contractors. He outlines the ways in which the Affordable Care Act will free disabled people from reliance on public assistance by offering affordable care options and eliminating the fear that entering the workforce might mean giving up guaranteed care. Harris goes on to describe the ways in which the Disability Empowerment Initiative (DEI) has partnered with other federal agencies to provide better service to its grantees and gives examples of the work said grantees have done with DEI investments. He closes with an endorsement of President Barack Obama's deficit reduction plan, and he highlights the ways in which an impending sequestration would negatively affect Americans with disabilities.

Good morning everyone and welcome to Washington, DC, and the US Department of Labor. Thank you so much, Kathy, for that generous introduction, but more importantly for your great leadership as Assistant Secretary for Disability Policy. The Disability Employment Initiative is, of course, a collaborative effort between Kathy's shop and our Employment Training Administration, so let me also recognize Assistant Secretary Jane Oates and her team for their hard work. The Labor Department is one of the federal government's most important resources for people with disabilities, and DEI is taking our support to the next level.

I'm very excited that you're all here—this gathering has been a long time coming—and even more excited to learn about the innovative work you're doing in your communities and the partnerships you're building to bring people with disabilities into the workforce. In just a few short years, DEI is already making a powerful difference in people's lives.

Delivered March 12, 2013, at the Disability Employment Initiative Grantee National Meeting, Washington, DC, by Seth D. Harris.

But let's face it—this is a difficult challenge and we have our work cut out for us. The new jobs numbers came out last Friday. And while there was some good news, the unemployment rate for people with disabilities is still 12.3 percent. Look at it this way: if you're a person with disabilities, you're living through a recession more devastating even than anything the nation as a whole experienced in 2008 and 2009.

It makes absolutely no sense to approach deficit reduction by cutting services to a population experiencing double-digit unemployment (like people with disabilities), instead of asking millionaires and billionaires to pay a little more by closing tax loopholes.

But the statistic that really jumps out at me is this one: only 20.7 percent of people with disabilities are participating in the labor force at all. Think about that: four out of every five individuals with a disability aren't working and aren't looking for work. It's a shocking waste of human capital, one that does violence to our nation's values. It should be a blaring wake-up call for all of us to do more.

There are millions of people with disabilities out there who *can* work, who *want* to work, who want nothing more than to enjoy the dignity of participating in the economy and contributing to their community. They don't want to spend their lives on SSI and SSDI. They have no higher aspiration than to wake up every morning, head to a job where they add value, and then take home a paycheck at the end of the week. They don't want to live in the shadows; they want to live in the economic mainstream.

There are three main obstacles to employment for people with disabilities. One of them is plain old-fashioned discrimination. We've come plenty far on that front, though with much further to go. Combating discrimination is largely the function of other government agencies like the Department of Justice and the Equal Employment Opportunity Commission. But we are doing our part—with the proposed regulations from our Office of Federal Contract and Compliance Programs that would, for the first time, set meaningful goals for employment of people with disabilities by federal contractors.

Health care is another obstacle, one that I'm proud to say is mitigated by implementation of the Affordable Care Act. The old health care system created perverse incentives—many people stayed on SSI and SSDI because it guaranteed them health care coverage. If they entered the job market, there was an excellent chance that the position they'd find would not come with health care benefits. Now, under health care reform, people with disabilities aren't trapped on public assistance—they can look for work knowing that they will have access to affordable health care options.

One great example of a DEI partnership on the federal level is our collaboration with the Social Security Administration. Our requirement that DEI grantees participate in SSA's Ticket to Work program as Employment Networks means that we're better able to improve the coordination of services to public workforce system clients who also receive SSA disability benefits.

DEI sites are having positive experiences with Ticket to Work and report its positive effects on serving customers with disabilities—including more follow-up with customers, and more thoughtful discussions about when to serve customers in-house and when to refer them to more specialized programs like vocational rehabilitation.

DEI sites are implementing new outreach strategies for customers with disabilities, particularly through the dedicated Disability Resource Coordinator, and bringing more Ticket to Work customers into the American Job Center to link them with a wider range of programs. DEI sites also reported having more staff capacity to serve customers with disabilities, both through new hires and through training.

You all are rising to the challenge. In three rounds we've invested $63 million, and you are using those resources to craft effective solutions tailored to your states and communities. Just a few examples: You've got Los Angeles American Job Center staff starting a monthly disability and Ticket to Work conference call to discuss outreach and promising practices resulting in a significant increase in the number of Tickets assigned to the Los Angeles Employment Network. Then there's New York developing local asset development coalitions to help people with disabilities manage and grow their financial assets as they become financially self-sufficient.

And Kansas has expanded state and local business networks that focus on hiring and supporting the employment of people with disabilities. I recently visited with the CEO Council of the National Organization on Disability, and I can tell you there are plenty of private sector employers who get it, who understand what an asset people with disabilities can be to their companies.

DEI is working. Analysis of Workforce Investment Act data show that people with disabilities are served in greater numbers in those states that have received DEI funding. WIA data from Program Year 2011 show that the percentage of exiters with disabilities in DEI states was 6.5 percent, compared to 4.3 percent for all states. Looking at DEI pilot sites within DEI states, the percentage of exiters with disabilities was even higher—7.9 percent.

In his State of the Union address, President Obama talked about skills acquisition as one of the keys to building an economy that grows from the middle class out and not from the top down. One of the cornerstones of his second-term agenda is to equip our citizens with the education and training they need to secure and succeed in twenty-first-century jobs.

But we can't do that without a robust federal government making smart investments. And that's why so-called sequestration threatens to undermine our progress.

"Sequestration"—it's our Washington version of March Madness. It's not even a term most people outside of Washington know or can relate to—unless you've been on a jury and you're locked away in a room with eight other strangers eating bad food.

But sequestration means that beginning the first of this month, we're seeing automatic, arbitrary across the board cuts throughout the federal government. Future funding for the DEI will be threatened. Across the federal government, persons with disabilities will see programs they rely on—from special education, to the Mental Health Block Grant, to vocational rehabilitation—all scaled back.

This is no way to get our fiscal house in order. The President has offered a balanced deficit reduction plan that asks the wealthy to do their fair share without targeting programs that middle-class families need. It makes absolutely no sense to approach deficit reduction by cutting services to a population experiencing double-digit unemployment (like people with disabilities), instead of asking millionaires and billionaires to pay a little more by closing tax loopholes.

It's just bad policy—bad for people with disabilities, bad for all workers, bad for the businesses that need skilled workers, bad for the whole economy.

Sequestration throws another obstacle in our path, but we must continue to do the best we can with the resources we have. The good news is that the first three rounds of DEI funding are secure, and you can continue to do your innovative work. I want to thank you again. You are meeting head-on one of the nation's most urgent civil rights challenges. But inclusion of people with disabilities in the mainstream of American life is more than a question of fundamental fairness; it's also an economic imperative. Our goal is not just freedom *from* discrimination—as important as that is—but also freedom *to* achieve self-sufficiency.

As President Obama put it when he called for more disability hiring in the federal government: "The fight for progress has never been about sympathy—it's about opportunity." Thank you for doing so much to create that opportunity. We are proud to partner with you, and we look forward to doing more together.

About Seth D. Harris

Seth D. Harris is the current United States deputy secretary of labor. He was nominated by President Barack Obama in February 2009 and was sworn in on May 26, 2009. Harris is the eleventh person to hold the title of deputy secretary of labor since the position was created in 1986. He was acting secretary of labor from January to July 2013, between the departure of Hilda Solis and the confirmation of Thomas E. Perez as secretary. Harris previously worked for the Department of Labor as counselor to the secretary of labor and as acting assistant secretary of labor for policy during the Clinton Administration. After leaving the department, Harris was a professor of law and director of labor and employment law programs at New York Law School. He received a bachelor's degree from the School of Industrial and Labor Relations at Cornell University, and attended the New York University School of Law, where he was editor-in-chief of the Review of Law and Social Change. *After completing his studies at NYU in 1990, he worked as a law clerk to Judge Gene Carter of the US District Court for the District of Maine, and Judge William Canby of the US Court of Appeals for the Ninth Circuit.*

Making It: My Address to the 2012 Women Entrepreneurs Festival

By Joanne Wilson

Entrepreneur and writer Joanne Wilson addresses the 2012 Women Entrepreneurs Festival. The event was held in New York City in January 2013 and hosted by New York University and the Tisch School of the Arts. The event focuses on women's involvement in start-up businesses, web-based companies, and high-tech industries. Wilson serves as a consultant and advisor to a variety of businesses, the majority of which were founded by women. These include the chocolatier Cacao Preito and the social commerce company Red Stamp. She has written for various blogs—often under the name Gotham Gal—since 1994. She is a founder of the Women Entrepreneurs Festival and served as cochair of the 2012 event. In her remarks, Wilson suggests that women entrepreneurs implement ideas that fulfill unmet needs in their lives. She recounts her own personal history as a businessperson and mother, speaking of her experience with the challenges of finding a balance between work and personal time. Wilson also discusses her experiences as a woman working in the corporate world. She implies that when starting a new business, remaining optimistic is important, but challenges should be expected. According to Wilson, women entrepreneurs need to take more risks and be less inclined to judge each other. She encourages festival attendees to network and learn from each other.

This year we chose the theme "making it" for the Women Entrepreneurs Festival. A maker is a person who creates something. Women tend to create businesses that fill a void in their lives. As women we tend to have this desire to take care of others. It is innate. It isn't surprising that a woman invented the stove, refrigerator, dishwasher, ironing board, liquid paper, Scotchguard, the Apgar test, disposable diapers, fire escapes, and, of course, chocolate chip cookies. There were many other innovations that came from women, but we weren't allowed to file for our own patents until 1840. How crazy is that? No doubt we have come pretty far since then.

Throughout my career I have made things. Even as a kid my first entrepreneurial venture was making cinnamon sticks and selling them to kids in my elementary school. I started off making profits for a large organization. I then moved into making clothing for the large sized women's market. During this time I was also making children which in turn meant creating a home. I struggled with the work-life balance, particularly after I had children, as many do.

I always thought that I was going to be the bread winner, yet after having two children I made the decision to stay home for a while while I baked chocolate chip cookies and made a variety of things with our children. I did love being home but mentally I yearned for more.

Life is a journey and the dots always seem to connect. I returned to the work force in a start-up where I got my mojo back. I was able to find my own identity again. Being a woman entrepreneur and the oldest one in the room at the time allowed me to create a structure that worked well for me and my

> *As women we need to lead and by leading we inspire others. Leading means supporting other women entrepreneurs in any way that we can. We should all do what we can to see more women running companies.*

family. Once I had created a structure that worked for me it was really hard to ever give it back. That is the beauty of being your own boss. It is the freedom that comes from being an entrepreneur.

I would bet that every woman in this room has dreamed of doing great things with their career. We want to follow our passions, feed our egos, and live our lives on all cylinders. We want to have it all. Technology is giving us a platform to do that but there is more to it than that.

First of all, building a business is hard work. There is no magic bullet and there is no such thing as an overnight success. Being a woman starting a company is even harder. We have to push boundaries to get our businesses off the ground. It is far from glamorous but it is seriously exhilarating. It is an emotional roller coaster and if somebody tells you it isn't, they aren't telling you the truth. If women want to change the ratio and proliferate women led businesses, then the change has to start with us.

When I started out my career, I was working in corporate America. I was truly blindsided by what I saw. Men moved up more quickly and women competed with each other in ways that men did not. Women did not look at their peers as people who could help them move forward but as another barrier to get through to their next promotion. That kind of mentality has changed over time but there is more work to do.

We need to collaborate and mentor each other. We need to find mentors and peer groups where we can learn from each other by picking each other's brains. It isn't about emulating your mentor; it is about learning from them so several are recommended. Those conversations will enable us to create the tool kits for our own business.

Women need to take more risks. The thing about risk is that it can lead to extraordinary success (and failure). This kind of success can only be achieved by being an entrepreneur and owning your own life and company. We need to be able to plunge in more often with two feet first and ask questions later. We are much more calculating about risk then men, and in order to be successful entrepreneurs we need to start shooting first and asking questions later. Our companies will evolve over time and what we think was going to happen won't and what we believe won't happen will.

At Techstars, both women and men were asked to be mentors for the start-up companies going through the program. Every man that was asked to be a mentor said yes without a question. Every woman asked what would be expected of them, how often would they have to come; they wanted to know the rules of the game before committing.

That was an opportunity to be part of the game. And the truth is you didn't necessarily need to show up every day. The men understood that. The women didn't. We need to be more self-confident with an independent mind-set about just going for it.

We need to build our businesses with teams that challenge us. We need to be strategic about our businesses from day one. We aren't building families here; we are building businesses. We must create the right team that is going to help us succeed in our businesses. We tend to be loyal to a fault. We have to hire competent trustworthy people. And we have to move people out of our businesses if they are not competent and trustworthy. We cannot put a priority on loyalty over performance.

How can we build businesses and brands that eventually will not need us? The value in a business comes from setting the right foundation from the start so that eventually every role can replaced with a new set of people. That includes you. That is how we should be thinking about our companies. Use yourself in the brand but create a separation between you and the brand of the company. When we think of Foursquare or Twitter we don't necessarily think about the entrepreneurs behind those companies, but when we think of Oprah and Martha Stewart you do. We need to build more Foursquares and Twitters.

I encourage you to use all of your assets. I learned this early on. When I was working as an assistant store manager at Macy's I worked for an amazing woman. She was smart, brilliant and she knew exactly how to get what she wanted. She was my mentor. She had the confidence that came from her belief that she was the smartest person in the room. We should all learn from that. Once every few months the big boys (yes, the men who happened to run the company) would come to the store to visit. As an assistant store manager I would walk the top management through my departments introducing them to the managers that reported to me as we recited the numbers of our business so they knew how on top of things we were. For my first visit, I got to the store early and, of course, wore my black suit. My boss called me to come upstairs to her office for a quick meeting before the boys showed up. I went upstairs and my mouth dropped because she was wearing a tight black leather miniskirt with a pair of 4-inch-high red pattern leather pumps and a tight black sweater. I couldn't believe it. I said to her, don't you know who is coming today? Her response . . .yes, I do. What was my take away? Know your audience and be a woman, not a man.

Don't be afraid to ask for something. And for god sakes we need to stop saying I'm sorry. Sorry for what, asking for what we deserve? Confidence is a choice or, as my son says, it is a necessity. Create your own path. Be successful at whatever it is you choose to do. As women we need to lead and by leading we inspire others. Leading means supporting other women entrepreneurs in any way that we can. We should all do what we can to see more women running companies. Here is what I do: I invest in those women. If I invest in ten women who are starting their own companies, then I have just changed the statistics. Now there are ten more women running companies. I'd like to see more women that have the means and also experience behind them do that. Help more women entrepreneurs be successful by mentoring them to navigate the waters of growing a company.

Recently I was interviewed at an event put on by 85 Broads. The room was filled with women who were mostly out of the finance industry. One woman got a little pissy with me about how I was championing women entrepreneurs in the start-up/ tech community and she was angry because in regards to her industry that she couldn't get any higher up the ladder and she wanted to run the place. I questioned her to why did she stay with that company? My advice to her was, here is a room of super successful women in the finance industry; at the end of the day only one person gets to run Goldman Sachs, so why doesn't she collaborate with a few other women that are movers and shakers and create your own Goldman Sachs? Now that would inspire other women. I bet they would do a better job too. As Janet Hanson said to me, at one point corporate America becomes rungless, so why continue trying to charge up that ladder. We need to take more risks and start our own companies that give us the ability to balance our own life between work, friends and family.

Here is one thing that women do that men don't. We are incredibly judgmental of each other. We need to stop judging others and start focusing on what is in front of us. We look at other women and say, where did she get those awful shoes, look at that haircut, yikes what an outfit, why is she flirting with that guy, how did she get that funding and I didn't? It has to stop. We have to stop it because who the hell really cares. I bet half of us in this audience can barely boil water. Does that matter? Does it make us less able to be successful at our chosen path? No.

What we need to do is applaud each others' efforts as we start our own companies, we need to help each other figure out how to find the perfect engineer, to share our rolodexes, to be champions of each other and be honest about how difficult it is to start a company and that includes sharing how you actually find time to buy groceries and get your hair cut.

This room is a cross section of women of all ages who have all come here today from a different path. Some of us have already started our own companies; others are thinking about jumping in the game. This is an environment for everyone to put their guard down and talk about the real deal. Last year on one of the panels somebody asked a panelist about the first year of her business. You hear from most entrepreneurs that everything is just great. There is this eternal optimism. The panelist said she pretty much cried every day of the first year. There was an audible sigh in the room.

Let's be champions of each other not only by the excitement of our ideas and the frustrations of raising money or finding the right hire but also by sharing our favorites websites so we can get [things] done and by sharing the fact that [we] haven't had time for a mani-pedi in over a month. Most important, today we need to meet as many people as we can in this community. We have put together the people in this room because you are leaders in the community. Use this event to network, create connections and use our collective intelligence to move our companies and ideas forward to be the makers of the next wave of women led start-ups.

About Joanne Wilson

Joanne Wilson is an angel investor and adviser who has invested time and money in more than thirty companies, including Food52, DailyWorth, Nestio, Blue Bottle Coffee Company, and Red Stamp. Many of the companies she invests in are owned and operated by women entrepreneurs. Previously, Wilson worked at Macy's as an assistant store manager and later a buyer. Wilson spearheaded sales for the Silicon Alley Reporter, an online publication that covers the tech scene in Manhattan's so-called Silicon Alley. She sat on the board of the nonprofit organization MOUSE (Making Opportunities in Upgrading Schools in Education) as well as the board of Hot Bread Kitchen and the High Line park. Wilson is the founder and cochair of the Women Entrepreneurs Festival in New York City, an annual event that celebrates women leaders in entrepreneurship. Published since 1994, Wilson's blog, Gotham Gal, covers a range of topics.

Capital Formation from the Investor's Perspective

By Luis Aguilar

In an address to the American Institute of Certified Public Accountants (AICPA), Commissioner Luis A. Aguilar of the United States Securities and Exchange Commission (SEC) discusses the issues of investor confidence in the securities markets. Aguilar discusses the role accountants play in assuring investors that capital markets are trustworthy. He reviews how the global financial crisis has led to a decrease in average daily trades and a loss of investment in securities. According to Aguilar, investor confidence has been negatively affected by failures of corporate governance and fraudulent behavior. Details related to the process of capital formation are reviewed. Aguilar expresses his view that the real economy is positively affected by investments in businesses instead of securities alone. SEC initiatives aimed at curbing instances of fraud and corruption are reviewed. The importance of regulatory controls and transparency in the market is discussed—including the accuracy of foreign audits. Aguilar suggests that foreign companies that are not willing to comply with American laws pertaining to transparency should not be allowed to trade in the American securities market. He reviews the work of the SEC's Public Company Accounting Oversight Board (PCAOB) in conducting audits of public companies to ensure their compliance with financial regulations. Aguilar expresses his belief that accountants play an important role in maintaining sufficient financial reporting. He describes the AICPA and its members as "gatekeepers" who must protect investors and ensure the integrity of capital formation.

Thank you for that kind introduction, and for the opportunity to be with you at the 40th annual AICPA Conference on Current SEC and PCAOB Developments. I note that this year also marks the 125th anniversary of the AICPA's founding. Congratulations on this milestone. Before I begin, let me issue the standard disclaimer that the views I express are my own, and do not necessarily reflect the views of the Securities and Exchange Commission, my fellow Commissioners, or members of the staff.

Today, I would like to use my time to talk about capital formation and the critical role that accountants play in that process. I want to particularly focus on capital formation from the investor's perspective. Too often, the investor perspective is lost in the discussion over capital formation. The companies, lawyers, and investment bankers that often dominate this discussion often see regulation only as an obstacle

---

Delivered December 12, 2012, at AICPA Conference on Current SEC and PCAOB Developments, Washington, D.C., by Luis Aguilar. Reprinted with permission. All rights reserved.

to be overcome. They focus the discussion on how to raise money quicker and more cheaply—but seem to forget that the money raised comes from the pockets of hard-working Americans. The capital raising process should not make investors more vulnerable, and attempts to raise money quicker and more cheaply should not come at the investor's expense. Today I want to put the focus on investors and examine how protecting investors facilitates capital formation by enhancing confidence, promoting integrity, and fostering transparency.

A Perfect Storm

Just five weeks ago, we witnessed the devastation of a "perfect storm." Images from coastal New Jersey and other areas affected by Superstorm Sandy make clear that, for many of our neighbors, recovery will be a long and difficult process.

Five years ago, we were hit with another type of "perfect storm" as the housing bubble burst and global credit markets began to freeze. The perfect storm of the financial crisis also led to a long, slow, and uneven recovery that left all too many Americans underwater.

One persistent after-effect of the financial crisis has been a loss of confidence in the securities markets among individual investors. A recent survey finds that only 17 percent of Americans trust the stock market.[1] Average daily trades in US stocks are about half their 2008 peak.[2] From 2006 through 2011, US domestic equity funds experienced a total outflow of half a trillion dollars.[3] Some of this shift may be a natural result of the aging population of baby boomers, but there may also be a decline in the willingness of even younger investors to invest in the stock market.[4] Looking back over a longer timeframe, the number of US IPOs fell sharply after the tech bubble burst in 2000 and never truly recovered, particularly in the case of smaller companies with sales of less than $50 million per year.[5]

To the list of factors contributing to the loss of confidence is the recurring news of household names being sued by the SEC for fraudulent behavior, dramatic breakdowns in corporate governance, or other misconduct.[6] It is understandable that investors feel uneasy. It's hard for them to know whether the capital markets are trustworthy.

Obviously, we need to turn this trend around. It is clear that if you want people to invest in the capital markets, you have to foster trust in the capital markets—and for that to happen, the capital markets must be trustworthy.

I know that the AICPA shares this perspective. As an organization responsible for setting ethical and professional standards for accountants, the AICPA is the public representative of a rigorous and noble profession. As financial statement preparers and auditors, accountants have a special responsibility to help make sure the capital markets are trustworthy. You are important "gatekeepers." Your professional training and experience prepare you for this role, and whether you work in industry or in public accounting, your clients and colleagues look to you for guidance. Investors count on you as well to make sure they get the information they need to make good investment decisions. The work of the accounting profession is critically important to investors and absolutely central to capital formation.

Understanding True Capital Formation

Before discussing the role that accountants play in maintaining investor confidence and in fostering fair and efficient capital markets, let's first make sure we're on the same page when we talk about capital formation. Capital formation is much more than just capital raising. By itself, selling a bond or a share of stock doesn't add a thing to the real economy, no matter how quickly or cheaply you do it. True capital formation requires that the capital raised be invested in productive assets—like a factory, store, or new technology—or otherwise used to make a business more productive. The more productive those assets are, the greater the capital formation from the investment—and, importantly, the more jobs created.[7]

Unfortunately, the reverse is true as well: When investor funds are diverted away from productive uses, capital is destroyed. Scam artists and promoters can be very effective at raising money, but accounting frauds, Ponzi schemes, and "casino capitalism"[8] are the black holes of capital formation. They attract investment dollars and make them disappear. We see this again and again in cases brought by the SEC and other regulators: All too often, by the time the fraudster is caught, investor funds have been dissipated and the defendant is judgment-proof. The result is that investors are left holding the proverbial bag—their money lost and their dreams shattered.

My experiences as an SEC Commissioner make it clear to me that rules to promote full and fair disclosure, reliable financial information, and accountability for market participants are absolutely necessary. When properly enforced, such rules help to deter fraud, protect investors and enable true capital formation. This happens in a variety of ways.

Investor Protection Is Necessary for True Capital Formation

First and foremost, protecting investors promotes true capital formation by providing investors with the confidence they need to invest.[9] Investors must have confidence in the integrity of the capital markets to invest their savings in stocks, bonds, mutual funds and other securities. They must have confidence that the markets are fair and that the rules are effectively enforced. And they must have confidence that the information available is meaningful, accurate, and complete.

Members of the accounting profession can help to promote this confidence, through your roles in a regulatory system that requires, among other things, accurate disclosure of financial and other material information, independent audit committees with financial expertise, effective and efficient internal controls, and diligent, independent and professionally skeptical auditors. These safeguards work together to ensure that public company financial statements are accurate, informative and reliable.

Second, true capital formation requires that investment decisions be based on reliable and useful information, so that investors can better price risk and determine value. This in turn increases the likelihood that capital will be invested productively. The goal of such transparency is not to eliminate risk—all investments carry a degree of risk. The essential thing is that investors are fully informed of the risks, so that they can decide where, when and how to put their money to work.

Third, widespread access to reliable financial information lowers the cost of capital by reducing the risk premiums demanded by investors. When a market has sufficient information, and confidence in that information, investors will tend to bid-up the price of quality investments, lowering the cost of capital for such issuers. However, if information is lacking, unreliable, or difficult to compare, investors will tend to "overpay" for low-quality securities and "underpay" for high-quality ones.[10] This interferes with the efficient allocation of capital and negatively impacts capital formation. When investors have no confidence that the market knows how to price a security, then no transactions in that security will take place.[11] This is a situation to be avoided, because when market information becomes unreliable, it is the honest and lower-risk businesses that, in effect, subsidize the dishonest or higher-risk businesses.[12]

In other words, true capital formation is best facilitated when investors and other capital providers have the information they need to make informed decisions.

However, experience tells us that it is not enough to simply require disclosure. Effective regulation also requires oversight, enforcement, and important procedural safeguards. For example, for publicly-traded companies, these built-in safeguards include, among many others, the independent audit, a system of internal control, and an audit committee comprised of independent directors. These safeguards, in particular, rely on the participation of accountants with, as established by the AICPA Code of Professional Conduct, a professional duty to "serve the public interest, honor the public trust, and demonstrate commitment to professionalism."[13] When members of the profession act with integrity, objectivity and due care—and when auditors in public practice are independent in both fact and appearance—that is when they can truly fulfill their role as gatekeepers, helping to protect the integrity of our capital markets.

Clearly, this is in the best interests of investors and our economy. There is no substitute for an environment where investors can rely on the integrity of published financial information.

US Investors Must Be Able to Rely on the Integrity of Foreign Audits

This is not just important in the United States. It is also important to recognize that capital formation is a global process. Many large US companies have operations all over the world, and businesses of all sizes from other countries come to the United States to access our capital markets. Accordingly, foreign operations of US issuers are often reviewed by foreign auditors, including the local affiliates of the major global accounting networks, as well as independent firms.

US investors rely on the work product of these foreign auditors when making investment decisions, often without knowing the role the foreign accounting firm played in the audit. This lack of transparency, made worse by news reports of audit failures in China and other countries, can create uncertainty in the capital markets. Last year, with a goal toward improving transparency, the Public Company Accounting Oversight Board (PCAOB) proposed amendments that, among other things, would require disclosure in the audit report of other accounting firms that took part in the audit, including foreign firms.[14] This transparency regarding the audit participants would be a step forward for investors.

In addition, I remain seriously concerned about the lack of effective oversight regarding foreign auditors that issue audit reports or participate in the audits of US issuers. Like US firms that audit public companies, these foreign audit firms must register with the PCAOB. As such, they are subject to periodic inspections, including review of work papers for selected audits.

One persistent after-effect of the financial crisis has been a loss of confidence in the securities markets among individual investors. A recent survey finds that only 17 percent of Americans trust the stock market. Average daily trades in US stocks are about half their 2008 peak.

Unfortunately however, although many foreign-based firms currently cooperate with the inspection regime, the PCAOB has been prevented from inspecting the audit work of accounting firms in certain European countries, China, and—to the extent their audit clients have operations in China—Hong Kong. Chinese regulators have resisted direct inspections by US regulators for years.

The PCAOB's inability to inspect the Chinese operations of registered accounting firms is a particular problem, given the number of claims in recent years regarding potential fraud or other irregularities at China-based companies traded on US markets. I have spoken before about my concerns regarding the many claims related to smaller companies that entered the US markets through reverse merger transactions, further reducing transparency.[15]

It has been widely reported that the PCAOB has been working to resolve this situation, and I commend the PCAOB for its efforts. In fact, just last month, for the first time, representatives of the PCAOB were able to observe audit inspections by Chinese regulators.[16] While this is by no means a substitute for a PCAOB inspection, I am hopeful it is a first step to achieving the ultimate goal of a full inspection.

A related issue has been the difficulty in obtaining access to accounting work papers and other documentation. It's no secret that the SEC has been investigating accounting irregularities at dozens of China-based companies that are publicly traded in the United States. However, those investigations have been hampered by the lack of access to relevant documents, many of which are located overseas.[17]

It is obvious that SEC enforcement staff often need access to audit work papers to investigate possible financial fraud claims. In fact, Section 106 of the Sarbanes-Oxley Act, as amended, requires foreign public accounting firms to provide audit work papers concerning US issuers to the SEC upon request. Unfortunately, when we made these requests of audit firms in China, it was an act of futility. As a result, in May of this year, the Commission filed an enforcement action against the Shanghai member firm of a Big Four global accounting network for its refusal to provide the Commission with audit work papers. This particular action related to a China-based company under investigation for potential accounting fraud against US investors.[18]

Commission staff had sought to obtain such documents for more than two years before bringing that action. The Shanghai-based auditor refused to provide the documents, citing Chinese law as the reason for its refusal.

Regardless of Chinese law, however, the fact remains that foreign auditors in China and elsewhere have voluntarily registered with the PCAOB and have chosen to perform audit work for US-listed issuers, knowing full well that US investors would be relying on their audit reports and other work product. If these firms are unable or unwilling to comply with US law, the question to ask is whether the companies they audit should be allowed to trade in the US securities markets.[19]

This is a question that must be answered with the needs of investors in mind—both to protect investors and to promote capital formation. Uncertainty regarding audited financial statements hurts investor confidence in the securities of all issuers whose operations are based in places opaque to regulatory oversight.[20]

This has been an open issue for some time, and it is past time that it be resolved.

The Role of the PCAOB

In this regard, I would like to recognize the important role of our regulator in this space, the Public Company Accounting Oversight Board. As this group knows well, the PCAOB was established in response to the Enron, WorldCom and other accounting scandals of the "dot-com bubble" era. These scandals were widely seen as a failure of the gatekeepers: Not just accountants and auditors, but boards of directors, securities analysts, credit rating agencies, and sophisticated institutional money managers as well—all of whom seemingly closed their eyes to complex financial frauds designed to maximize the company's stock price by any means available, regardless of the underlying economic reality.[21]

Under the Sarbanes-Oxley Act of 2002, the PCAOB is charged with overseeing the audits of public companies to protect the interests of investors and to further the public interest in the preparation of informative, accurate, and independent audit reports.

As you likely know, this summer marked the 10th anniversary of the Sarbanes-Oxley Act. Over this period, the PCAOB has conducted nine annual inspection cycles, and the largest accounting firms—that is, those that issue audit reports for 100 or more public companies—are audited annually, so there is a wealth of information about audit quality that can be analyzed.

Unfortunately, the available data raise serious issues about the quality of many audits. For the 2010 inspection cycle—the most recent year for which complete results are available—the PCAOB issued inspection reports for all eight accounting firms in the "annual inspections" category.[22] In the aggregate, these firms are responsible for auditing the financial statements of the great bulk, by market capitalization, of public issuers.[23] In each case, the PCAOB identified multiple audits with deficiencies, and multiple deficiencies that rose to the level of audit failures. Moreover, the evidence suggests that these results were not an aberration. Many common deficiencies cited in these recent inspection reports were also identified as frequent weaknesses in the PCAOB's report on audit risk areas affected by the economic crisis, which focused on the 2007, 2008 and 2009 audit cycles.[24] Moreover, early results from the 2011 cycle also indicate an unacceptable level of audit deficiencies.[25]

The audit failures revealed by the PCAOB damage investor confidence, discourage investment, and impede the efficient allocation of capital required for true capital formation.

I know you will agree with me that this is not acceptable. In light of these concerns, the PCAOB is currently considering a wide range of potential approaches for improving audit quality.[26] I appreciate the work that the PCAOB does to protect investors and promote financial transparency and I look forward to its recommendations. I encourage the AICPA and its members to be active participants in this dialogue, and I know many already are.

The Importance of Internal Controls

As we consider the critical role that accountants play in promoting transparency, protecting investors and facilitating true capital formation, it is also useful to consider the importance of effective internal control over financial reporting (often referred to as ICFR).

It has long been recognized that effective systems of internal controls are fundamental to reliable financial reporting. For more than 70 years, the Commission's rules for certifying financial statements have required independent auditors to consider the adequacy of the issuer's internal control system in determining the scope of their audits.[27] As far back as 1940, the Commission found that an accountant's determination regarding the effectiveness of the client's internal controls was a "cornerstone of any examination of financial statements."[28] And for a quarter of a century, companies subject to SEC reporting have been required to maintain internal control systems sufficient to provide reasonable assurance that their financial reporting is reliable.[29]

Given the importance of an issuer's internal controls to effective auditing, investors should know about any material deficiencies or weaknesses in those controls. And given the importance that accurate financial statements have to investors, it is regrettable that Section 404(b), and its requirement for auditor attestation of internal controls, have so often been a target for criticism. The argument critics make against auditor attestation is that the costs outweigh the benefits, particularly for small and medium-sized companies. However, there is ample evidence to rebut that argument.

First, evidence shows that independent attestation of internal controls promotes good financial reporting. Last year, as required by the Dodd-Frank Act, the SEC's Office of Chief Accountant completed a study and recommendations on Section 404(b) for issuers with a public float between $75 million and $250 million.[30] The study concluded that "financial reporting is more reliable when the auditor is involved with ICFR assessments" and that "investors generally view the auditor's attestation on ICFR as beneficial."[31]

In particular, the Study found evidence that auditor testing of internal controls has generally resulted in the disclosure of control deficiencies that were not previously disclosed by management. Auditor testing also appears to have a positive effect on the quality of financial reporting generally. The Study stated that issuers that only filed Section 404(a) reports—that is, management certification, without 404(b) auditor attestation—were significantly more likely to restate their financial statements than issuers that complied with both Section 404(a) and Section 404(b).[32] The benefits of auditor attestation are confirmed by other commenters as well, including the Council of Institutional Investors, the Center for Audit Quality, and the AICPA.[33]

Second, it has been generally reported that the cost of complying with Section 404(b) has moderated substantially in the years since first implemented.[34]

However, despite evidence of Section 404(b) benefits to investors and the public interest, and despite evidence that the costs of this requirement are manageable and declining, there have been repeated efforts to limit the auditor attestation requirement. In 2010, the Dodd-Frank Act permanently exempted all smaller reporting companies from the requirements of Section 404(b).[35] This year, the JOBS Act expanded the list by exempting so-called "emerging growth companies" from Section 404(b).[36] This is a very broad exemption, as the definition of "emerging growth company" includes businesses with up to $1 billion in annual gross revenue, for up to five years after their initial public offering.[37] I am concerned that the rollback of Section 404(b) will be harmful for both investors and the capital markets. Uncertainty regarding the reliability of financial reporting is likely to damage investor confidence. This could actually reduce demand for the securities of these companies, raising their cost of capital and harming, rather than helping, the market for IPOs.[38]

In fact, there is data to back this up: Researchers have found that companies that voluntarily comply with Section 404(b) experience a lower cost of capital, including a decline in the cost of equity and debt capital in the first year of compliance.[39] In other words, auditor attestation of internal controls enhances financial transparency, protects investors and promotes true capital formation.

Given this evidence, I strongly support retaining the benefits of Section 404(b) for all companies currently subject to it. The SEC and PCAOB should also continue to monitor the financial reporting and internal controls of those issuers that have already been exempted from Section 404(b), and we should not hesitate to call for the reinstatement of that obligation if necessary to promote capital formation and protect investors.

Conclusion

As gatekeepers, the AICPA and its members have a meaningful opportunity to protect investors, promote true capital formation, and uphold the integrity of the capital markets. The auditing profession has a proud history of working to improve audit quality for the benefit of investors and the public interest. Your commitment to providing accurate, meaningful, and reliable accounting, auditing and financial reporting is one of the reasons that the American economy is the envy of the world. In an increasingly global society, I believe that the work of the AICPA will have a positive impact not only in the United States but around the world. I know that you recognize your responsibility to investors and other financial statement users—and how essential your role is to the proper functioning of our capital markets.

I thank you for having me here today, and I wish you a productive conference.

Notes

1. Chicago Booth/Kellogg Financial Trust Index (September 2012), available at http://www.financialtrustindex.org.
2. Nathaniel Popper, "Stock Trading Is Stall Falling After '08 Crisis," *The New York Times* (May 7, 2012), p. A1, available at http://www.nytimes.com/2012/05/07/business/stock-trading-remains-in-a-slide-after-08-crisis.html?pagewanted=all. Editorial: "End of the Affair?" *The New York Times* (May 15, 2012); Joe Light, "An About-Face for Investors," *The Wall Street Journal* (May 29, 2012), p. C1; Sal Arnuk and Joseph Saluzzi, "Here's Why Investors Are Pulling Money Out of the Market," http://www.cnbc.com/id/47710901 (June 7, 2012); Reuters, "Facebook IPO mishandling hurt investor confidence: TD Ameritrade" (June 8, 2012), http://in.reuters.com/article/2012/06/08/us-facebook-investors-tdameritrade-idINBRE8560SN20120608.
3. *Investment Company Institute, 2012 Investment Company Fact Book*, 52nd ed. (2012), p. 27, available at www.ici.org. Other data also show a relative decline in the domestic equity markets. U.S. equity market volumes have generally declined over the past three years, since reaching a monthly peak in March 2009. Popper, op cit., citing Crédit Suisse Trading Strategy; BATS Global Markets. This year, average daily trading volume on the New York Stock Exchange is about 3.8 billion shares, down from about five billion in early 2010. Light, op. cit, at p. C2.
4. *2012 Investment Company Fact Book*, Figures 2.5 and 2.6.
5. Statement of Jay R. Ritter, Cordell Professor of Finance, University of Florida, before the Senate Committee on Banking, Housing, and Urban Affairs, Tuesday, March 6, 2012, p. 1, available at http://banking.senate.gov/public/index.cfm?FuseAction=Files.View&FileStore_id=a5ded25c-135d-484a-943a-bfa52fba3206. ("The market is not failing when firms with poor investment prospects are unable to get funding. The market is working when firms with good prospects are able to get funded at reasonable cost and grow, and firms with poor prospects are deprived of capital that would be wasted." Id. at p. 10.)
6. See, e.g., SEC Press Release No. 2010-123, "Goldman Sachs to Pay Record $550 Million to Settle SEC Charges Related to Subprime Mortgage CDO," July 15, 2010, http://www.sec.gov/news/press/2010/2010–123.htm; SEC Press Release No. 2010–136, "SEC Charges Citigroup and Two Executives for Misleading Investors About Exposure to Subprime Mortgage Assets," July 29, 2010, http://sec.gov/news/press/2010/2010–136.htm; SEC Press Release No.

2011–7, "SEC Charges Schwab Entities and Two Executives With Making Misleading Statements," (Jan. 11, 2011) http://sec.gov/news/press/2011/2011-7.htm; SEC Press Release No. 2011–22, "SEC Charges Merrill Lynch for Misusing Customer Order Information and Charging Undisclosed Trading Fees," (Jan. 25, 2011) http://sec.gov/news/press/2011/2011–22.htm; SEC Press Release No. 2011-81, "SEC Charges Satyam Computer Services with Financial Fraud," (Apr. 5, 2011) http://sec.gov/news/press/2011/2011–81.htm; SEC Press Release No. 2011-83, "SEC Announces Securities Laws Violations by Wachovia Involving Mortgage-Backed Securities," (Apr. 5, 2011) http://sec.gov/news/press/2011/2011–83.htm; SEC Press Release No. 2011-131, "J.P. Morgan to Pay $153.6 Million to Settle SEC Charges of Misleading Investors in DCO Tied to U.S. Housing Market," (June 21, 2011) http://sec.gov/news/press/2011/2011-131.htm; SEC Press Release No. 2011–214, "Citigroup to Pay $285 Million to Settle SEC Charges for Misleading Investors About CDO Tied to Housing Market," (Oct. 19, 2011) http://sec.gov/news/press/2011/2011-214.htm; SEC Press Release No. 2012–189, "SEC Charges New York Stock Exchange for Improper Distribution of Market Data," (Sept. 14, 2012) http://www.sec.gov/news/press/2012/2012-189.htm; SEC Press Release No. 2012–231, "BP to Pay $525 Million Penalty to Settle SEC Charges of Securities Fraud During Deepwater Horizon Oil Spill," (Nov. 15, 2012) http://www.sec.gov/news/press/2012/2012–231.htm.

7. UN Conf. on Trade and Development, Macroeconomic Policies to Promote Growth and Job Creation (New York, March 12–13, 2012), p.3. ("There is also a strong positive correlation between investment in fixed capital and employment creation in developed countries." Chart: Growth of Employment and Gross Fixed Capital Formation in Developed Countries, 1971–2010.) http://www.un.org/esa/ffd/ecosoc/springmeetings/2012/Unctad_BGNote.pdf.

8. See John Maynard Keynes, *General Theory of Employment, Interest, and Money* (Cambridge, 1936), p. 159. ("When the capital development of a country becomes a by-product of the activities of a casino, the job is likely to be ill-done.")

9. Luigi Guiso, Paola Sapienza, and Luigi Zingales, "Trusting the Stock Market," 63 *The Journal of Finance*, No. 6 (Dec. 2008), available at http://www.kellogg.northwestern.edu/faculty/sapienza/htm/trusting_stock.pdf. ("The decision to invest in stocks requires not only an assessment of the risk–return trade-off given the existing data, but also an act of faith (trust) that the data in our possession are reliable and that the overall system is fair.")

10. See George A. Akerlof, "The Market for 'Lemons': Quality Uncertainty and the Market Mechanism," *The Quarterly Journal of Economics* (August 1970).

11. Id. ("There may be potential buyers of good quality products and there may be potential sellers of such products in the appropriate price range; however, the presence of people who wish to pawn bad wares as good wares tends to drive out the legitimate business. The cost of dishonesty, therefore, lies not only in the amount by which the purchaser is cheated; the cost also must include the loss incurred from driving legitimate business out of existence.")

12. Ricardo N. Bebczuk, *Asymmetric Information in Financial Markets, Introduction and Applications* (Cambridge Univ. Press, 2003), pp. 15–16.

13. AICPA Code of Professional Conduct, ET Section 53—Article II, The Public Interest, available at http://www.aicpa.org/Research/Standards/CodeofConduct/Pages/et_section_53__article_ii_the_public_interest.aspx.

14. PCAOB Release no. 2011–007, Improving the Transparency of Audits: Proposed Amendments to PCAOB Auditing Standards and Form 2 (Oct. 11, 2011). In addition, the proposed amendments would require that accounting firms disclose the name of the engagement partner in audit reports and PCAOB annual report forms.

15. SEC Commissioner Luis A. Aguilar, "Facilitating Real Capital Formation," remarks to the Council of Institutional Investors (April 4, 2011) http://www.sec.gov/news/speech/2011/spch040411laa.htm.

16. Tammy Whitehouse, "PCAOB Gains First View of Chinese Audit Work," *Compliance Week* (Nov. 9, 2012), available at http://www.complianceweek.com/pcaob-gains-first-view-of-chinese-audit-work/article/267678/.

17. See, Shen Hu and Zheng Fei, "SEC probes hit a wall in uncooperative China," *MarketWatch, The Wall Street Journal, Caixin Online* (June 11, 2012), http://www.marketwatch.com/story/sec-probes-hit-a-wall-in-uncooperative-china-2012-06-11; Aruna Viswanatha and Dena Aubin, "UPDATE 2-US SEC delays court action seeking Deloitte China audit papers," Reuters (Jul. 18, 2012), http://www.reuters.com/article/2012/07/18/sec-deloitte-idUSL2E8II6OH20120718.

18. Release No. 66948, Administrative Proceeding File No. 3-14872, In the Matter of Deloitte Touche Tohmatsu Certified Public Accountants Ltd., Second Corrected Order Instituting Administrative Proceedings Pursuant to Rule 102(e)(1)(iii) of the Commission's Rules of Practice and Notice of Hearing (May 9, 2012), available at http://www.sec.gov/litigation/admin/2012/34-66948.pdf.

19. See, "Judge Questions U.S. Legal Authority on Deloitte Shanghai," Reuters (Oct. 14, 2011) (quoting law professor and former SEC Commissioner Roberta Karmel, "Should the SEC allow any companies that are audited by auditors who refuse to produce information in U.S. courts to be listed on an exchange to be sold to U.S. persons? [...] Should the New York Stock Exchange allow a company to be listed under circumstances where its auditors are not going to be forthcoming with information if problem arises?")

20. See, Shen Hu and Zheng Fei, "SEC probes hit a wall in uncooperative China," *MarketWatch, The Wall Street Journal, Caixin Online* (June 11, 2012), http://www.marketwatch.com/story/sec-probes-hit-a-wall-in-uncooperative-china-2012-06-11.

21. See, John C. Coffee Jr., *Gatekeepers: The Role of the Professions and Corporate Governance* (Oxford Univ. Press, 2006), Ch. 2.

22. PCAOB Release No. 104-2012-071, Inspection of BDO USA, LLP (January 31, 2012); PCAOB Release No. 104-2011-290, Inspection of Deloitte & Touche LLP (December 7, 2011); PCAOB Release No. 104-2011-319, Inspection of Ernst & Young LLP (November 30, 2011); PCAOB Release No.

104-2012-109, Inspection of Grant Thornton LLP (March 29, 2012); PCAOB Release No. 104-2012-095, Inspection of McGladrey & Pullen, LLP (February 28. 2012); PCAOB Release No. 104-2012-110, Inspection of MaloneBailey, LLP (April 5, 2012); PCAOB Release No. 104-2011-288, Inspection of KPMG LLP (November 8, 2011); PCAOB Release No. 104-2011-289, Inspection of PricewaterhouseCoopers LLP (November 8, 2011). Each of the foregoing is available at http://pcaobus.org/Inspections/Reports/Pages/default.aspx.

23. See, United States Government Accountability Office, Report to Congressional Addressees, Audits of Public Companies: Continued Concentration in Audit Market for Large Public Companies Does Not Call for Immediate Action (January 2008), available at http://www.gao.gov/assets/280/270953.pdf ("According to our analysis, the largest accounting firms audit 98 percent of the more than 1,500 largest public companies—those with annual revenues of more than $1 billion. In contrast, midsize and smaller firms audit almost 80 percent of the more than 3,600 smallest companies—those with annual revenues of less than $100 million.")

24. PCAOB Release No. 2010-006, Report on Observations of PCAOB Inspectors Related to Audit Risk Areas Affected by the Economic Crisis (September 29, 2010) http://pcaobus.org/Inspections/Documents/4010_Report_Economic_Crisis.pdf. See, also PCAOB Rel. No. 2008-008, Report on the PCAOB's 2004, 2005, 2006, and 2007 Inspections of Domestic Annually Inspected Firms, at 2, (Dec. 5, 2008).

25. See, Floyd Norris, "Bad Grades Rising At Audit Firms," *The New York Times* (August 24, 2012), B2.

26. See, Docket 29: Improving Transparency Through Disclosure of Engagement Partner and Certain Other Participants in Audits, http://pcaobus.org/Rules/Rulemaking/Pages/Docket029.aspx; Docket 30: Proposed Auditing Standard on Communications with Audit Committees and Related Amendments to PCAOB Standards, http://pcaobus.org/Rules/Rulemaking/Pages/Docket030.aspx; Docket 034 : Concept Release on Possible Revisions to PCAOB Standards Related to Reports on Audited Financial Statements and Related Amendments to PCAOB Standards, http://pcaobus.org/Rules/Rulemaking/Pages/Docket034.aspx; Docket 037 : Concept Release on Auditor Independence and Audit Firm Rotation, http://pcaobus.org/Rules/Rulemaking/Pages/Docket037.aspx. See also, James R. Doty, Chairman, PCAOB, "The Relevance of Audits and the Needs of Investors," remarks at the 31st Annual SEC and Financial Reporting Institute Conference, Pasadena, CA (May 31, 2012), http://pcaobus.org/News/Speech/Pages/05312012_DotyAuditsInvestors.aspx, and Doty, "Looking Ahead: Auditor Oversight," remarks at the Council of Institutional Investors 2011 Spring Meeting, http://pcaobus.org/News/Speech/Pages/04042011_DotyLookingAhead.aspx.

27. Howard L. Kellogg, Assistant Chief Accountant, "The S.E.C. Looks at Internal Control, " address to the New York Chapter, Institute of Internal Auditors (Mar. 27, 1951), pp. 1–3, www.sec.gov/news/speech/1951/032751kellogg.pdf.

28. United States of America before the Securities and Exchange Commission in the Matter of McKesson & Robbins, Inc., pursuant to Section 21(a) of the Securities Exchange Act of 1934, Report on Investigation, available at the SEC Historical Society, Virtual Museum & Archive of the History of Financial Regulation, www.sechistorical.org/museum. The financial markets were rocked by the fraud at McKesson & Robbins, a New York Stock Exchange-listed drug distributor, which had gone undiscovered by McKesson's auditors for several years. The McKesson & Robbins scandal and resulting SEC report led to auditing reforms by the AICPA, including requirements to test inventory and receivables. See, John C. Coffee, Jr., *Gatekeepers: The Role of the Professions and Corporate Governance, Clarendon Lectures in Management Studies* (Oxford Univ. Press, 2006).

29. Securities and Exchange Act of 1934, §13(b)(2)(b), 15 U.S.C. §78m(b)(2)(B), added by Section 102 of the Foreign Corrupt Practices Act of 1977, Pub. L. No. 95–213, 91 Stat. 1494 (1977).

30. Office of the Chief Accountant, Securities and Exchange Commission, Study and Recommendations on Section 404(b) of the Sarbanes-Oxley Act of 2002 for Issuers with Public Float Between $75 and $250 Million (the "2011 Staff Study") http://www.sec.gov/news/studies/2011/404bfloat-study.pdf.

31. Id., p. 7. These conclusions were based on analyses by staff in the SEC's Chief Accountant's office; public comments from issuers, investors and other interested parties; and a review of prior academic and other research on Section 404.

32. Id., pp. 6, 39–40, 72–73, 85, 86.

33. See, Letter from Cindy Fornelli, Center for Audit Quality, and Jeff Mahoney, Council of Institutional Investors, to the Hon. Spencer Bachus, Chairman, and the Hon. Barney Frank, Ranking Member, Committee on Financial Services, U.S. House of Representatives (November 29, 2011), http://www.aicpa.org/Advocacy/Issues/DownloadableDocuments/404b/CAQ-CII_404_letter_11-29-11.pdf; Letter from Barry C. Melancon, AICPA, to Chairman Bachus, Ranking Member Frank, and the Hon. Scott Garrett, Chairman, and the Hon. Maxine Waters, Ranking Member, Subcommittee on Capital Markets and Government Sponsored Enterprises, U.S. House of Representatives (October 4, 2011), http://www.aicpa.org/Advocacy/Issues/DownloadableDocuments/404b/10_4_11-404SubcommitteeLetter.pdf.

34. Domestic accelerated filers were first required to provide auditor attestation of ICFR with respect to fiscal years ending after November 15, 2004. Smaller reporting companies have never been required to comply with Section 404(b). Since 2007, the costs of complying with Section 404(b) have tended to moderate, reflecting both increased clarity over the requirements of Section 404(b), resulting from the implementation of PCAOB Auditing Standard 5, the Commission's Interpretive Release, and other guidance on compliance provided by the PCAOB, by the Commission, and by the Committee of Sponsoring Organizations of the Treadway Commission ("COSO"), as well as operational efficiencies resulting from experience and the development of best practices. See,

2011 Staff Study; See also, the letter from Fornelli and Mahoney and the letter from Melancon, referred to in note 33, supra. COSO is currently in the process of reviewing and updating its Integrated Framework for internal controls.

35. Dodd-Frank Wall Street Reform and Consumer Protection Act ("Dodd-Frank") §989G(a), Pub. L. No. 111–203, 124 Stat. 1376 (2010).

36. Jumpstart Our Business Startups Act ("JOBS Act") §103, Pub. L. No. 112–106, 126 Stat. 306 (April 5, 2012).

37. Section 101(a) of the JOBS Act amends the Securities Act of 1933 to define "emerging growth company" as any issuer that had total annual gross revenues of less than $1 billion during its most recently completed fiscal year. An issuer that is an emerging growth company as of the first day of a fiscal year continues to qualify as such until (A) the last day of the fiscal year in which it has annual gross revenue of $1 billion or more, (B) the last day of the fiscal year following the fifth anniversary of its initial registered public offering, (C) such issuer has issued more than $1 billion in non-convertible debt over a three-year period, or (D) such issuer becomes a large accelerated filer (i.e., has a $700 million public float, measured as of the end of the company's most recent prior second fiscal quarter). More than three-quarters of all active filers today have less than $1 billion in revenue. It has been estimated that 98 percent of all IPOs since 1970 would have fit into that category. See, Statement of Lynn E. Turner before the Senate Committee on Banking, Housing, and Urban Affairs on Spurring Job Growth Through Capital Formation While Protecting Investors, Part II (March 6, 2012), at 12, citing Audit Analytics. http://banking.senate.gov/public/index.cfm?FuseAction=Files.View&FileStore_id=5aaabb66-36eb-4b1e-8195-3cbeda832814.

38. See, Statement of Professor Ritter (March 6, 2012), at 8 (note 5 infra). Statement of Professor John C. Coates IV, John F. Cogan, Jr. Professor of Law and Economics, Harvard Law School, before the Subcommittee on Securities, Insurance, and Investment of the Committee on Banking, Housing, and Urban Affairs, United States Senate, on Examining Investor Risks in Capital Raising (December 14, 2011), at 2. http://banking.senate.gov/public/index.cfm?FuseAction=Files.View&FileStore_id=1d24b42e-3ef8-4653-bfe8-9c476740fafa.

39. Cory A. Cassell, Linda A. Myers and Jian Zhou, "The Effect of Voluntary Internal Control Audits on the Cost of Capital" (January 2, 2011), http://papers.ssrn.com/sol3/papers.cfm?abstract_id=1734300.

About Luis A. Aguilar

Luis A. Aguilar is currently a Democratic commissioner of the US Securities and Exchange Commission (SEC). He was appointed by President George W. Bush and took office in 2008. He was reappointed by President Barack Obama in 2011. Aguilar was born in November 1953 in Cuba and immigrated to the United States in 1960. After earning his bachelor's degree from Georgia Southern University in 1976, he attended the University of Georgia Law School, graduating in 1979. He also received a master of law degree in taxation from Emory University in 1985. Aguilar was an attorney for the SEC starting in 1979 but left in 1982 to work at the Georgia law firms Powell Goldstein and Kilpatrick & Cody. He later worked at INVESCO, where he served as general counsel, executive vice president, and corporate secretary. He departed INVESCO in 2002 to join the law firm Alston & Bird LLP as a partner and subsequently became a partner with McKenna Long and Aldridge, LLP, an international law firm, in 2005. From September 2006 to July 2008, he served as the president of the Hispanic National Bar Foundation.

The Power of Socially and Environmentally Engaged Companies

By Bill Novelli

Professor Bill Novelli of Georgetown University's McDonough School of Business addresses the Charities at Work Annual Best Practices Summit on Employee Engagement in Corporate Citizenship. The event took place on April 3, 2013, in New York City. Charities at Work is an initiative that was formed by four nonprofit federations—America's Charities, Community Health Charities, EarthShare, and Global Impact. The initiative, which represents over 2,000 charities, works with businesses worldwide in the effort to enhance charitable practices. The subject of Novelli's speech is employee engagement in social enterprise. He discusses his belief that effecting positive social change takes consolidated, consistent effort. He reviews the ways in which companies worldwide are becoming more involved in social and environmental issues. According to Novelli, this involvement offers businesses the opportunity to increase revenues, save money, and provide benefits to their customers and shareholders. He theorizes that the most talented employees want to be involved in businesses that value the greater social good and recognize the economic and environmental benefits of sustainable practices. Novelli remarks on a passage from the book The Coming Jobs War *by Jim Clifton. Various examples of corporate social enterprise programs are discussed, including examples from IBM, Bank of America, and Procter & Gamble. Novelli believes that employees of socially and environmentally engaged companies help improve productivity, increase profit margins, and enhance stock performance.*

I've had the opportunity to do a number of things in my career, in business and in public service. Now I'm at Georgetown University, in the business school—a different setting for me, but in my mind a continuation of public service.

Outside the school, I am co-chairing a large and growing coalition to reform advanced illness and end-of-life care in the US. It is called C-TAC, for the Coalition to Transform Advanced Care, and several companies here today, including Aetna and United HealthGroup, are active members.

Some years ago, I was on my way to speak to a class at Columbia University, and I asked a student for directions to the building. She inquired who the professor was, and when I told her, she said, "Oh, he's famous." I said, "Really, what for?" And she replied, "He's famous for being a great teacher." That really stuck with me. What wonderful praise. I admire great teachers, and now I aspire to be one.

Delivered April 3, 2013, at Charities at Work Annual Best Practices Summit on Employee Engagement in Corporate Citizenship, New York, New York, by Bill Novelli.

But no matter what you're doing these days, teaching, managing companies and lines of business, working in government or nonprofits or anything else, these are challenging times.

Climate change, combined with environmental difficulties like clean water, food security and deforestation, debt and deficit problems at home and abroad, unsustainable health care costs, major risk factors like diabetes, smoking and obesity, chronic poverty in many parts of the world and many other problems are all right here and right now.

I have a favorite haiku that goes like this: "Problems worthy of attack, prove their worth by attacking back." These are the big ones, the problems that don't lend themselves to sitting back or muddling through.

I saw an article that said that scientists think there may be a mysterious bacterium that is eating a lot of the oil from the Gulf oil spill. If it's true, wouldn't that be great? And wouldn't it be great if we had a bug that could eat our enormous national debt, our health care inefficiencies and our carbon emissions, and maybe a few other things as well?

But it's almost surely not going to happen. Life doesn't work that way. So we need to act, to create change, to work to solve big social and environmental problems. A useful definition of positive social change is the sustainable transformation of systems and institutions to create a safer, healthier, more prosperous and more equitable society.

My own career goal is to make significant contributions to solving major social problems. Those are the big ones from the haiku—the ones that attack us back.

There are many challenges to achieving real and sustainable change, including scaling up to a meaningful level, acquiring and marshaling resources, the need for continuity, problems in measuring impact and a lack of basic knowledge about what works, such as with the difficulties we face in controlling today's obesity epidemic.

And there are many contributing factors to achieving positive social change. But perhaps the most important one is leadership—in the private sector, in government and in civil society. Someone once said that leadership is the cause, and all else is effect.

You don't have to be at the top to lead. You can lead from anywhere in the ranks. Colin Powell recognized this. He said, "Have you ever noticed that people will personally commit to certain individuals who, on paper or on the organization chart, possess little authority, but instead possess …drive, expertise and genuine caring for teammates and products?" He's right. We've all seen it. Many people are leaders from all parts of an organization.

Today, corporations are taking more and bigger roles in tackling social and environmental problems around the world. There are many labels for this: corporate social responsibility, corporate citizenship, triple bottom line, shared value and others. I prefer to call it corporate social enterprise.

You know a lot about this, so in a way I feel like I'm carrying coals to Newcastle in talking to you experts. But let me give you my point of view.

Why are companies getting more involved in social and environmental issues? For several reasons:

- Because they can. Large modern corporations have the talent and the resources and skills to do amazing things. And there is a certain moral imperative to use those resources to serve the planet and its people.

- But, of course, companies are required to serve shareholder interests, and so altruism isn't enough. There has to be a good business case for engaging in social enterprise.

- Companies can increase revenues through strategies of doing well by doing good. Look at Philips, the global company, which sees the world's aging population and the opportunity to create and sell technologies to enable people to age in place, which usually means at home. Philips has a strong revenue interest in this, and at the same time—through enabling people to be at home as they age—Philips can create enormous social value for adult children, for the elderly themselves, and for taxpayers who don't have to foot the bill for institutionalized care.

- Companies can also save money, which flows to the bottom line. An often cited example is Wal-Mart's successful efforts to reduce packaging costs and volume and to encourage its suppliers to do the same. The result is substantial savings for the company and a cleaner environment, with less waste in landfills around the world.

- And then there are potential advantages with consumers. We've all seen the surveys that show that consumers favor companies they believe are socially responsible. Of course, you need to have products and services people want to buy, but all things being equal, customers appear to gravitate to companies that care.

- In addition, there are other stakeholders who may respond favorably to good corporate citizenship, such as regulators, legislators, the media, financial analysts and foreign governments. Procter & Gamble's water purification program was said to be the catalyst for having the government of Malawi open the country to more P&G products because, as one government official put it, "You are the company doing the good water work." Coca Cola demonstrates similar stakeholder value with its clean-up program on the Galapagos Islands, where it utilizes hundreds of volunteers in working with the Galapagos Ecuador Foundation.

These are all good business reasons for companies to be more strategically involved in creating both economic and social value.

You're no doubt aware of this trend and are contributing to it. What I want to do now is to zero in on some other aspects of social enterprise that are specific to employee engagement and the focus of this conference.

Let's start with the truism that there is nothing more important to a company's success than its employees. In his book, *The Coming Jobs War,* Jim Clifton, the chairman of Gallup, writes that his firm has analyzed many surveys from many countries to answer the question: "What do people around the world invariably want?" The answer is a good job. This is—or should be—the currency for all world leaders, of countries and companies.

Talented people gravitate to countries and organizations that offer the opportunity to be entrepreneurial, to achieve, to excel and to feel positively about where they work. These employees are engaged and involved, and they are as direct a connection as there can be to business success.

Towers Watson's 2012 Global Workforce Study surveyed employees at 50 global companies on how well their employers engage them in the workplace. It's no surprise that the companies with sustainable, holistic engagement programs did best, including better financial performance compared to peer companies with less employee engagement.

Towers Watson defined "engaged" as intensity of connection to the organization, based on commitment to achieving work goals, a supportive environment for productivity and the promotion of well-being.

Where do these talented, committed employees come from? From all over the world, drawn to multinational companies. And many of them come through business schools like Georgetown. To appeal to these prospective employees, companies offer a variety of inducements, as you know so well: good salaries, the opportunity for advancement, location, corporate reputation and more.

One of the most powerful inducements, I believe, is to appeal to today's students' demand for, and strong interest in, global social enterprise—the idea of doing well by doing good and making a difference on those big problems I talked about earlier—as a core social value and a key contributor to the bottom line.

Business students are hard-eyed realists, for the most part. They believe in free enterprise and in the rewards of capitalism. But they also want to understand the environmental dependencies of human society and modern business and the effects of economic activity on the environment.

They want to know the business case for sustainability. They are interested in socially beneficial business practices. And they want to know about how government and business intersect in these matters. In other words, they are attracted to financial performance—and more.

There are some who want an MBA or undergraduate business degree as preparation for government or nonprofit work, or who are motivated primarily by altruism. One of them approached a pharmaceutical executive on campus who was talking about malarial drugs in Africa. The student said, "I want to come to work for you and save the world." He replied, "Saving the world is good, but I need people who understand supply chains." Again, economic and social value are key.

At Georgetown, we take the position that our business faculty, students and graduates are in service to business and society. Our Global Social Enterprise Initiative—you have the handout at your tables—develops partnerships with corporations, government and nonprofits—and across these sectors—to tackle big social issues and provide the leadership and practical training for future business leaders

Talented people gravitate to countries and organizations that offer the opportunity to be entrepreneurial, to achieve, to excel and to feel positively about where they work. These employees are engaged and involved, and they are as direct a connection as there can be to business success.

in economic and social value creation. An example is our partnership with the State Department and the Tides Foundation, along with numerous corporations and NGOs regarding corporate investment to advance international development.

What do you employers think? In the current issue of *BizEd Magazine,* there is an article that looks across a number of surveys to identify what employers say they're looking for in graduate hires and what business schools say they are teaching. In both instances, social responsibility, as well as leadership and business ethics, rank high.

Many of you compete hard for these young workers. PWC's most recent survey of business leaders worldwide found that CEOs say that, in order to gain access to a continuing supply of skilled and enthusiastic employees, attracting and keeping younger workers is one of their biggest talent challenges.

And several studies of millennial generation employees indicate that, after they leave the university and enter, or re-enter, employment, they continue to want social impact opportunities. The 2011 Deloitte Volunteer IMPACT survey of workers aged 21 to 35 showed that those who participate in workplace volunteer activities are twice as likely to be very satisfied with the progression of their careers.

They tend to want to be involved in causes. That's a big reason why Blue Cross/ Blue Shield, United HealthGroup, Adobe and other companies work with KaBoom! to build neighborhood playgrounds in partnership with communities all over the country.

Bank of America also has a major commitment to community development, along with philanthropic giving and investing in environmental initiatives.

America's Charities report on *Trends and Strategies to Engage Employees in Greater Giving* finds that young workers are arriving in organizations with different expectations of their employers. "They want their giving experiences to be engaging, empowering and catalyzing. These new expectations are causing employers to . . . find new ways to meaningfully engage Millennials in giving their time, talent and money."

Cone Communications' studies also support these findings about participation in volunteering and giving.

As I see it, there are strong connections between employee engagement and global social enterprise. First, employee engagement contributes to a companies' ability to create both economic and social value for stockholders and other stakeholders, at home and abroad.

In addition, employee engagement benefits from a corporation's work and success in social enterprise. As a P&G brand manager said about her companies' clean water program in Africa, "It's amazing when you know your work is serving a higher purpose." She wasn't talking about her brand manager initiatives; she was referring to the water program. But for her, it was the same company, and she was proud of it.

I use a case in one of my courses about IBM's Corporate Service Corps. It sends employees to various developing and emerging markets for four-week assignments that are pre-screened by partner NGOs. The IBMers work on a variety of social and economic problems. The company believes that it gets a number of benefits from this employee engagement, with one of them being increased retention of valuable workers.

As important as motivated employees are to the financial and overall success of a company, you would think that employee engagement programs would be even better funded and utilized. They have great value, which is shown time and time again.

Employee engagement can, or should be, a strong competitive advantage, which everyone—management, stockholders, prospective employees and workers themselves—can recognize. In making this advantage as visible and valued as possible, there are three good business reasons to be made:

- Productivity gains: Gallup studied over 150 organizations across numerous industries and countries, and found that productivity was some 18 pecent higher at companies where employees were more engaged (reported in the Harvard Business Review blog).

- Operating margins increase: The Towers Watson study I referred to earlier claimed that companies with high engagement scores had an average one-year operating margin of 27 percent versus 14 percent for companies with traditional levels of employee engagement and 10 percent for those with low engagement.

- Stock performance: The Pamassus Workplace Fund—which is a portfolio of stocks of companies with outstanding workplaces—was reported in *Fast Company* to outperform the S&P Index by a substantial margin.

These benefits are supported by the study, *Driving Business Results Through Continuous Engagement,* by WorkUSA, which reported that companies with engaged employees experience 26 percent higher revenue per employee, 13 percent higher total returns to shareholders and a 50 percent higher market premium.

A good way to improve employee engagement acceptance inside and outside a company may be better integration. I mean this two ways: first, improved alliances and integration of employee programs within overall corporate social enterprise initiatives. And second, better integration and alignment of employees into the core business, strategies and practices of the company.

In the IBM Corporate Service Corps example I mentioned, the company sees employee engagement as a component within its globally integrated business to serve clients around the world.

A former CSR executive of a Fortune 500 company recently told me, "Corporate citizenship is about engaging employees to integrate the social agenda into their day-to-day work on behalf of the company." She went on to offer this idea: "If a company wants to truly think of itself as socially responsible, it needs to hold its employees accountable for socially responsible behavior." She gave, as an example, energy conservation and other eco-friendly behaviors.

That is a challenging idea. For employees to be engaged and accountable for social enterprise, like anything else for which we hold people accountable, they would need the opportunity, the resources and the support to perform. I think they would rise to the occasion.

I was at a business conference talking about all this, and the subject came up about the challenge of social impact coming into conflict with the everyday demands of running a business.

The COO of a large company said it was unfortunate that "we can't all do what we love" (referring to social issues and causes), and "so we have to learn to love what we do" (meaning business operations).

But what if management and employees could do both—economic and social performance and results? And what if they were integrated and aligned? Employee engagement in corporate social enterprise can help make this happen. More and more companies are figuring it out. And you are a big reason why.

Thanks very much.

About William D. Novelli

William D. Novelli is an American businessman who served as the chief executive officer of AARP (formerly the American Association of Retired Persons) from 2001 to 2009. Prior to his leadership of AARP, Novelli was the vice president of CARE (Cooperative for Assistance and Relief Everywhere), an international nongovernmental relief agency dedicated to humanitarian aid and economic development. He holds a bachelor's of arts degree from the University of Pennsylvania and a master's of arts degree from the University of Pennsylvania's Annenberg School for Communication. He also pursued doctoral studies at New York University. Novelli began his career at Unilever, a consumer goods marketing company; he then became the director of advertising and creative services for the Peace Corps. In 1972 Novelli cofounded Porter Novelli, an international public relations firm, where he served as president. He retired from the firm in 1990 and began to focus on public service. Novelli taught at the University of Maryland's MBA program for ten years. He is currently a professor at the McDonough School of Business at Georgetown University.

Grassroots Economics

By William C. Dudley

William C. Dudley, president and chief executive officer of the Federal Reserve Bank of New York and vice chairman of the Federal Open Market Committee (FOMC), addresses the Business Council of Fairfield County, Connecticut. The speech was given on July 2, 2013, in Stamford. The subject of Dudley's remarks is the near-term growth and development of the American economy. He discusses the impact of Hurricane Sandy on businesses and communities in the northeastern United States in 2012. He also remarks on efforts being undertaken to address storm damage and head off damages from future natural disasters. Macroeconomic data pertaining to the Great Recession are reviewed. Dudley remarks that, although the American labor market remains troubled, household net worth has increased while debts have decreased. According to Dudley, consumer spending and retail sales remain depressed, in part because of fiscal policy. He states his belief that the United States economy will experience measured growth in 2014. Dudley reviews recent actions undertaken by the FOMC to maintain modest growth and claims that increases in the Fed's short-term interest rates will likely not occur before 2015. Details related to the Connecticut economy are also discussed— including jobs data, consumer debt, the regional housing market, and the economic impact of Hurricane Sandy. The increase in debt-per-person in the state is discussed, as are the economic benefits of Connecticut's proximity to New York City.

Good afternoon. I am pleased to be here with the Business Council of Fairfield County. I am told that your meetings are very inclusive—that you routinely invite education professionals, executives of local not-for-profit agencies and community leaders as well as business leaders. In doing so, you assemble the type of broad Main Street audience that I most enjoy addressing. So, thank you for inviting me here today.

Today I want to talk a bit about the outlook for the nation and the region. As many of you know, I was scheduled to speak at this forum on October 29 of last year but that meeting had to be postponed because of the arrival of Superstorm Sandy, which hit on that very day. The region covered by the New York Fed was at the center of the storm, and Fairfield County, as well as parts of the Connecticut shoreline, suffered extensive damage.

Immediately following the storm, our Regional and Community Outreach function worked with all of the affected areas as part of a needs assessment. We asked: "How can the New York Fed best leverage our resources to help our community?"

Delivered July 2, 2013, at the Business Council of Fairfield County, Stamford, Connecticut, by William C. Dudley.

We heard that it could be challenging to find key recovery information and advice online. So we pulled key resources under one roof—or I should say under one URL. We developed our Sandy Information Center with the best information we could find for residents and businesses impacted by Sandy—including key deadlines along with expert legal, finance and insurance guidance.

Conditions are not entirely back to normal, and restoration and repair activities continue in a number of hard-hit neighborhoods. Connecticut, along with New York, New Jersey, Maryland, and Rhode Island, have been appropriated federal funding for relief efforts and this should help move the area's recovery forward. I am confident that these areas will recover over the course of the year. The legislation also contains funding for helping coastal communities to prepare to weather future storms better.

My meeting with you today is part of our continuing efforts to understand what is going on at the grassroots level of our economy. Let me offer a few examples from this trip. Yesterday evening I met with some of Stamford's business leaders to discuss the local state of economic and business conditions. This morning I met with Mayor Finch and key economic development staff to discuss Bridgeport's re-development initiatives. Local efforts such as these and your business council are essential complements to the Fed's support for economic recovery. I applaud the efforts of state and local governments and community leaders to bolster the recovery in Bridgeport, Stamford and elsewhere in the district.

I also met with Joan Carty from the Connecticut Housing Development Fund. We discussed innovative approaches for addressing the foreclosure crisis here and across the state. Housing has been a major impediment to a more rapid economic recovery and we at the Fed have been working hard to help homeowners and the overall housing market recover. Afterwards, I spoke with small business leaders about the opportunities and challenges they are facing today. I traveled to Sikorsky Aircraft Corporation with several goals in mind. I wanted to learn how sequestration was affecting ground-level operations, to understand the local and regional economic impact of Sikorsky, and to view state-of-the-art manufacturing at work.

After this program, I will be meeting with Joseph Carbone of The Wo to discuss best practices and emerging approaches to workforce development, particularly his innovative program for the long-term unemployed, which I understand he is piloting in five different cities across the nation. At the end of the day I will be meeting with University of Connecticut (UConn) Stamford campus staff, your own executive director Chris Bruhl and other officials to learn about the ecosystem that is being created to spur further economic development locally. I'll end the day with a meeting with Governor Malloy to better understand the complex issues and opportunities facing the state.

The agenda for these visits is always packed, but that's part of the point—to meet with a diverse array of representatives in order to get a comprehensive picture of what's happening on Main Street and its interaction with state and national developments. At the end of my talk I will be happy to answer any questions you have about the economic outlook from my perspective.

As always, what I have to say reflects my own views and not necessarily those of the Federal Reserve System or the Federal Open Market Committee, also known as the FOMC.

National Economic Conditions

I would like to begin by taking stock of where we are at the moment. Then I will address my expectations for the performance of the economy over the remainder of 2013 and into 2014.

Since the end of the Great Recession in mid-2009, we have had 15 consecutive quarters of positive growth of real GDP. However, the average annual growth rate over that period has been just 2.1 percent. Although the unemployment rate has declined by 2.5 percentage points from its peak of 10 percent in October of 2009, much of this decline is due to the fact that the labor force participation rate has fallen by 1.5 percentage points over this period. Recall that discouraged workers who do not actively look for work are regarded as not participating in the labor force and so are not counted as unemployed even though they are without jobs. Using an alternative measure, the employment to population ratio, which is not influenced by changes in the number of discouraged workers, there has been limited improvement in labor market conditions. Job loss rates have fallen, but hiring rates remain depressed at low levels. Taken together, the labor market still cannot be regarded as healthy. Numerous indicators, including the behavior of labor compensation and household assessments of labor market conditions, are all consistent with the view that there remains a great deal of slack in the economy.

That being said, I see persuasive evidence of improved underlying fundamentals for much of the private sector of the US economy. Key measures of household leverage have declined and are now at the lowest levels they have been in well over a decade. Household net worth, expressed as a percent of disposable income, has increased back to its average of the previous decade, reflecting rising equity and home prices and declining liabilities. Banks are beginning to ease credit standards somewhat after a prolonged period of tightness. As a result, we are now experiencing a fairly typical cyclical recovery of consumer spending on durable goods. For example, lightweight motor vehicles sold at a seasonally-adjusted annual rate of 15.3 million in May, not far from the 16.1 million sales in 2007.

Similarly, after five years in which housing production was well below what is consistent with underlying demographic trends, it now appears that we have worked off the excess supply of housing built up during the boom years of the last decade. Housing starts and sales are now on a clear upward trend, and a widely followed national home price index is up around 12 percent over the twelve months ending in April. Indeed, anecdotal reports suggest that this higher-than-expected increase in home prices is due to a lack of homes for sale.

Unfortunately, the improvements in consumer spending on durable goods and housing are not yet showing through in the overall GDP growth rate due to the significant headwinds that we continue to face. First, federal fiscal policy has recently become quite contractionary. Estimates from the Congressional Budget

Since the end of the Great Recession in mid-2009, we have had 15 consecutive quarters of positive growth of real GDP. However, the average annual growth rate over that period has been just 2.1 percent.

Office (CBO) indicate that this fiscal restraint is on the order of 1.75 percentage points of potential GDP this year. In the period since 1960, there have been only two previous episodes of fiscal contraction of this order of magnitude—1969 and 1987—both of which occurred when the economy was on a more solid footing than it is today. Second, the euro area is experiencing a protracted recession and growth in many of the largest emerging economies has slowed. This has resulted in a very sharp slowing of US exports, with an associated slowing in production and employment growth in the US manufacturing sector.

Thus, I continue to see the economy as being in a tug-of-war between fiscal drag and underlying fundamental improvement, with a great deal of uncertainty over which force will prevail in the near-term. This tug-of-war is clearly seen in the monthly employment data. Over April and May, the average monthly gain in employment in the private service-providing sector has been well maintained at 175,000. In contrast, employment in the manufacturing sector and the federal government declined a combined 20,000 per month. And the resulting uncertainty is, I believe, an important contributing factor behind the relatively sluggish pace of business investment spending.

My best guess is that growth for all of 2013, measured on a Q4/Q4 basis, will be about what it has been since the end of the recession. But I believe a strong case can be made that the pace of growth will pick up notably in 2014. The private sector of the economy should continue to heal, while the amount of fiscal drag will begin to subside. I also see some indications that growth prospects among our major trading partners have begun to improve, for example, the rise in the June euro area composite Purchasing Managers' Index. And this combination of events is likely to create an environment in which business investment spending will gather strength.

Finally, I believe this tug-of-war analogy is useful in explaining the recent inflation dynamics. As is well known, total inflation, as measured by the personal consumption expenditures (PCE) deflator, has slowed sharply over the past year and is now running below the FOMC's expressed goal of 2 percent. Softness in energy prices, resulting from the weakening of global growth mentioned earlier combined with increased energy production here in the US has contributed to the slowing of total inflation. However, it is also the case that core inflation, that is, excluding food and energy, has slowed sharply as well. A decomposition of core inflation reveals that some of the decline is due to slowing in the rate of increase in prices of non-food and non-energy goods. This probably is due in large part to the softening of global demand for goods and the modest appreciation of the dollar that has occurred since mid-2011.

In the service sector, the rate of increase in prices of medical services and "non-market" services—the latter includes some financial services—also has slowed notably recently. In contrast, the rate of increase in prices for other non-energy services has been relatively stable. Comparing this set of conditions to that in 2010, the recent slowing of inflation has been less widespread across core goods and core services, and inflation expectations so far have declined less appreciably than they did in 2010. Thus, my best guess is that core goods prices will begin to firm in the months ahead as global demand begins to strengthen and inventories get into better alignment with sales.

As is always the case, there is substantial uncertainty surrounding this forecast. Moreover, there is always the possibility of some unforeseen shock. Thus, we will be monitoring US and global economic conditions very carefully and will adjust our views on the likely path for growth, inflation and the unemployment rate accordingly in response to new information.

At its recent meeting, the FOMC decided to continue its accommodative policy stance. It reaffirmed its expectation that the current low range for the federal funds rate target will be appropriate at least as long as the unemployment rate remains above 6.5 percent, so long as inflation and inflation expectations remain well-behaved. It is important to remember that these conditions are thresholds, not triggers. The FOMC also maintained its purchases of $40 billion per month in agency MBS and $45 billion per month in Treasury securities, with a stated goal of promoting a substantial improvement in the labor market outlook in a context of price stability.

In its statement, the FOMC said that it may vary the pace of purchases as economic conditions evolve. As Chairman Bernanke stated in his press conference following the FOMC meeting, if the economic data over the next year turn out to be broadly consistent with the outlooks that the FOMC sees as most likely, which are roughly similar to the outlook I have already laid out, the FOMC anticipates that it would be appropriate to begin to moderate the pace of purchases later this year. Under such a scenario, subsequent reductions might occur in measured steps through the first half of next year, and an end to purchases around mid-2014. Under this scenario, at the time that asset purchases came to an end, the unemployment rate likely would be near 7 percent and the economy's momentum strengthening, supporting further robust job gains in the future.

As I noted last week in our regional press briefing, a few points deserve emphasis. First, the FOMC's policy depends on the progress we make towards our objectives. This means that the policy—including the pace of asset purchases—depends on the outlook rather than the calendar. The scenario I outlined above is only that— one possible outcome. Economic circumstances could diverge significantly from the FOMC's expectations. If labor market conditions and the economy's growth momentum were to be less favorable than in the FOMC's outlook—and this is what has happened in recent years—I would expect that the asset purchases would continue at a higher pace for longer.

Second, even if this scenario were to occur and the pace of purchases were reduced, it would still be the case that as long as the FOMC continues its asset purchases it is adding monetary policy accommodation, not tightening monetary policy. As the FOMC adds to its stock of securities, this should continue to put downward pressure on longer-term interest rates, making monetary policy more accommodative.

Third, the Federal Reserve is likely to keep most of these assets on its balance sheet for a long time. As Chairman Bernanke noted in his most recent press conference, a strong majority of FOMC participants no longer favor selling agency MBS securities during the monetary policy normalization process. This implies a bigger balance sheet for longer, which provides additional accommodation today and continuing support for mortgage markets going forward.

Fourth, even under this scenario, a rise in short-term rates is very likely to be a long way off. Not only will it likely take considerable time to reach the FOMC's 6.5 percent unemployment rate threshold, but also the FOMC could wait considerably longer before raising short-term rates. The fact that inflation is coming in well below the FOMC's 2 percent objective is relevant here. Most FOMC participants currently do not expect short-term rates to begin to rise until 2015.

To reiterate what I said last week, some commentators have interpreted the recent shift in the market-implied path of short-term interest rates as indicating that market participants now expect the first increases in the federal funds rate target to come much earlier than previously thought. Setting aside whether this is the correct interpretation of recent price moves, let me emphasize that such an expectation would be quite out of sync with both FOMC statements and the expectations of most FOMC participants.

Regional Economic Conditions

Turning to the regional economy, my colleagues and I at the New York Fed continually track conditions in our District, and we have a number of tools we use for that purpose.

To promote growth in our local communities, we publish extensive data and analysis on the local economy. We provide outreach initiatives, such as our workshops on access to global markets to help small businesses learn about loan programs and sources of credit enhancements. We also run an annual video festival for college students in the Second District. In this program student teams produce videos aimed to help young adults make sound personal financial decisions. A panel of advertising and video professionals selects winning video productions for screening in local movie theaters.

As you know, even states as wealthy as Connecticut have large pockets of poverty. So we target some of our work specifically to low- and moderate-income groups.

We have worked hard to help neighborhoods that face high foreclosure rates. This work is important obviously because foreclosures are a terrible event for those who lose their homes. But beyond that, this work is important because high levels of foreclosures affect neighbors' home values, the local tax base and economic vitality more broadly. We have provided housing counselors and community groups with the latest information on mortgage conditions via mortgage briefs, roundtables, presentations and an interactive web tool that shows very local monthly delinquency and foreclosure conditions. This past fall we hosted a conference on distressed residential real estate to share new expert analysis with senior policymakers and practitioners from across the nation. Your new Commissioner of Housing—whom I note, formerly worked at the New York Fed—attended that conference.

We also conduct a periodic poll about the credit needs of small businesses, which are an important source of new jobs in the District. If you represent a small business and would like to participate in our next poll, please pass your business card to my colleagues, who are in the audience, or see me after the speech. And if your business is somewhat larger, I urge you to consider becoming one of our business contacts—just indicate your interest to us on your business card.

So how is the region doing? I want to begin by pointing out that Fairfield County has a number of strengths, beginning with a highly-educated workforce: Two in five adults in the county hold a college degree, nearly twice the nationwide average. It also has an array of fine educational institutions, including Fairfield University, UConn Stamford, the University of Bridgeport, Sacred Heart University, Western Connecticut State University, Housatonic Community College, and Norwalk Community College.

The industry mix here is quite diverse, with a good representation of jobs in the high-paying finance sector. In fact, roughly 35,000 jobs in the county, about 9 percent of total employment, are in the finance and insurance industry, a share almost twice as large as in the nation and even slightly higher than in New York City. Although the sector has shed jobs over the past two years, it remains an important and valuable component of the local economy. There are also numerous corporate headquarters in the county and a notable manufacturing presence, particularly in the pharmaceuticals, electrical equipment and aerospace industries.

In addition, the whole tristate region has benefited from its proximity to New York City, where the rebound in the economy—and also in employment—has been much stronger. Fairfield County's connection to New York City is not quite as strong as Long Island's or the lower Hudson Valley: About 7 percent of working residents in the county commute to New York City compared to about 20 percent in those areas. Still, the city's strong pace of job creation during the current recovery is supporting incomes in the county.

Turning to the recent performance of the economy, this area is growing pretty much in line with the nation, at least in terms of employment. That's a bit of an improvement from 2012 when, after solid gains in 2010 and 2011, job creation in both Fairfield County and Connecticut had stalled. Some sectors, such as education, health, and professional and business services were adding jobs; but those were offset by job losses not only in finance, but also in the goods-producing and distributing sectors.

And at the end of October, Superstorm Sandy hit the region, causing major damage and disruption. While most of the news focused on New York City, Long Island and New Jersey, parts of Fairfield and New Haven counties—cities and towns like Bridgeport, Stamford, Milford, and Fairfield—were severely affected as well.

Thankfully, Sandy's disruptive effect on the region's economy seems to have been short-lived. Fairfield County did see some job losses during the winter months, and Sandy likely contributed to that. But in the spring this area saw a strong and broad-based rebound in employment. In fact, in May employment in Fairfield County surged to a more than four-year high.

Even with this recent surge in employment, however, the county has recouped only about 60 percent of the 36,000 jobs lost during the last downturn, whereas the nation has recouped close to three-quarters of its job losses and New York City has more than fully rebounded. And, at more than 7 percent, the county's unemployment rate remains high.

Another dimension of the local economy where we have seen modest improvement is housing. Homebuilding, as measured by housing permits issued, languished from 2008 through 2011, but last year, multi-family construction picked up noticeably, and this year single-family construction has begun to move up as well. Home values have also begun to recover. After falling about 25 percent between 2006 and early 2012, home prices have risen by 5 percent in Fairfield County and 3 percent across Connecticut overall. While this upturn in home prices is encouraging, it has been considerably weaker than in other parts of our region and also weaker than nationally.

The New York Fed's measures of regional credit conditions suggest continued financial challenges for families here. As of the first quarter of 2013, average debt per person was about $60,000 in Connecticut and over $90,000 in Fairfield County—little changed over several years. The county's delinquency rate on that debt is now 5.7 percent, similar to the national average. And the mortgage crisis continues to take a toll on local homeowners. As of the first quarter, about 6 percent of mortgage debt in Fairfield County was 90-plus days delinquent, slightly higher than the national delinquency rate.

It is also important to recognize the county's strengths that will support recovery and the rise in household income over the longer term—over and above just being close to a thriving New York City. In particular, the above-average educational attainment of residents and the numerous educational institutions position the area well to move into the expanding knowledge-based economy. Also, its diverse industry mix has a good representation of jobs in high-paying sectors and the area maintains its attractiveness as a location for corporate headquarters.

Thank you for your kind attention and I will now be happy to take a few questions.

About William C. Dudley

William C. Dudley has been the president and chief executive officer of the Federal Reserve Bank of New York since 2009, and he serves as the vice chairman and permanent member of the Federal Open Market Committee. Previously, he was the executive vice president of the Markets Group at the New York Federal Reserve and managed the System Open Market Account. Dudley earned his bachelor's of arts degree from New College of Florida in 1974, and his doctorate in economics from the University of California, Berkeley, in 1982. He was the vice president of the Morgan Guaranty Trust Company, and an economist at the Federal Reserve Board from 1981 to 1983. In 1986, he joined Goldman Sachs, becoming a partner and managing director during his tenure. He also served as a member of the Technical Consultants Group to the Congressional Budget Office from 1999 to 2005. In 2007 he left Goldman Sachs when he was appointed to the Federal Reserve Bank of New York. Dudley was chairman of the Committee on Payment and Settlement Systems of the Bank for International Settlements from 2009 to 2012, when he was designated chairman of the BIS Committee on the Global Financial System.

Immigrants and America's Innovation Economy

By Luis Arbulu

Entrepreneur and venture capitalist Luis Arbulu addresses the United States Senate Committee on Commerce, Science, and Transportation. The speech took place on May 8, 2013, in Washington, DC. The subject of the speech is immigrant entrepreneurs in the United States and how they will be affected by the Senate immigration bill known as S.744. Arbulu is best known for his work at Google Inc., where he worked in business development. In April 2013, he was appointed "entrepreneur in residence" by the White House and the Department of Homeland Security. Working with US Citizenship and Immigration Services, he helps spearhead efforts to grow job creation in the public and private sectors of the American economy. Arbulu begins his remarks with a brief review of his personal history and professional experience. He discusses his work as a board member with Engine Advocacy, which works to provide government funding to immigrant entrepreneurs throughout the United States. The crucial roles played by STEM (science, technology, engineering, and mathematics) workers in the American economy is discussed. Arbulu also discusses details related to the H-1B nonimmigrant visa program, which allows employers in the United States to employ foreign workers on a temporary basis. According to Arbulu, reforms should be made to the H-1B system to ensure that immigrant entrepreneurs are able to grow their businesses in the United States.

Dear Chairman Rockefeller, Ranking Member Thune, and Members of the Committee, thank you for the opportunity to submit testimony to the committee.

Born and raised in Peru, I came to the US to study engineering through the Fulbright program. I worked as an engineer building large-scale infrastructure projects in the US and abroad, was the head of engineering operations at a startup and then held a number of senior roles at Google. As a founder and managing director at Hattery, a seed stage investment fund and ideas and innovation lab based in San Francisco, I work with entrepreneurs from all around the world who have come the United States to start their businesses. Recently, I was appointed as an Entrepreneur in Residence with the US Citizenship and Immigration Services in order to help the agency understand the realities and nuances of high impact entrepreneurship when they look to adjudicate visas. I understand the trials of these struggling entrepreneurs because I have lived them; that's why I support the Senate's efforts to pass comprehensive immigration reform.

Delivered May 8, 2013, at the United States Senate, Washington, DC, by Luis Arbulu.

Startups, the Drivers of Our Economy

As a result of my experiences, I joined the Board of Engine Advocacy. Engine's mission is to create an environment where technological innovation and entrepreneurship thrive by educating and working with startups and lawmakers to construct smarter public policy. Engine has more than 500 members, from young companies making products ranging from semantic search tools to heart scanning technologies, to MIT physicists building satellites and thriving businesses such as Yelp. Across the country, Engine members are driving our economy.

"High growth entrepreneurial companies" are responsible for all new net job growth since 1980, according to research from the Kauffman Foundation. Our own Tech Works research[1] has found that employment in the STEM occupations of science, technology, engineering, and mathematics has been continually robust, gaining twenty-seven jobs for every one job gain in all other occupations between 2002 and 2011. These jobs have also boosted local communities; for every job created in the high-tech sector, 4.3 additional jobs are projected to be created in the local goods and services economy, including barbers, lawyers, and health care professionals.

INVEST Visa

As risky investments, startups are unlikely to receive, or even investigate the possibility of receiving, conventional bank loans. Instead, startups rely on angel investors and venture capitalists who are willing to take the financial risk in exchange for equity. To ensure that these fledgling businesses can prosper, angels and VCs will often offer advice and mentoring in addition to financial investment. Investors steer companies toward success by literally being present as the startup grows. These interactions, together with hard work and late nights, grow truly innovative companies.

These networks and access to capital and talent are the reasons why so many of the world's entrepreneurs flock to the US to start and grow their companies. Unfortunately, our current immigration system makes this prohibitively difficult. Fabien Beckers, for example, has created a 3D heart imaging system that could revolutionize the way we diagnose and treat heart disease. He has a PhD from Cambridge and an MBA from Stanford. Despite having funding contingent on his ability to stay in the country, Fabien was not technically employed and so did not fit the requirements for an H class visa. Instead of working on his product, Fabien had to spend months being rejected by visa category

[T]he number of H1B applications correlates with economic growth; in good growth years, there are more applicants than during recession years. It is for this reason that Engine advocates for an H1B system that is responsive to the needs of the marketplace rather than arbitrary caps.

after visa category. Finally, he proved he was "exceptional" enough in his ability (as defined by the visa class) to receive an O visa that allowed him to stay in the country.

Columbia business school graduate Sumit Suman, on the other hand, has not been as fortunate. His online mentoring startup Mentii is being used by universities around the country to help better connect alumni networks. In order to qualify for an H1B visa, Sumit had to relinquish control of his company to a member of his Board. But Sumit lost out in this year's visa lottery so he was forced to return to India. Though still building Mentii from Delhi, Sumit is no longer able to meet possible clients and actively build the community.

Foreign-born startup founders continually struggle to stay in the country. Some, like Fabien, eventually find a visa category that fits. Some, like Sumit, however, relinquish control of their companies. Still others use L visas to travel back and forth from their home country as their business demands. But this is one of the costliest visas because startup founders must incorporate their business, and maintain staff and offices, in two countries.

The INVEST visa remedies this problem by allowing startup entrepreneurs with funding to stay here and grow their businesses. We believe that the requirements in S.744 are reasonable: an investment of $100,000 in the previous three years for a nonimmigrant visa. This investment can be easily verified by the regulatory and enforcement agencies.

Highly Skilled Workers

As startups grow, it is also important to make sure that they are able to hire the right talent. A recent study by Engine Advocacy shows that STEM workers continue to be in high demand. Inflation adjusted wages for STEM workers have grown faster than for non-STEM over the last two decades, despite the recession. The number of computer and math and science jobs has also increased by 5.2 percent annually over the last decade, with an unemployment rate below 1 percent and a job openings rate of around 8 percent.[2] Moreover, despite claims that foreign workers are paid less than their American counterparts, foreign born IT workers earn 6.8 percent more than those with US Citizenship.[3]

According to USCIS data, the number of H1B applications correlates with economic growth; in good growth years, there are more applicants than during recession years. It is for this reason that Engine advocates for an H1B system that is responsive to the needs of the marketplace rather than arbitrary caps.[4] While the comprehensive immigration bill makes great strides toward reducing the burden on the H1B system, the existence of a cap and the preference for workers with graduate degrees will continue to cause difficulties for startups. For startups, the *right* talent is not defined by what degree they have.

As startups struggle to find highly skilled workers who can lead the technology revolution, each H1B worker makes a substantial impact on the growth of the business. According to a 2011 GAO report, the H1B caps did not impact larger firms who were able to move workers to a foreign office and then use L visas to join their team in the United States as needed.[5] Startups, on the other hand, do not have the flexibility to locate their workers around the world. The same GAO study noted that for startups, being denied an H1B visa could mean moving the whole company abroad or abandoning the startup entirely.

Conclusion

S.744 makes great strides towards reforming the current immigration system. The INVEST visa allows entrepreneurs from around the world to start their businesses in the United States. Reforms to the H1B system, however, stop short of allowing these businesses to prosper. Startups can power the next generation of growth in the American economy if we let them. Entrepreneurs and innovators need congressional support to continue to build the businesses of the future. We hope that you will consider these measures that will allow for that future, our future, to be prosperous.

Notes

1. https://s3.amazonaws.com/engineadvocacy/TechReport_LoRes.pdf
2. http://engine.is/blog/posts/itsallrelativestemworkersareinhighdemand
3. http://www2.itif.org/2010h1bvisa.pdf
4. http://www.engine.is/blog/posts/howthegangofeightimmigrationbillimpactsstartups
5. http://www.gao.gov/new.items/d1126.pdf

About Luis Arbulu

Luis Arbulu is a founding and managing partner at Hattery, a startup incubator and product development and investment firm located in San Francisco, California. He also currently works as the director of the Open Innovation (venture investing) department at Samsung Electronics. Previously, he held a number of high-ranking positions at Google, including the head of finance and analytics for AdSense, the company's multi-billion-dollar online ad syndication business. Arbulu was born in Peru, but he came to the United States on a Fulbright Scholarship to study engineering at the University of Kansas, earning his bachelor of science degree in mechanical engineering. He also studied at the University of Pennsylvania's Wharton School, where he received his MBA. In addition to Google, Arbulu worked as a consultant at Booz Allen Hamilton, an engineer at Black and Veatch, and a product manager with Alton Geo (acquired by TRC). Arbulu was recently appointed a resident entrepreneur with the US Citizenship and Immigration Services.

Leveraging Private Sector Investment in the Developing World

By Jim Yong Kim

In a speech delivered at the International Economic Forum of the Americas in Montreal, Quebec, World Bank Group president Jim Yong Kim describes the many ways in which private sector investment in developing nations can help lift populations out of extreme poverty while simultaneously generating profit and growth for investors. He begins by describing how, after a career of working with nongovernmental organizations, he realized the important role the private sector can play in the developing world. He talks of his time in Haiti and describes the handful of Canadian companies that remained active there after the 2012 earthquake. He shares an anecdote about how an investment from the World Bank's International Finance Corporation helped build a successful energy provider in post-earthquake Haiti. In Canada, Kim says, the extraction industry comprises a formidable chunk of the Canadian economy, employing over three hundred thousand people and generating a $36 billion portion of the national GDP. He speaks about the investment potential for mining companies in resource-rich African countries that don't have the proper infrastructure or economic participation to capitalize on that potential and points to the Canadian mining industry's successful foreign investments in Latin America. To assuage investor concerns, Kim outlines the insurance and investment treaty programs the World Bank Group has to safeguard against political instability or foreign nationalization of resources. He closes by urging the private sector to join in the fight to end extreme poverty.

[Dr. Kim is speaking in French.]

Now, I apologize to my actual French-speaking friends—French is my fourth language. And it still needs a lot of work.

I've been working in development for the whole of my professional life. My background was rooted in the world of NGOs, working in some of the most difficult environments in the world, ranging from rural poverty in the central plateau of Haiti, to the prisons of Siberia, where we treated a form of drug-resistant tuberculosis that persists to this day.

I was implementing our programs, but I was also an activist—pushing establishments like the World Health Organization to develop policies that were grounded in the principles of providing quality health care access to all, especially the poorest.

The institution that I now lead, the World Bank Group, is at the forefront of so many issues in development—ranging from gender equality, to climate change, to

Delivered June 11, 2013, at the International Economic Forum of the Americas, Montreal, Canada, by Jim Yong Kim.

helping lead the efforts to end poverty by 2030. And it's now also at the forefront of leveraging private sector investment in the developing world. And that's what I'd like to talk to you about today.

I can give you many examples, but I'll pick one, in a country that has a very close connection to Canada, and to Haiti. By the way, I want to thank the Minister for those fantastic announcements that the World Bank failed to make, but it's extremely welcome. And, as you know, we are deeply committed to private sector investment in fragile and conflict affected states.

> *[M]any people living in developing countries are not seeing results of the extraction of their countries' natural resources. The so-called "natural resource curse," where natural resources are abundant, but economies don't grow and people don't participate, doesn't have to happen.*

But let's get back to Haiti. Canada is home to more than 200,000 Haitians. And Haiti is home to many Canadian businesses. The country's commitment to helping Haiti rebuild—whether it's through government aid, Haitian-Canadians sending money back home, or the private sector's investments—have been incredible. More than a half-dozen Canadian businesses that were operating in Haiti before the January 12, 2012, earthquake have maintained their operations. They include the Bank of Nova Scotia; Air Canada; the Desjardins Group, the largest cooperative financial group in Canada; and Gildan Activewear, a clothing manufacturer and marketer.

The impact from private sector investment is often overlooked. But let me tell the story of one business that I visited on my trip to Haiti.

The E-Power story is truly inspirational. A group of young Haitian entrepreneurs decided that they wanted to do something about the fact that only 25 percent of the people in Haiti have access to electricity. But they also wanted to do something about the cost of electricity in Haiti which, at the time, was around four times what you pay here in Montreal. IFC, our private sector group, invested $29 million in starting E-Power. But then the earthquake hit. And, rather than stop, they decided that they were going to build E-Power right next to Cité Soleil, the infamous slum area that is both unsafe and mired in deep, deep poverty. When I went there, I found out that they were in an area that was thought before as being completely vulnerable and hopeless.

Not only have they been able to increase the overall supply of electricity in Port-au-Prince by 35 percent, but they reduced the cost almost in half. This is the potential of the private sector.

And so the first message I want to bring to you today is that the private sector is essential if we're going to meet our goals of ending poverty by 2030 and building shared prosperity so that the bottom 40 percent of any population shares in economic growth.

Foreign assistance alone is not enough—the Minister said it very well. Foreign assistance now stands at $125 billion a year. And, as my good friend (inaudible) from (inaudible), for the first time in a very long time it has gone down for two years in a row.

But when I look at the prospects for ending poverty, I'm extremely optimistic. Because while official development assistance might be limited, there is so much capital sitting on the sidelines right now, and we want to make the case that investing in the developing world is not only the smart thing to do economically, but you can get so many other benefits for the poorest people on the earth with the work that you do.

Let's just take a quick example—$125 billion a year, that would be overall (inaudible) growth for official development assistance. India, over the next five years, is facing a $1 trillion infrastructure deficit, $200 billion a year over the next five years. So, all foreign assistance couldn't even meet India's requirement for infrastructure development.

In our World Development Report this past year, we pointed out that, globally, 90 percent of all jobs are created in the private sector. What do people around the world want more than anything else? The Gallup Institute, now based in Washington, D.C., has been doing surveys of the poorest women on the planet. And, guess what—what they want more than anything else is a good job.

So, if 90 percent of jobs are created in the private sector, and there's all this capital sitting on the sidelines, I look at this as an extraordinary opportunity to do well and to do good at the same time.

We need to help to create a favorable environment in which it's easier to start a formal business. Improved regulation and technology can help. Between 2007 and 2012, the time required to start a business had fallen from 50 days to 34 days in developing countries as a whole. Some countries have made major advances. In Georgia or Macedonia, anyone can create a business in about two days. But in other countries—in Latin America, Asia, and Africa—it takes more than two months to create a business.

Poor logistics remain a key constraint to trade in Africa. Today, it takes two weeks, and costs up to 21 cents per ton, per kilometer, to transport a container between the port of Douala, in Cameroon, and N'Djamena, in Chad—21 cents—compared to only 5 cents in the United States. And this doesn't take into account the two to three weeks' delay at the Port of Douala, or the 70 to 150 checkpoints along the way. These costs are ultimately transferred to the population through higher food prices—prices for food and goods—and they contribute to poverty.

With our "Doing Business Report," the World Bank Group monitors the conditions in which the private sector operates in specific countries. We're committed to this work, because we want to help governments focus on areas which can help the private sector create jobs. We also want countries to be able to know where they stand with regard to other countries, especially countries they're competing with.

Now, I can tell you that focusing specifically on trying to improve the ratings in the "Doing Business Report," countries in Africa and developing countries have made extraordinary advances in getting rid of just these kinds of barriers to doing business. And our intention, going forward, is to help them even more with even more effective and well-researched "Doing Business" reports in the future.

The second point I want to make is that many leaders in the developing world are actively looking for ways to work more closely with private sector. I was just in Tokyo, at the Tokyo International Conference on African Development, and I met many heads of state from Africa. But one meeting in particular struck me. The great Ellen Johnson Sirleaf, the first woman head of state in Africa, winner of the Nobel Peace Prize, we sat down, and here's the story she told me.

She said, you know, we've had peace for 10 years now. And when I took over as president, we had zero megawatts of installed capacity. The World Bank came in and immediately put in 5 megawatts, but now we only have 21. Now, I would guess that a couple of city blocks in Montreal consume about that much energy.

And what she told me was, "I need your help today. I need to quintuple my energy supply right away, because what I want most is for the private sector to invest so that we can have jobs for former combatants." She said, "I have 30-year-old men who've done nothing but fight their whole lives. And the one thing that will keep them off the battlefield would be the jobs. I need your help in building energy, and I need the private sector to invest."

Another important area for the private sector, of course, is investment in the extractive industries. Canada has a long mining tradition, and the extractive industry is an important part of your economy. The Mining Association of Canada reported that 308,000 employees work in mineral extraction, smelting, fabrication, and manufacturing as of 2010, and are contributing $36 billion to the national GDP. Or Latin America, for instance, 60 percent of total mining investments come from Canadian investors.

The extractive industry is important to us, because an estimated 3.5 billion people live in resource-rich countries, and many of those poorest countries, including several in Africa, have under-exploited mining resources. These resources could have a transformative impact to boost economic growth and alleviate poverty. In Mozambique, Niger, Sierra Leone, and Zambia, recent discoveries of oil, natural gas, copper, and other minerals, or the possible expansion of existing mines, have brought fantastic new growth opportunities.

However, many people living in developing countries are not seeing results of the extraction of their countries' natural resources. The so-called "natural resource curse," where natural resources are abundant, but economies don't grow and people don't participate, doesn't have to happen. In Botswana, for example, we've seen how mining revenues, when they are well used, when they are invested by countries in health and education, can help boost development. In Sub-Saharan Africa, Botswana is both the country which is the most dependent on minerals, and the country that has the highest ranking in the human-development index.

We need Canadians and other international firms to invest in the developing world. Canada is an international hub for many mining companies, including several IFC clients, such as Guyana Goldfields, working in Guyana; Unigold, working in the Dominican Republic; and Sama Resources, working in Côte d'Ivoire.

Many Canadian firms are among the world's leaders in corporate and social responsibility. In fact, the government of Alberta's International Development Office recently launched an initiative to connect the private sector with the development community. This will help transfer knowledge from Canadian companies and firms to the developing world.

At the World Bank, we're trying to help countries get the most out of their mineral resources. We're managing the Extractive Industries Transparency Initiative to ensure the transparent handling of government revenues from the mining and hydrocarbon sectors. Twenty-three countries are already in compliance with this initiative, and 16 additional ones are candidates.

My last point is that we at the World Bank are ready to be the best possible partner for all of you in investing in developing countries. The International Finance Corporation, our private sector arm, last year invested $20.4 billion in 103 developing countries and, moreover, in the last seven or eight years, we have increased our investments in Africa tenfold. And we're doing it because we believe in both the growth potential and the development impact of the investments we're making.

You know, the average return on investment for our equity investments over the last 15 years at IFC—and this includes during the last 5 years—has been, on average, 20 percent. We made good investments, we do well, and we also help countries meet their development targets.

We're also very proud that one part of the World Bank Group, the International Center for the Settlement of Investment Disputes, which is led by Meg Kinnear—a Canadian—they register almost 40 cases a year, and contribute to enforcing investment treaties, and to improving the investment climate for foreign direct investments.

In concluding, I'm often asked how my perspective on development has changed in the last few years. And one group of high school students particularly asked me: What have you learned over the last 20 years? Is there anything that you've really changed your mind about in all of your work in development? And my answer is that for far too long I grossly underestimated the power and importance of the private sector in helping develop potential to lift people out of poverty.

It's not a question of whether you are for or against the private sector in development. It's simply a question of how high your aspirations are for lifting people out of extreme poverty.

We cannot reach our goal without the private sector.

I'd like to ask all of you to look more closely at opportunities in the developing world. I know that the reaction from some is that it's too risky, or that you don't necessarily know where to find promising investments.

But we at the World Bank, we can help. We have MIGA, the Multilateral Investment Guarantee Agency, which provides political risk insurance in developing countries. We do everything we can to prevent countries from nationalizing (inaudible), but if that happens, we provide insurance.

And we have many experts at IFC who, for decades, have been making this private sector work in some of the most difficult settings. And we've made investments that, as I've mentioned, have been extremely profitable.

You know, we have a historic opportunity. The developing world has been the engine of growth, or one of the most important engines of growth in the economic crisis that began five years ago. More than half of the world's growth in the last couple of years has come from the developing world.

There are clearly opportunities for business to be profitable in many developing countries, but you have another opportunity here as well. You have a chance to join the government of Canada, the World Bank, and many other countries in multilateral organizations to help lift millions of people out of poverty. Think about that. You can satisfy your shareholders, and you can lift people out of extreme poverty.

"Extreme poverty" was described by one of my predecessors, Robert McNamara, in a speech in Nairobi some 40 years ago. He called it "a condition of deprivation that falls below any rational definition of human dignity." Let me repeat that: A condition of deprivation that falls below any rational definition of human dignity.

You can be part of this global movement to end extreme poverty within a generation. We need the private sector to help bring energy to Liberia. We need the private sector to help rebuild Haiti. We need you to help bend the arc of history and banish extreme poverty from this earth.

We look forward to working with you.

Thank you very much. Merci beaucoup. (Applause.)

About Jim Yong Kim

Jim Yong Kim is the current president of the World Bank Group, having replaced Robert B. Zoellick in July 2012. Born in South Korea in 1959, Kim moved to Muscatine, Iowa, at the age of five. He graduated magna cum laude from Brown University with a bachelor's degree in human biology in 1982, received his MD from Harvard Medical School in 1991, and earned a PhD in anthropology from Harvard in 1993. Kim cofounded Partners in Health—a Boston-based health care organization that provides services to some of the world's poorest communities—in 1987. Kim was instrumental in the 2003 launch of the World Health Organization's (WHO) 3 by 5 Initiative—a global effort to treat three million new HIV patients by 2005—and was the director of the WHO's Department of HIV/AIDS from 2004 to 2006. In 2006, Time magazine placed Kim on its 100 Most Influential People list in recognition of his work with 3 by 5, and for his efforts battling drug-resistant tuberculosis in Peru. He was named president of Dartmouth College in 2009, becoming the first Asian American president of an Ivy League institution. President Barack Obama nominated Kim to head the World Bank in March 2012.

Index

❖